GREAT BRITISH MENU

Great British Menu is an Optomen Television Production

LONDON, NEW YORK, MUNICH, MELBOURNE, DELHI

Writer Paul Lay
Project Manager and Editor Norma MacMillan
Art Direction and Text Design Smith & Gilmour, London
DTP Designer Louise Waller
Production Controller Elizabeth Warman
Operations Publishing Manager Gillian Roberts
Art Director Peter Luff
Creative Publisher Mary-Clare Jerram
Publisher – Special Projects Stephanie Jackson
Publisher Corinne Roberts
Senior Jacket Creative Nicola Powling
Jacket Editor Anna Stewart
Photographers Dan Jones (food), Noel Murphy (locations),
Chris Bairstow, Steve Sklair, Jessica North (chefs)

First published in Great Britain in 2006 by Dorling Kindersley Limited
80 Strand, London WC2R ORL

A Penguin Company
2 4 6 8 10 9 7 5 3 1

By arrangement with Optomen Television
Optomen logo © Optomen Television 2006
Optomen Television Production Team: Executive Producer Nicola Moody,
Series Producer Bernice Daly, Researcher Annina Vogel, Studio Producer
Sophie Seiden, Assistant Producer Jackie Baker, Personal Assistant
Vanessa Land, Home Economist Lisa Harrison

By arrangement with the BBC
BBC logo © BBC 1996
The BBC logo is a registered trademark of the British Broadcasting Corporation and is used under licence.

A CIP catalogue record for this book is available from The British Library

ISBN-13: 978 1 4053 1650 7
ISBN-10: 1 4053 1650 0

Colour reproduction by GRB, Italy
Printed and bound by Mohn media, Germany

Discover more at
www.dk.com

CONTENTS

The BBC TWO television series Great British Menu has gathered together 14 of the country's finest chefs to compete for the chance to be part of the winning team creating a special lunch for the Queen on her 80th birthday. The competition celebrates not only this personal milestone, but also the United Kingdom's remarkable culinary renaissance. The recipes created by the chefs for the competition, and reproduced here, reflect brilliantly the range and quality of ingredients, produce and cuisine found in these diverse and bountiful islands.

We have come a long way. When Queen Elizabeth II succeeded to the throne in 1952, the end of food rationing was still two years away. Britain, broken and impoverished by the sacrifices of the Second World War, and in retreat from its once mighty Empire, was a grey, austere place, where food and drink was widely regarded as little more than a necessity endured. The puritan was in the ascendant during those years of austerity, the cavalier within us would have to wait.

The pleasures of the table were never entirely neglected. Elizabeth David raised sights with her magisterial paeans to unpretentious and honest food, albeit conjured from the then elusive produce of the Mediterranean, those "blessed lands of sun and sea and olive trees". But in many ways, this celebration of all things distant only encouraged the further diminution of Britain's culinary heritage, though a few lonely voices could be heard in the wilderness. Among them was that of Jane Grigson, whose boundless, brilliantly articulated love for the food of these islands fed an optimism that refused to lie down "even when confronted with perceived realities".

Her optimism was not misplaced. For, over a quarter of a century after she penned those words, Britain is a serious food nation once more. Greater affluence has seen many more of us dining out with regularity, educating our palates, taking pleasure in food, demanding ever higher quality. A remarkable openness to new ideas, encouraged by widespread travel and postwar immigration, has seen the people of Britain embrace cuisines from every corner of the world which, in turn, have fused with native traditions to create a vibrant food culture, peopled by world-class chefs, entrepreneurs and producers who are making the most of Britain's extraordinarily diverse larder.

There is another important ingredient in the mix, a new-found passion for our past, the rediscovery of the very best of Britain's regional dishes and produce. Some politicians have tried – and failed – to present Britain as a young country. It is not. It is an ancient one and at its best when it embraces both the past and the future, seeking the best of both worlds. Nowhere is this more evident than in the way food producers, many of them featured in these pages, have used the internet to market the finest traditional products, from choice cuts of Aberdeen Angus beef, to the revival of mutton, to the ever growing array of artisanal cheeses, to the varieties of fruit and vegetables we had turned our back on in the sterile pursuit of conformity.

The realm over which Queen Elizabeth II still reigns has undergone a revolution in its eating habits, marked by the marriage of technology and tradition. Escaping its puritan past, the United Kingdom is now a land of plenty, peopled by culinary cavaliers, a "blessed plot" indeed.

Alan Kennedy (pictured on the right, with James Culley) is a butcher who knows his beef, and his customers are confident that all meat he sells is fully traceable.

CHAPTER ONE **THE SOUTH EAST**
GARY RHODES & ATUL KOCHHAR

When we talk of the food of London we talk of the food of the world, because alongside New York City, London offers a greater variety of cuisines than can be found anywhere else on earth. Every area of London, it seems, has its own particular ethnic speciality: Soho's Chinatown, Brick Lane's Bangla Town, the Turks of Dalston, Vietnamese in Hackney, Portuguese in Lambeth, the Poles of Ealing, Italians in Clerkenwell... the list goes on, with new arrivals bringing strange new combinations and sensations to jaded palates.

Within this wealth of styles, does it make sense to talk of a traditional London cuisine? For much of its history, the traditional food of London was street food, sold by costermongers who made a living hand to mouth, and who've long disappeared, victims of the great Victorian clean-up that brought police to the capital's streets. Those who today complain about the eating of fast food on the tube will echo the thoughts of Horatio Busino, chaplain to the Venetian ambassador, who in the early 17th century made this observation of Londoners: "Between meals one sees men, women and children always munching through the streets, like so many goats."

What those Londoners were munching was probably whitebait, the fry of sprats and herrings fished from the Thames, deep-fried whole and livened up with lemon and a dash of cayenne pepper. It was a dish that attracted, in the words of the 18th-century Welsh traveller Thomas Pennant, "a vast resort of the lower order of epicures to the taverns". But the whitebait were fresh, and wholesome, and so it is safe to judge that the fast food of our forebears was better than that of today.

PIES, MASH, EELS, TEA
If there is one dish associated with London, and the Cockney in particular, it is the jellied eel, like whitebait a diminished fruit of the Thames. Boiled with herbs, the eels cool to form their own gelatine, and taste rather like rollmops. The soft, slithery texture puts off many, and its partaking is a badge of cultural identity to Eastenders and South Londoners, who frequent the distinctive London pie shops. In truth, even the pie shops owe much to immigrants.

The oldest remaining one in London, and a fine exemplar of the form, with its green tiling and meat and fruit pies stacked in the window, is M Manze, which has occupied its site on Tower Bridge Road for over a century. The founder, Michele Manze, was born well beyond the sound of Bow Bells – in the southern Italian hill town of Ravello – and his grandson, Geoff, admits a liking for curry, ubiquitous in nearby Brick Lane. The Manze's menu, unchanged in generations, makes bald reading: "pies, mash, eels, teas, sarsaparilla", the latter a drink made of a plant from the West Indies, a taste of another world in which London indulged.

TO MARKET
As well as being popular with dockers, pie and mash shops also found favour with stall holders at London's great markets – Billingsgate, for fish, Covent Garden, for vegetables, Smithfield, for meat. Ian Nairn, the great chronicler of London, whose book *Nairn's London*, though 40 years old, remains the best guide to the city's temper, wrote of the dual function of the capital's markets: "London can't do without buying it, and the counties can't do without selling it." A visit to the new Billingsgate and Covent Garden markets, now tucked away in the appendix of Docklands, remain fascinating experiences, though one will need to rise early to catch the action.

But it is to Southwark one must go to witness a more revealing aspect of the changing face of Britain's food culture. There one finds Borough Market, a celebrated foodie heaven. It takes place on the site of one of the oldest settlements in London, close to Shakespeare's Globe theatre. Mention of a 'Borough' market dates back to 1276, and this is

where London's ancient market traditions meet the new revolution in British food. It does have its critics, however. It is overwhelmingly a middle-class phenomenon, a snap shot of the capital's chattering classes at play.

Southwark was the destination of Kentish men, whose county's low rainfall and mild climate conspired to make it 'the garden of England'. Some of Britain's most famous fruits originated in Kent, including the archetypal English apple, the Cox's Orange Pippin, as well as the Bramley's. Pears abound too, and the Romans introduced cherries like the Morello and Kentish Red. They also introduced hops, so we owe a debt to Latin Europe for warm English bitter. Through the 19th and much of the 20th century, every September, as the hop picking season began, thousands of working class Londoners would head south, escaping the polluted air for the freshness of Kent, where they would provide casual labour for the hop growers.

London's Borough Market brings together under one roof and a few side streets some of the country's, and the world's, finest artisanal producers.

A NATIONAL TREASURE

There is more to the rural South East than orchards and oast houses. Further south, on the Kent/Sussex border, lies Romney Marsh, one of the most beautifully desolate landscapes in England, where the 800-year-old church of St Mary in the Marsh stands in eerie isolation. The 2500-hectare flatland is famous for its sheep, a longwool breed noted for its salty flesh. At the edge of the marsh, on the coast where smugglers once swapped wool for French brandy, Dungeness nuclear power station casts its shadow on an English Channel famed for fish like dab, halibut (a favourite of that most distinguished of all immigrants, novelist Joseph Conrad), turbot and, above all, the aristocratic Dover sole, a fish that, grilled with a little butter, even a fool could make a feast of, a treasure from the very edge of the realm.

10

GARY RHODES

When a 13-year-old Gary Rhodes made a Sunday roast for his family, followed by a steamed lemon sponge pudding from a recipe by Marguerite Patten, he knew the path his life should take. "I felt like the lord of the manor," he recalls. "That was it. I wanted to cook." After training at Thanet technical college, he became commis chef at the Amsterdam Hilton and a sous chef at the Reform Club before developing his abiding passion for British food at the Castle Hotel, Taunton, where he retained, at the age of 26, its Michelin star. Another star followed when he became head chef at Mayfair's Greenhouse Restaurant. Alongside his broadcasting career, he also managed to pick up another two stars at City Rhodes and Rhodes in the Square.

His passionate commitment to British produce is especially evident at Rhodes Twenty Four, located in the City of London's tallest building, where dishes like braised oxtail and bread and butter pudding are regular fixtures. "At Rhodes Twenty Four, we keep as close to the seasons as possible," he says. "Around 80 per cent of our produce is British. I'm very much for the return of the local greengrocer but you must give supermarkets some credit for the way they've introduced the public to a wider range of tastes."

To introduce seasonality back into the high street, Rhodes suggests that the first line of every supermarket should have a certain amount of local produce. "That way we would be supporting the nation's produce."

MENU ONE
> Cured Salmon with Sweet Citrus Asparagus and Dill Hollandaise
> Buttered Turbot with Leeks and Whitstable Champagne Oysters
> Roast Duck with Crispy Duck Hash and Beer Gravy, Spring Greens and Orange Curd Carrots
> Kentish Apple Mousse with Toasted Honey Syrup Apples

MENU TWO
> English Salad Plate
> Seared Red Mullet with Rosemary-scented Mussels
> Slow Roast Pork with Kentish Apple Tart, Leeks and Cauliflower Cream
> Strawberry Champagne Trifle

ATUL KOCHHAR

Born in the city of Jamshedpur in eastern India, and trained in the kitchens of New Delhi's prestigious Oberoi Hotel, Atul Kochhar came to London in 1994 and, as head chef at Tamarind, became the first Indian to gain a Michelin star. In 2003, he remained in London's Mayfair to open Benares, named in honour of India's great spiritual centre on the banks of the Ganges. Kochhar's menu is a genuinely all-Indian experience, influenced by the remarkably diverse regional styles of the sub-continent.

What is remarkable is that, to any lover of Indian food, many of the dishes will be – at least in name – familiar from Britain's traditional Indian restaurants. Kochhar's Murg Makhani is his take on chicken tikka, arguably Britain's most popular dish, and classics like rogan josh, lamb braised in cinnamon, ginger and chilli, are fixtures of every high street tandoori. It's just that Kochhar's spicing of the curries is so much more subtle, the fish stews are so much more delicate, and the pilau rice is so much more airy and fluffy.

An acknowledged master of spice, Kochhar returns again and again to his homeland to research new dishes. The result, served within the opulent surroundings of his Berkeley Square restaurant, is Indian food at its most authentic.

MENU ONE
> Crisp Soft Shell Crab, Crab Salad and Tandoor Smoked Salmon Mousse with Kumquat and Spicy Plum Chutneys
> Sea Bass in Coconut Milk and Ginger Sauce with Curry Leaf Potatoes, topped with Asparagus Cress
> Tandoori Chicken with Black Lentil Sauce and Herb Pulao, Mango-Apple-Rocket Salad and Peshawari Naan
> Passion Fruit Bhapa Doi with Dark Chocolate Mousse and Pistachio Kulfi

MENU TWO
> Lobster Ke Panje
  (Tandoori Lobster Claws with Aubergine Fritters and Pear Chutney)
> Hari Machchi
  (Pan-Fried John Dory Marinated in Green Spice Paste with Oven-roasted Baby Tomatoes)
> Murg ki Biryani
  (Chicken Cooked with Rice)
> White Chocolate Mousse with Red Raspberry Coulis

12

CURED SALMON
WITH SWEET CITRUS ASPARAGUS
AND DILL HOLLANDAISE

SERVES 4
450g salmon fillet (preferably middle cut)
25g coarse sea salt
25g caster sugar
1 tsp crushed white peppercorns
finely grated zest of 1 lemon
salt and pepper

SWEET CITRUS DRESSING
50g caster sugar
juice of 2 lemons
strip of lemon zest
1 star anise
1 stick lemongrass, finely chopped
150ml olive oil

DILL HOLLANDAISE
2 tbsp white wine vinegar
2 tsp caster sugar
175g unsalted butter
2 egg yolks
juice of 1 lemon
2 tsp Dijon mustard
2 tbsp chopped dill

ASPARAGUS
8 asparagus spears, peeled
handful of watercress sprigs

1 Lay the salmon fillet skin side down on a large sheet of cling film. Remove any pin bones. Mix together the salt, sugar, pepper and lemon zest until well combined. Spread over the salmon, then wrap it in the cling film. Place the salmon on a tray, salted side up. Put another tray on top and place a weight on this roughly equal to the weight of the salmon. Refrigerate for 24 hours to complete the curing process: the salt and sugar will dissolve into the salmon, leaving a 'cooked' finish.

2 To make the sweet citrus dressing, boil together the sugar and 50ml water. Once the sugar has dissolved, add the lemon juice and zest, star anise and lemongrass. Simmer the syrup for several minutes. Remove from the heat and leave to infuse for several hours. Then strain and whisk in the olive oil and seasoning to taste. (This makes about 150ml; it can be kept in an airtight jar in the fridge for several weeks.)

3 For the hollandaise, rapidly simmer the vinegar and sugar until reduced by half. Set aside. Melt the butter in a saucepan and simmer for 2 minutes; cool until warm. It will separate into milky white solids at the bottom and clear clarified butter on top.

4 Place the yolks, lemon juice and 2 tbsp water in a blender and blend briefly. While blending, slowly add the warm clarified butter to make a thick, creamy consistency. Whisk in the reduced vinegar, mustard, dill and seasoning. Keep warm.

5 Plunge the asparagus into a pan of boiling salted water and cook until just tender. Drain and refresh quickly in iced water. Cut each spear into four or five pieces.

6 To serve, unwrap the salmon and wipe off any lemon zest, then cut into 12 slices. Season the asparagus and watercress with salt, pepper and a little citrus dressing. Arrange the salad and salmon on the plates. Add a small dish of hollandaise to each.

BUTTERED TURBOT
WITH LEEKS AND WHITSTABLE CHAMPAGNE OYSTERS

SERVES 4

8 oysters
1 shallot, shredded
200ml Champagne
2 tbsp double cream
100g butter
squeeze of lemon juice
4 portions of turbot fillet, each 75–100g,
   skinned

1 large or 2 small leeks, finely
   shredded
1 heaped tbsp chopped chervil
salt and pepper

1 First open the oysters, saving all the juices. In a small saucepan, gently warm the oysters in their juices for a minute or two, then remove from the heat.

2 Put the shallot and Champagne into a saucepan, bring to the boil and reduce by half. Strain the oyster juices into the pan and continue to boil until once again reduced by half.

3 Add the cream and, once simmering, whisk in 75g of the butter, in small pieces, a few at a time. Finish with a squeeze of lemon juice and a seasoning of salt and pepper. Keep the sauce to one side.

4 Divide the remaining butter between two frying pans. Once sizzling, place the turbot in one pan and the shredded leeks in the other. Season both with salt and pepper. Gently fry both for a few minutes, allowing the turbot to take on a light golden colour before turning, and softening the leeks.

5 Warm the sauce, adding the oysters and chervil.

6 To serve, divide the leeks among four bowls and add an oyster to each. Place the turbot on top and finish with a second oyster, then spoon the sauce over.

Illustrated overleaf

ROAST DUCK
WITH CRISPY DUCK HASH AND BEER GRAVY
SPRING GREENS AND ORANGE CURD CARROTS

SERVES 4
4 ducks
goose fat (optional)
salt and pepper

BEER GRAVY
groundnut oil
2 large onions, sliced
1 tbsp brown sugar (preferably Muscovado)
250ml beer (preferably Shepherd Neame 'Spitfire')
300ml chicken stock
200ml veal or beef gravy/glace or canned beef consommé

CRISPY DUCK HASH
50g shallots, finely chopped
olive oil
3 large baking potatoes, baked until cooked
2 knobs of butter

ORANGE CURD CARROTS
675g carrots, thickly sliced or cut into barrel shapes
2 tbsp orange curd
knob of butter

SPRING GREENS
450g spring greens, stalks removed and leaves torn into pieces
large knob of butter

1 Preheat the oven to 150°C/gas 2. Remove the legs from the ducks and place in a roasting tin. Slow roast for 1–1 1/2 hours or until completely tender. (Alternatively, for a richer flavour, submerge the duck legs in goose fat before roasting them for 1 1/2–2 hours.) Remove the meat from the leg bones, discarding any skin and fat, and keep to one side for the hash.

2 Chop away the central leg carcass from each bird, leaving the two breasts attached to the breast bone. Reserve the breasts.

3 To make the beer gravy, trim all fat from the carcasses, then chop them and roast in some groundnut oil in a saucepan until well coloured. Add the sliced onions and continue to fry over a moderate heat to a rich golden brown. Stir in the sugar, then pour the beer on top. Bring to the boil and reduce by three-quarters before adding the chicken stock. Continue to boil until reduced by half.

4 Add the veal or beef gravy (if using consommé, you will need to thicken the sauce with cornflour once it is completed). Bring back to a simmer, then cook for a further 30 minutes, skimming off any excess fat. Strain. Should the gravy be too thin, simply boil to a sauce consistency, but take care not to allow the flavour to become too strong. Set aside. (The gravy can be made well in advance and refrigerated until needed.) Reheat for serving.

5 To cook the duck breasts, preheat the oven to 200°C/gas 6. Gently begin to fry the

Buttered turbot (recipe on page 13)

duck breasts, skin side down, on top of the stove. As they fry the fat will melt away, leaving a thinner and crisper finish. Continue to fry for 10–15 minutes or until all the breasts are a rich, golden brown colour. Turn skin side up and place in the oven to finish cooking for 6–10 minutes, depending on the size of the breasts. Once roasted, allow to rest in a warm place.

6 While the breasts are cooking, make the duck hash. Sweat the chopped shallots in a little olive oil until tender. Scoop the potato flesh from the skins and mix it with the cooked shallots and duck leg meat. Season with salt and pepper.

7 Divide the duck hash into four portions and press into buttered rectangular or round moulds to shape; or simply shape into cakes with your hands. Melt the butter in an ovenproof pan and pan fry the hash until golden brown on the base. Turn over and transfer the pan to the oven. Roast for 8–10 minutes or until warmed through and with a crispy edge.

8 Meanwhile, prepare the orange curd carrots. Cook the carrots in boiling salted water until tender. Drain off most of the water, leaving a few tbsp in the pan. Set aside. Just before serving, add the orange curd and butter and heat, stirring gently, until they are completely melted and each slice of carrot is glazed. Season to taste with salt and pepper.

9 While the carrots are cooking, plunge the spring greens into a large pan of boiling water and cook for a few minutes until tender. Drain well. Place the butter in the pan in which you cooked the greens. Once the butter has melted, stir in the spring greens and season with salt and pepper.

10 To serve, remove the duck breasts from the bone and cut each into three or four slices. Place the duck hash towards the top of each warm plate, with the carrots and spring greens on either side beneath. Arrange the duck breasts on top of the greens and offer the gravy separately.

Kent's reputation for fine apples and other fruits was sown when Richard Harries, Henry VIII's fruiterer, planted the first pippins at Teynham in 1533. London provided an eager, insatiable market.

KENTISH APPLE MOUSSE
WITH TOASTED HONEY SYRUP APPLES

SERVES 4-6

ALMOND SPONGE BASE
75g unsalted butter, diced
75g caster sugar
75g ground almonds
2 tbsp plain flour
1 egg

ITALIAN MERINGUE
175g caster sugar
15g liquid glucose
3 egg whites

MOUSSE
4 large apples, peeled, cored and diced
butter
200ml apple juice
50ml Calvados
3 egg yolks
20g caster sugar
2 gelatine leaves, soaked in cold water
    for at least 10 minutes
150ml whipping cream, whipped to a soft peak

JELLY TOPPING
200ml sweet wine
75ml orange juice
juice of ½ lemon
75g caster sugar
1 whole clove
2 English apples, chopped
gelatine leaves (see method)

TOASTED HONEY SYRUP APPLES
300ml sweet cider
2 apples
squeeze of lemon juice
Demerara or caster sugar to glaze
50g raisins
75g clear honey

1 Preheat the oven to 180°C/gas 4. Butter a 20cm loose-bottomed cake tin and line the bottom with baking parchment.

2 First make the almond sponge. In a food processor blend together all of the ingredients until thoroughly mixed. Spread the mixture in the bottom of the cake tin. Bake for 9–10 minutes or until the sponge is firm to the touch. Remove from the oven and leave to cool.

3 Next make the Italian meringue for the mousse. Bring the sugar, glucose and 50ml water to the boil and boil until the syrup reaches the thread stage (110°C on a sugar thermometer). At this point, whisk the egg whites in an electric mixer until firm. As soon as the syrup reaches the hard ball stage (118–120°C), remove the pan from the heat. Turn the mixer to its lowest speed, then pour the syrup into the egg whites in a thin stream. Once all the syrup has been added, continue to whisk the meringue until only just warm. Reserve. (This will make twice as much meringue as you need for the mousse; divide the remainder and bake in a low oven until crisp outside with a soft centre.)

4 For the mousse, cook the diced apples gently in a little butter until softened, then purée in a blender or food processor until completely smooth.

5 Boil the apple juice and Calvados together until reduced by half. Meanwhile, in an electric mixer, whisk the egg yolks and sugar together to a creamy ribbon stage. Pour on the hot apple juice while whisking, then return the mixture to the saucepan. Cook gently, stirring constantly, until thick enough to coat the back of the spoon. It is important the custard does not boil. Remove from the heat.

6 Squeeze dry the gelatine leaves, then add to the custard and stir until completely melted. Cool until just warm, then stir in the apple purée. Fold in 100g of the Italian meringue and the softly whipped cream. Spoon the mousse into the cake tin and smooth the top. Chill in the fridge to set.

7 To make the jelly, put the wine, orange juice, lemon juice, sugar, clove and chopped apples in a pan and simmer until the apples have softened. Strain through a sieve and measure the finished quantity of liquor; you need 1 gelatine leaf for every 100ml liquor. Soak the gelatine in cold water for 10 minutes, then gently squeeze dry and add to the pan. Stir until completely melted. Leave to cool. Once the mousse has set, pour the cold jelly on top, then return to the fridge to set the jelly.

8 For the toasted honey syrup apples, pour the cider into a saucepan and bring to the boil. Meanwhile, peel, halve and core the apples, then cut each half into three or four wedges. Squeeze the lemon juice over the apples to prevent them from discolouring. Add the apples to the cider and bring back to a simmer. Cook for 1–2 minutes or until tender. Remove the apples from the pan and keep to one side. When needed, dip one side of each wedge in sugar and glaze to a rich golden brown under a preheated grill or with a blow torch.

9 Add the raisins and honey to the cider, return to the boil and reduce to a syrup consistency. Pass through a sieve, pushing through all the juices from the raisins. Allow to cool before serving.

10 Loosen the mousse from the tin by quickly blasting a blow torch around the sides or pressing and moving a warmed knife between the mousse and tin. Ease the ring away from the bottom of the tin.

11 To serve, cut the mousse into wedges and place on the plates with the toasted apples side by side. Drizzle the apples with the honey syrup.

ENGLISH SALAD PLATE

SERVES 4

BEETROOT DRESSING
200ml ruby Port
2 tbsp red wine vinegar
1 medium raw beetroot, peeled and
    finely grated
50ml groundnut oil
50ml walnut oil
salt and pepper

BEETROOT SALAD WITH PORT
3–4 medium to large raw beetroots
50g soft goat's cheese
1 tbsp single cream or crème fraîche
    (optional)
whole or snipped chives

CELERIAC AND PEAR SALAD
1 small celeriac
1 large or 2 small pears
juice of 1 lime
2 heaped tbsp mayonnaise
1–2 tsp wholegrain mustard

BLUE CHEESE CAESAR GEM SALAD
50ml mayonnaise
100ml crème fraîche
100g blue cheese, at room temperature,
    broken into small nuggets
1 small garlic clove, crushed
1 tsp Dijon mustard
1 tsp capers
1 tbsp lemon or lime juice
2 Little Gem lettuces

GARNISH (OPTIONAL)
rocket, watercress or chives
olive or walnut oil

1 First make the beetroot dressing. Boil the ruby Port until reduced to 50ml. Whisk together the reduced Port, red wine vinegar, 2 tbsp water and the grated beetroot. Mix the two oils, then whisk them into the beetroot mixture. Season with salt and pepper. Leave to infuse while you cook the beetroots for the salad. Before using the dressing, pass it through a sieve.

2 Cook the beetroots either by boiling for 1 hour until tender, or by wrapping in foil and baking on sea salt in a preheated 180°C/gas 4 oven for up to 2 hours. Once cooked, leave to cool. Peel the beetroots and cut each into four or five slices. The slices can now be shaped into neat rounds of the same size using a round cutter. Place in a bowl, season and top with the beetroot dressing. Set aside.

3 Beat the goat's cheese until smooth. If still slightly grainy and dry, stir in the chosen cream and season with salt and pepper, if needed. Add the chives. Mould the cheese between two spoons to create four oval 'quenelle' shapes. Keep in a cool place until serving time.

4 To serve the beetroot salad, lift the beetroot slices from the dressing and layer them into four stacks, set on the plates and drizzle with a little more dressing. Place the cheese quenelles on top just before serving.

5 Next prepare the celeriac and pear salad. Peel the celeriac and thinly slice, then cut each slice into matchsticks. Peel and grate the pear, stirring in the lime juice to prevent discoloration. Mix with the celeriac and season with coarse sea salt and pepper. Mix the mayonnaise with the preferred quantity of mustard, then stir into the celeriac and pear mixture to bind. Refrigerate until required. The celeriac and pear flavour will become stronger as it rests.

6 Finally, prepare the blue cheese Caesar Gem salad. In a small food processor, blitz together all of the ingredients, except 50g of the cheese and the lettuces, until smooth. Season with a twist of pepper. The dressing can be left with a slight coarse consistency, or blitzed for a smooth finish. If too thick, whisk in water to loosen.

7 Discard the outer leaves of the lettuces and separate the remaining leaves. To serve, mix the remaining blue cheese nuggets amongst the leaves and arrange in piles on the plates. Drizzle with the dressing.

8 To assemble, arrange a portion of each salad on the four plates. Scatter rocket, watercress or chive sticks on top and finish with a trickle or two of olive or walnut oil.

Long-neglected, beetroot is now a fashionable 'superfood'. Low in fat and rich in vitamins and minerals such as zinc and iron, it even contains a compound – betaine – which is said to fight depression.

22

SEARED RED MULLET
WITH ROSEMARY-SCENTED MUSSELS

SERVES 4
200ml white wine
1 onion, sliced
a few sprigs of rosemary
1kg fresh mussels, debearded and washed
100ml double or whipping cream
squeeze of lemon juice
4 fillets of red mullet
2 tbsp olive oil
knob of butter + 25g butter, diced
salt and pepper

MASHED POTATOES (OPTIONAL)
2 large, floury potatoes, preferably
    Maris Piper, peeled and quartered
25g unsalted butter
a few tbsp single cream or milk to loosen

1 Boil together the white wine, onion and some rosemary sprigs. Add the mussels. Cover with a tight-fitting lid and cook for 4–5 minutes, shaking the pan occasionally, until the mussels have opened. Drain in a colander set over a large bowl or saucepan. Discard any mussels that have not opened. Remove the mussels from their shells and keep to one side.
2 Simmer the mussel cooking liquor, whisking in the cream with a fresh sprig of rosemary, and cook for a few minutes. Season with salt, pepper and a squeeze of lemon juice. Pass the sauce through a fine sieve or muslin cloth. Set aside.
3 If serving the fish with mashed potatoes, cook the potatoes in boiling salted water for 20–25 minutes, depending on size. When the potatoes are tender, drain off all water and replace the lid. Shake the pan vigorously, which will start to break up the boiled potatoes. Add the butter and cream or milk, a little at a time, while mashing the potatoes to a smooth consistency. Season with salt and pepper to taste. Keep hot.
4 Remove any pin bones from the mullet fillets, then season with salt and pepper. Heat the olive oil in a frying pan. Once hot, add the mullet fillets, skin side down, and fry for several minutes or until golden brown and crisp. Add the knob of butter to the pan and turn the fillets. Baste with the frothy butter, then remove from the heat and allow the fish to continue its cooking with the residual heat left in the pan.
5 Meanwhile, warm the mussel sauce, whisking in the diced butter until totally absorbed. Add the mussels to the sauce and warm gently.
6 To serve, spoon or pipe mashed potato into the centre of each warm large bowl or plate. Spoon the mussels and creamy sauce around the potatoes and arrange the red mullet fillets on top.

SLOW ROAST PORK
WITH KENTISH APPLE TART
LEEKS AND CAULIFLOWER CREAM

SERVES 4
1 piece of pork belly, 1–1.2kg
vegetable oil
coarse sea salt
salt and pepper

GRAVY
knob of butter
1 carrot, roughly diced
1 large onion, roughly diced
2 celery sticks, roughly diced
sprig of thyme
1 bay leaf
2 Bramley's apples, roughly diced
100ml Calvados (optional)
300ml chicken stock
300ml veal or beef gravy/glace
(or canned beef consommé)

APPLE TARTS
2 English onions, sliced
Demerara sugar
a few sage leaves, chopped
2 apples, peeled, halved and cored
4 puff pastry discs, each about
11cm diameter

CAULIFLOWER CREAM
1 cauliflower, cut into florets
milk to cover
25g butter
squeeze of lemon juice

SMOKY LEEKS
100g streaky smoked bacon, diced
or cut into strips
3 medium leeks, sliced or shredded
knob of butter

1 Preheat the oven to 160°C/gas 3.

2 Season the meat side of the pork belly with salt and pepper. Place the pork skin side up on a rack in a roasting tray. Brush the rind with oil and scatter coarse sea salt liberally over the top. Roast the joint for 2–2 1/2 hours or until completely tender.

3 Meanwhile, make the gravy. Melt the knob of butter in a saucepan. Once sizzling, add the chopped carrot, onion and celery along with the thyme and bay leaf. Cook over a moderate heat, stirring from time to time, until the vegetables are a rich golden brown and beginning to soften. Add the diced apples and continue to cook for 5–10 minutes.

4 Pour in the Calvados, if using, and boil until reduced by three-quarters. Add the stock and gravy (or consommé) and bring to a simmer. Leave to simmer, skimming from time to time, until reduced to about 400ml, then reserve. (If using consommé, the gravy will need to be thickened with cornflour before serving.)

5 Next make the apple tarts. Place the sliced onions in a large saucepan or frying pan with 1 tbsp of water and cook slowly on a moderate heat until softened and the natural sugars begin to caramelise the onions. To help speed up the caramelisation, you can add 1 tsp of Demerara sugar to the onions. Once at a golden caramelised stage, remove from the heat and season with salt and pepper. Allow to cool, then stir in the chopped sage.

6 Butter four 9cm non-stick moulds and dust them with Demerara sugar. Place an apple half, flat side down, in each mould. Spoon the caramelised onion on top of the apple. Cover with the puff pastry discs, ensuring they are firmly pressed in and neatly edged. Pierce the pastry with a skewer to release steam during baking. Set aside until ready to cook.

7 For the cauliflower cream, place the cauliflower florets in a saucepan with just enough milk to cover. Bring to a simmer and cook for 15–20 minutes or until the cauliflower is completely tender. Spoon the florets with just a trickle of milk into a liquidiser and blitz until smooth. Add the butter and season with salt, white pepper and lemon juice. Quickly blitz again until completely emulsified and smooth. If the cauliflower creeam is slightly grainy, simply push it through a fine sieve. Set aside in a saucepan, and reheat for serving.

8 Once the pork is cooked, remove it from the oven. Lift the joint on to a board and leave to rest in a warm place. Turn the oven up to 180°C/gas 4 and bake the apple tarts for 15–20 minutes or until the pastry is golden brown. When baked, allow to rest for about 30 seconds before removing from the moulds.

9 While baking the tarts, prepare the smoky leeks. Warm a large frying pan or wok, then add the streaky bacon and fry over a moderate heat until just beginning to colour, leaving the pieces tender. Add the leeks and butter, and season with a twist of pepper. Stir the leeks for several minutes until softened. Remove from the heat and set aside. Reheat for serving.

10 Pour away any fat from the roasting tray and place it over a moderate heat. Add the gravy. This will now collect any residue, adding a natural pork edge. Simmer for several minutes, stirring well, then pass through a fine sieve. Keep hot.

11 To serve, cut the rind from the joint, cutting or breaking it into crisp bites. Carve the pork into slices or four large pieces. Arrange the pork, apple tarts and smoky leeks on the warm plates, and offer the cauliflower cream and gravy separately.

STRAWBERRY CHAMPAGNE TRIFLE

26

SERVES 4
3–4 punnets of early season English
   strawberries
100–150ml double cream, whipped
   to a soft peak, to serve

SPONGE BASE
3 eggs
100g caster sugar
1 tsp honey
125g plain flour, sifted
2 tsp baking powder
125g butter, melted and cooled
strawberry jam

CHAMPAGNE JELLY
175g sugar
300ml Champagne or sparkling wine
strip of lemon zest
strip of orange zest
5 gelatine leaves, soaked in cold water
   for at least 10 minutes

VANILLA CUSTARD
100g custard powder
1.2 litres milk
3 vanilla pods, split lengthways,
   or 1 tbsp vanilla essence
50g caster sugar

1 Preheat the oven to 180°C/gas 4.

2 First make the sponge base. In an electric mixer, whisk together the eggs, sugar and honey to a thick creamy consistency. Gently fold in the flour and baking powder, followed by the melted butter. Divide the mixture between two greased 18–20cm sponge tins lined with baking parchment, spreading evenly. Bake for 6–8 minutes or until firm with a spongy finish. Remove from the oven and leave to cool.

3 Once cold, sandwich the two sponge layers with strawberry jam and press into a 2 litre glass serving bowl.

4 To make the Champagne jelly, boil 200ml water with the sugar for a few minutes, then add the Champagne and lemon and orange zests. Simmer for a few more minutes, then remove from the heat. Gently squeeze dry the soaked gelatine, then stir into the liquid until completely melted. Leave to cool before passing through a sieve. Chill in the fridge to a thick pouring consistency.

5 Trim the strawberries, then lay them side by side on top of the sponge. Pour half of the jelly over the berries and refrigerate to set before topping with the remaining jelly. Return to the fridge to set.

6 For the custard, in a bowl mix the custard powder with enough of the milk to loosen. Put the remainder of the milk in a saucepan and scrape in the seeds from the vanilla pods. Add the pods too. Bring just to the boil, then pour a little of the hot milk on to the loosened custard powder, whisking constantly. Pour this mixture back into the pan and continue to whisk as the custard comes to the boil. At this point, add the sugar and simmer for a few minutes before straining into a bowl or jug. Cover closely with greaseproof paper or cling film and leave to cool.

7 Pour the custard on top of the set Champagne jelly and refrigerate to set.

8 When serving, top each portion with a dollop of whipped cream.

CRISP SOFT SHELL CRAB
CRAB SALAD AND TANDOOR SMOKED SALMON MOUSSE WITH KUMQUAT AND SPICY PLUM CHUTNEYS

SERVES 4

KUMQUAT CHUTNEY

100g kumquats, sliced

30g palm sugar

20ml white vinegar

½ tsp toasted cumin seeds

½ tsp toasted coriander seeds, crushed

1 red chilli

1 tsp melon seeds

salt

SPICY PLUM CHUTNEY

1kg red plums, stoned and roughly chopped

300g brown or palm sugar

500ml red wine vinegar

3 star anise

½ tsp garam masala

1 dried red chilli

½ tsp crushed black peppercorns

MARINADE FOR SALMON

20 garlic cloves, peeled

small bunch of coriander leaves

knob of fresh ginger, lightly crushed

4–5 lime leaves

1 tbsp grated lime zest

2 tbsp lime juice

1 tbsp red chilli powder

½ tbsp garam masala

50ml vegetable oil

1 tbsp gram flour

100g plain yoghurt

SALMON MOUSSE

400g salmon fillet with skin, cut into
    4cm cubes

knob of butter for smoking (optional)

2 tbsp melted butter for basting

2 tbsp single cream

1 tbsp set plain yoghurt

1 tbsp chopped mint leaves

1 lime leaf, finely chopped

1 tsp finely chopped fresh ginger

1 tsp lime juice

¼ tsp garam masala

SOFT SHELL CRAB FRITTERS

½ tbsp ginger-garlic paste

1 tsp ground turmeric

1 tsp ground coriander

½ tsp red chilli powder

1 tbsp finely chopped fresh ginger

2 tbsp chopped coriander leaves

1 tbsp lime juice

2 tbsp rice flour

4 small soft shell crabs

vegetable oil for deep frying

CRAB SALAD

3 tbsp vegetable oil or coconut oil

1 ½ tsp mustard seeds

10 curry leaves, chopped

1 tsp chopped fresh ginger

½ tsp chopped green chilli

100g chopped onions

300g white crab meat, flaked

1 tsp ground turmeric

3 tbsp coconut milk

1 tsp chopped coriander leaves

1 tbsp freshly grated coconut or
    desiccated coconut

GARNISH

mustard cress

julienne of plums tossed in oil

1 First make the kumquat chutney. Heat all the ingredients together with 1 tsp salt and cook to a thick chutney-like consistency, stirring from time to time. Remove from the heat and allow to cool.

2 Next make the plum chutney. Heat all the ingredients with 1 tsp salt and simmer for 30 minutes or until the plums are soft. Pass through a fine sieve. (This makes more chutney than you need for 4 servings; the remainder can be kept in the fridge for up to 3 months.) Warm through before serving.

3 To make the marinade for the salmon, blend together the garlic, coriander, ginger, lime leaves, lime zest and juice, the spices and 1/2 tbsp salt to make a fine paste. Heat the oil in a pan, add the gram flour and cook, stirring, to make a roux, without burning. Allow to cool, then mix the spice paste and roux with the yoghurt. Add the cubes of salmon, turning them to coat all over, then leave to marinate for 1 hour.

4 To prepare the soft shell crabs, mix together the spices, herbs, lime juice and rice flour, then marinate the crabs for 30 minutes.

5 While the salmon and crabs are marinating, make the crab salad. Heat the oil in a heavy-bottomed pan and sauté the mustard seeds until they splutter. Add the curry leaves and sauté, then stir in the ginger and green chilli. Add the chopped onions and sauté until translucent. Add the crab meat with the turmeric and 3/4 tsp salt and sauté for 2 minutes, then mix in the coconut milk, coriander and coconut. Remove from the heat and set aside to cool.

6 If you want to smoke the salmon before cooking it, you can use a special smoker, if you have one, or fashion a makeshift smoker with a deep bowl or saucepan that has a tight-fitting lid. Put the salmon in the bowl or pan and set a small metal bowl of burning charcoal in the middle. Drop a knob of butter on the charcoal and put on the lid so that no smoke can escape. Leave to smoke for 30–40 minutes. Remove the charcoal bowl and discard.

7 Preheat the oven to 200°C/gas 6 or the grill to high.

8 Cook the salmon in the oven or under the grill for 10–15 minutes, basting once or twice with melted butter to keep the fish moist. Allow to cool to room temperature. Remove the skin from the salmon and break up the flesh with a fork.

9 To finish the salmon mousse, whisk together the remaining ingredients, then lightly mix in the salmon. Keep in the fridge until required.

10 Just before serving, cook the soft shell crabs. Heat oil in a wok to 180°C, then deep fry the crabs until they are crisp and golden brown on both sides. Remove and drain on kitchen paper.

11 To serve, use rectangular plates if possible. Place a quenelle of salmon mousse, a neat mound of crab salad (shaped in a 4cm metal ring) and a crisp soft shell crab in a line on each plate. Drizzle the warm plum chutney on the plate and spoon the kumquat chutney near the salad. Garnish the plate with mustard cress and plums.

SEA BASS IN COCONUT MILK

AND GINGER SAUCE WITH CURRY LEAF POTATOES
TOPPED WITH ASPARAGUS CRESS

SERVES 4

4 small fillets of sea bass or sea bream,
  each 80-100g
vegetable oil
salt and pepper

COCONUT AND GINGER SAUCE

1 tbsp coconut or vegetable oil
¼ tsp mustard seeds
10 curry leaves
1 tsp finely chopped fresh ginger
3 garlic cloves, sliced into fine strips
2 green chillies, slit lengthways
2 onions, finely sliced
1 ½ tsp ground turmeric
1 tsp ground coriander
¼ tsp ground black pepper

2 tbsp freshly prepared tamarind extract
  (made by soaking tamarind slab in
  water and passing through a sieve)
400ml coconut milk

CURRY LEAF POTATOES

200g Jersey Royal potatoes, peeled
1 tbsp vegetable oil
¼ tsp finely chopped fresh ginger
¼ tsp black gram lentil
¼ tsp mustard seeds
10 curry leaves, deep fried and crushed
1 tbsp finely chopped coriander leaves

ASPARAGUS CRESS SALAD

asparagus cress
mustard cress
coriander cress
curry leaf oil (see page 35)

1 First make the sauce. Heat the oil in a flat pan and sauté the mustard seeds
and curry leaves until they splutter. Add the ginger, garlic, green chillies and sliced
onions and sauté until the onions are translucent. Reduce the heat to low and stir
in the ground spices. Pour in 120ml water and add the tamarind extract. Once the
sauce comes to a simmer, add the coconut milk and 1 ½ tsp salt. Simmer until the
sauce is thick. Remove from the heat and set aside. Reheat for serving.

2 Cook the potatoes in boiling salted water until just tender; drain. Heat the oil and
sauté the ginger, gram lentil and mustard seeds until spluttering. Add the potatoes
and stir well to mix, crushing them roughly, then add the curry leaves and ½ tsp
salt. Cook for a further 2–3 minutes. Remove from the heat and keep warm. Add
the chopped coriander just before serving.

3 Pan fry the fish in some hot oil, making the skin very crisp.

4 Meanwhile, mix all the cresses together and dress with a little curry leaf oil.

5 To serve, place the potatoes in the centre of the warm plates and spoon the sauce
around them. Place the fish on top of the potatoes and garnish with the cress salad.
Drizzle with a little more curry leaf oil.

TANDOORI CHICKEN
WITH BLACK LENTIL SAUCE AND HERB PULAO
MANGO-APPLE-ROCKET SALAD AND PESHAWARI NAAN

SERVES 4
4 chicken breasts on the bone, skin removed
mixture of melted butter and oil for basting
1 ½ tsp lime juice
1 tsp chaat masala
salt
4 Peshawari naan to serve

FIRST MARINADE
1 tbsp ginger-garlic paste
1 tsp red chilli powder
2 tbsp lemon juice

SECOND MARINADE
250g thick plain yoghurt
1 tsp garam masala
100ml vegetable oil
½ tsp ground cinnamon
½ tsp red chilli powder
a pinch of edible red colouring (optional)

BLACK LENTIL SAUCE
200g black lentils
4 tbsp vegetable oil
1 tbsp finely chopped fresh ginger
2 garlic cloves, peeled
2 green chillies
1 tsp cumin seeds
1 tbsp ginger-garlic paste

½ green chilli, chopped
2 tbsp tomato paste
½ tsp each red chilli powder, ground
    coriander, ground turmeric, garam
    masala and fenugreek leaf powder
30g butter
2 tbsp single cream
1 tbsp chopped coriander leaves

HERB PULAO
15g butter
2 tsp vegetable oil
100g sliced onions
2.5cm cinnamon stick
2 black cardamoms
1 blade mace
500g Basmati rice, washed and soaked
    for 10–20 minutes
3–4 tbsp puréed spinach, coriander
    and mint
2 tbsp mascarpone cheese or cream

MANGO-APPLE-ROCKET SALAD
20g baby rocket leaves
1 Granny Smith apple, cut into julienne
1 green mango, cut into julienne
vinaigrette made with lime juice

1 Make three or four deep incisions in each chicken breast, without cutting all the way through. Mix together the ingredients for the first marinade with 1 tsp salt. Rub all over the breasts, then leave in the fridge for 20 minutes so the juices can drain.
2 Mix the ingredients for the second marinade with 1 tsp salt. Add the chicken and turn to coat, then leave in a cool place for 2–3 hours.
3 Meanwhile, make the black lentil sauce. Put the lentils, 2 tbsp oil, the ginger, garlic and whole chillies in a pan and cover with water. Bring to the boil, then simmer gently until the lentils are soft. Discard the garlic and chillies.
4 Prepare the seasoning by sautéing the cumin seeds, ginger-garlic paste and chopped chilli in the remaining oil until soft. Stir in the tomato paste and spices.

5 Add the cooked lentils to the seasoning and simmer for 10–15 minutes. Add the butter, cream and coriander with salt to taste. Blend with a hand blender to give a sauce consistency. Set aside, and reheat for serving.

6 Preheat a tandoor until moderately hot or preheat the oven to 200°C/gas 6.

7 Next make the pulao. Heat the butter and oil in a saucepan and fry the onions with the cinnamon, cardamom and mace until golden brown. Add the rice and 1 litre of water with 1 tsp salt. Bring to the boil, then cover the pan tightly and cook until the rice is tender and all liquid has been absorbed. Add the spinach purée and cheese or cream just before serving.

8 While the rice is cooking, skewer the chicken breasts and cook in the tandoor for 10 minutes. If using an oven, place the breasts on a non-stick baking tray and cook for 3 minutes; reduce the oven heat to 160°C/gas 3 and cook for a further 15 minutes.

9 Baste the chicken breasts with the butter and oil mixture and cook for a further 5 minutes. Remove from the tandoor or oven, baste the chicken again and sprinkle with the lime juice and chaat masala. Keep hot.

10 Toss all the ingredients for the salad together.

11 To serve, ladle the sauce on to four large round plates and spread out to cover. Place a large quenelle of herb pulao in the centre of each plate, set a tandoori chicken breast on the rice and garnish with the rocket and mango salad. Serve with naan.

PASSION FRUIT BHAPA DOI
WITH DARK CHOCOLATE MOUSSE AND PISTACHIO KULFI

SERVES 4

PISTACHIO KULFI
200ml milk
good pinch of ground cardamom
40g granulated sugar
30g pistachio nuts, lightly toasted and ground
2–3 drops screwpine flower essence

BHAPA DOI
150ml condensed milk
200g plain Greek yoghurt
30ml passion fruit purée (sieved pulp)
2 passion fruits, cut in half and pulp scooped out
raspberry coulis
raspberries

DARK CHOCOLATE MOUSSE
125g dark chocolate (55% cocoa)
60g egg yolks
280ml double cream
30g ground pistachio nuts
20ml Cointreau or other orange liqueur

PASSION FRUIT CHUTNEY
200ml passion fruit purée (sieved pulp)
60g palm sugar
3/4 tsp crushed red chillies
1 tsp salt
1/4 tsp cornflour mixed with water
1/2 tsp lime juice

1 First make the pistachio kulfi. Put the milk and cardamom in a heavy-bottomed saucepan and bring to the boil, then turn down the heat. Reduce the milk, stirring constantly, until it is about one-third of the original quantity and has a granular consistency. Remove from the heat, add the sugar and toasted nuts and mix well. Return to a low heat and stir until the sugar has dissolved. Allow the mixture to cool, then stir in the essence. Chill in the refrigerator.

2 Churn in an ice cream machine for 30–45 minutes or until softly set (this will produce a good texture), then spoon into two 8cm conical moulds (or four smaller moulds) and freeze until firm. Alternatively, just spoon the mixture into conical moulds and freeze it.

3 Preheat the oven to 140°C/gas 1.

4 Next make the bhapa doi. Whisk the condensed milk and yoghurt with the passion fruit purée, mixing well. Line four ramekins with muffin papers and spoon some passion fruit pulp into each. Pour in the yoghurt mixture.

5 Set the ramekins in a baking tray and pour enough hot water into the tray to come one-quarter of the way up the sides of the ramekins. Place the tray in the oven and bake for 30–40 minutes. Remove the ramekins from the tray and allow to cool, then place in the refrigerator to chill.

6 To make the mousse, melt the chocolate in a heatproof bowl set over a pan of simmering water. Remove the bowl and stir the chocolate until smooth, then set aside. Set another bowl with the egg yolks on the pan of hot water and whisk to a ribbon consistency. Remove from the pan of hot water.

7 Whip the double cream to soft peaks, then fold in the melted chocolate and whisked egg yolks. Mix in the ground pistachios and liqueur. Leave to set in the refrigerator for 2–3 hours.

8 For the passion fruit chutney, heat together the passion fruit purée, sugar, chilli flakes and salt. Reduce to three-quarters of the original quantity. Add the cornflour and stir until thickened. Remove from the heat and allow to cool, then add the lime juice. Chill before serving.

9 To serve, turn out the bhapa doi on to four square plates and peel off the muffin papers. Turn out a kulfi (or half of a larger kulfi) alongside and add a large quenelle or ball of mousse. Drizzle with raspberry coulis and passion fruit chutney. Finish each plate with 3–5 raspberries on the bhapa doi.

34

LOBSTER KE PANJE
TANDOORI LOBSTER CLAWS WITH
AUBERGINE FRITTERS AND PEAR CHUTNEY

SERVES 4
4 large lobster claws
mixture of vegetable oil and melted butter
chaat masala to sprinkle
1 tbsp finely chopped coriander leaves
½ tsp lime juice
coarsely crushed Szechuan pepper
salt

PEAR CHUTNEY
3 large pears, peeled, cored and sliced
1 large cooking apple, peeled, cored and sliced
1 tbsp raisins
1 small cinnamon stick
¼ tsp black peppercorns
½ tsp five spice powder
75g brown sugar
75ml rice wine vinegar

AUBERGINE FRITTERS
2 tbsp gram flour
¼ tsp each toasted cumin seeds, red
   chilli powder, garam masala, chaat
   masala and fenugreek leaf powder
½ tsp finely chopped fresh ginger
1 tbsp finely chopped coriander leaves
vegetable oil for deep frying
2 small, round baby aubergines

MARINADE
100g plain yoghurt
½ tsp each lightly toasted ajwain seeds,
   ginger-garlic paste and garam masala
¼ tsp each ground coriander, ground
   cinnamon and red chilli powder
50ml vegetable oil
1 tsp finely chopped fresh ginger

1 First make the chutney. Place all the ingredients in a pan with ¼ tsp salt and cook on a moderate heat for 30–40 minutes or until the pears and apple are reduced to a mushy consistency. Remove from the heat and leave to cool.

2 Next make the fritter batter. Mix together the gram flour, spices, coriander and ¼ tsp salt with enough water to make a dropping consistency. Set aside.

3 To prepare the lobster, wash well in running water and crack the shells lightly with a small hammer. Whisk together all the ingredients for the marinade with ¼ tsp salt and rub it on to the cracked lobster claws. Leave to marinate for 5–10 minutes.

4 Preheat a tandoor to hot or preheat the oven to 180°C/gas 4. Also heat oil for deep frying in a deep pan or wok to 180–190°C.

5 Skewer the lobster claws and cook in the tandoor for 3–4 minutes; baste with oil and butter, then cook for further 3 minutes. If cooking in the oven, place on a baking tray and cook for 2 minutes; turn over, baste and cook for another 2 minutes.

6 For the aubergine fritters, cut each aubergine into four wedges. Dip in the batter to coat well, then drop into the hot oil and fry until light golden and the aubergine is well cooked. Drain on kitchen paper.

7 To serve, place a lobster claw on each plate (rectangular if possible) and sprinkle with chaat masala, chopped coriander and lime juice. Arrange two aubergine fritters on each plate and add a spoonful of pear chutney. Sprinkle with Szechuan pepper.

HARI MACHCHI
PAN-FRIED JOHN DORY MARINATED IN GREEN SPICE PASTE WITH OVEN-ROASTED BABY TOMATOES

SERVES 4
4 fillets of john dory
2 tbsp lemon juice
4 tbsp vegetable oil
salt and pepper

CORIANDER OIL
small bunch of coriander leaves
100ml olive oil

GREEN SPICE PASTE
50g mint leaves
50g coriander leaves
10g peeled fresh ginger
2 green chillies
1 1/2 tsp fenugreek leaf powder
2 tsp chaat masala
1 tsp red chilli powder
2 tbsp gram flour

CORIANDER-INFUSED MUSHROOMS
1 tbsp vegetable oil
2 tbsp finely chopped onion
1/2 tsp coriander seeds, lightly crushed

100g shiitake mushrooms, thinly sliced
1/4 tsp red chilli powder
1/4 tsp ground turmeric
1 tbsp finely diced tomatoes
1 tbsp finely chopped coriander leaves

OVEN-ROASTED TOMATOES
1 tbsp vegetable oil
1/2 tsp each onion seeds, cumin seeds, sesame seeds, finely chopped fresh ginger and green chilli
24–30 baby plum or cherry tomatoes on the vine, separated into 4 portions on the vine
1/4 tsp each fenugreek leaf powder, red chilli powder, ground coriander and ground turmeric
coarsely crushed black pepper

GARNISH
lemon juice
50g asparagus cress or mustard cress
12–16 sprigs of coriander

1 First make the coriander oil. Shock-blanch the coriander in boiling water, then drain and refresh. Squeeze dry in kitchen paper. Blend the coriander with the oil until smooth. Strain through a muslin cloth, then set aside. The oil can be kept in the fridge for 2 days. (You can make other herb oils in the same way.)

2 Place the fish fillets in a colander and sprinkle with the lemon juice and 1/2 tsp salt. Leave for 15 minutes to drain the excess moisture.

3 Meanwhile, make the green spice paste. Blend all the ingredients together with 1/2 tsp salt in a blender or food processor. Transfer to a shallow dish.

4 Pat the fish dry and put into the spice paste. Leave to marinate for 40 minutes.

5 Next prepare the mushrooms. Heat the oil in a pan and sauté the onion with the coriander seeds until translucent. Add the mushrooms and sauté for 2–3 minutes. Stir in the spices and sauté for 2 minutes, then add the tomatoes and 1/4 tsp salt. Cook for 1–2 minutes. Remove from the heat and set aside, ready to reheat. Stir in the chopped coriander before serving.

6 Preheat the oven to 180°C/gas 4.

7 To prepare the tomatoes, heat the oil in a heavy-bottomed pan and sauté the onion,

cumin and sesame seeds with the ginger and green chilli until the seeds begin to pop. Add the tomatoes and sauté until they are slightly bruised by the heat and the skins burst open. Sprinkle with the spices, $1/4$ tsp salt and coarse pepper to taste, then transfer to the oven to roast for 3–4 minutes.

8 Meanwhile, cook the fish. Heat the oil in a flat pan. Shake off excess paste from the fillets, then place in the hot oil, flesh side down. Shallow fry for 3–4 minutes, then turn the fillets and fry the other side until the fish is cooked. Remove the fish from the pan and place on kitchen paper to remove the excess oil. Keep warm.

9 Make a dressing by mixing 2 tbsp of the coriander oil with lemon juice and seasoning to taste. Toss the cress and coriander sprigs in some of the dressing.

10 To serve, place the roasted tomatoes (still on the vine) in the centre of the warm plates. Place the pan-fried fish on the tomatoes and top with the mushrooms. Garnish with the cress salad and drizzle over the remaining coriander oil dressing.
Illustrated left

MURG KI BIRYANI
CHICKEN COOKED WITH RICE

SERVES 4
500g skinned and boned chicken thighs,
    cut into 2.5cm pieces
5 tbsp vegetable oil
3 dried red chillies
500g Basmati rice, washed and drained
salt

MARINADE
6 medium onions, finely sliced
vegetable oil for deep frying
200g set plain yoghurt, whisked until smooth
1 tbsp ginger-garlic paste
1 tsp ground turmeric

APPLE RAITA
250g plain Greek yoghurt
1 tsp toasted cumin seeds
$1/4$ tsp crushed red chilli
1 tbsp finely chopped mint
pinch of caster sugar
1 Granny Smith apple, cored and finely chopped

RICE SEASONING
5cm piece of cassia bark or cinnamon
6 green cardamoms
1 tsp cumin seeds
4 cloves
10 black peppercorns

TO ASSEMBLE
45g melted butter
2 tsp garam masala
1 tbsp finely chopped mint leaves
1 tbsp finely chopped coriander leaves
pinch of saffron strands, soaked in
    100ml tepid milk
2 tbsp mixed whole almonds, cashew
    nuts and raisins, deep fried to
    a light brown colour
4 puff pastry discs, each 10cm diameter
milk to glaze
1 tbsp mixed sesame seeds and
    onion seeds

1 First make the marinade. Deep fry the onions until crisp and brown; drain on kitchen paper. Save 3–4 tbsp of the onions for the garnish; purée the remainder with the yoghurt in a blender or food processor to make a fine paste. Mix this paste with the ginger-garlic paste, turmeric and 1 1/2 tsp salt. Mix the chicken into the marinade, then set aside in a cool place for 2 hours.

2 Meanwhile, make the apple raita. Whisk the yoghurt with the spices, mint and sugar. Stir in the apple. Keep in the fridge until required.

3 Heat 2 tbsp oil in a heavy-bottomed pan and sauté the whole dried red chillies for 1 minute. Add the marinated chicken and cook on a low heat for 10 minutes or until almost cooked. Remove from the heat and keep hot.

4 While the chicken is cooking, heat the remaining 3 tbsp oil in a saucepan and add the rice seasoning ingredients. Sauté for a few minutes until the spices splutter. Add the rice and sauté for 2 minutes, then add 1.5 litres of water. Bring to the boil. Boil the rice for 12–15 minutes or until almost cooked. Drain the rice, then spread out on a tray in a 2.5cm thick layer to cool a bit. Pick out the cassia, cardamom, cloves and peppercorns and discard.

5 Preheat the oven to 180°C/gas 4.

6 Brush four individual biryani pots or ovenproof soup bowls with melted butter. Add the chicken in a single layer. Cover with half of the rice and sprinkle with garam masala, herbs and butter. Spoon the remaining rice evenly on this and sprinkle with the rest of the garam masala and butter and the saffron milk. Scatter over the fried nuts and raisins and the reserved crisp fried onions.

7 Cover the pots or bowls with the puff pastry discs and seal the edges. Glaze with milk. Sprinkle the pastry with the sesame and onion seeds. Bake for 8–12 minutes or until the pastry is golden brown.

8 Serve each pot, sitting on a napkin on a plate, with the apple raita.

WHITE CHOCOLATE MOUSSE
WITH RED RASPBERRY COULIS

SERVES 4
1 tsp powdered gelatine
4 tbsp milk
150g white chocolate, broken up
350ml double cream

RASPBERRY COULIS
200g frozen raspberries
juice of 1/2 lemon
4 tbsp caster sugar
2 tbsp icing sugar, sifted
1 tbsp Grand Marnier or other
   orange liqueur (optional)

GARNISH
raspberries
dark and white chocolate shavings

1 First make the coulis. Purée the berries and lemon juice in a blender. Pass through a sieve, pressing with the back of a spoon. Add the caster sugar, icing sugar, 120ml water and the liqueur. Mix well.

2 Place in a saucepan over a moderate heat and bring to the boil, stirring frequently. Reduce the heat and continue stirring for 1 minute. Remove from the heat and leave to cool.

3 In a glass measuring jug, sprinkle the gelatine over 4 tbsp water, then allow the mixture to soften for 1–2 minutes. Microwave on high for 20 seconds. Allow to stand for 2 minutes or until the gelatine granules are completely dissolved. (Alternatively, place the jug in a bowl of hot water and stir until the gelatine has completely dissolved.)

4 Put the milk in a small saucepan and bring to simmering point. Remove from the heat and add the chocolate. Stir until the chocolate has melted and the mixture is smooth. Add the gelatine to the chocolate mixture and mix well. Refrigerate for about 10 minutes or until slightly thickened but not set.

5 Whip the cream until peaks will hold their shape. Fold the white chocolate mixture into the whipped cream.

6 Beginning with the raspberry coulis, make alternate layers of coulis and mousse in tall parfait glasses. Chill for 1–2 hours.

7 To serve, garnish with fresh raspberries and dark and white chocolate.

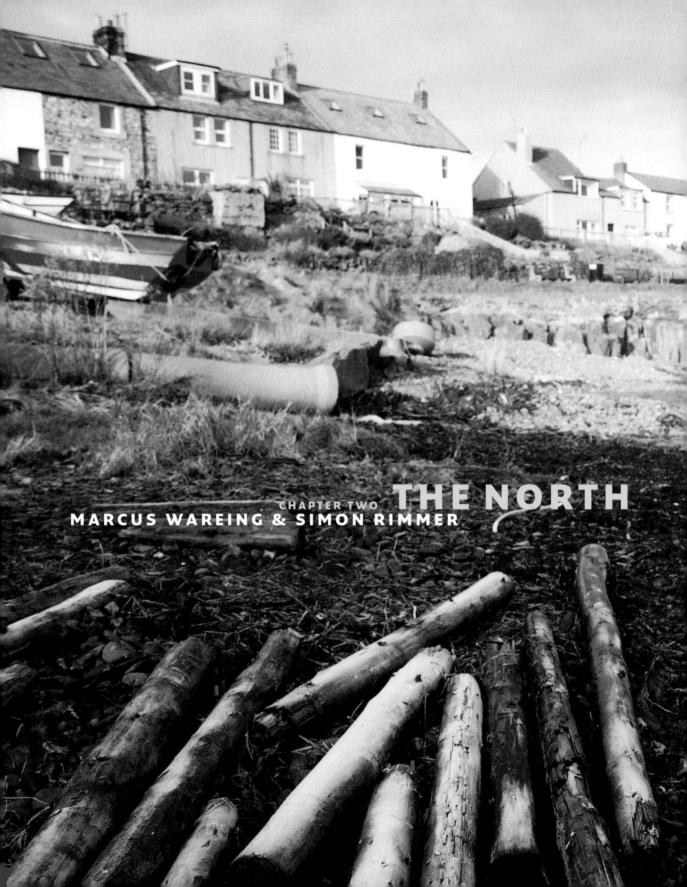

CHAPTER TWO **THE NORTH**

MARCUS WAREING & SIMON RIMMER

One of the reasons offered for Britain's supposedly limited cuisine, at least in comparison with those of France, Italy and Spain, is that the nation industrialised earlier than those countries and so lost its peasantry, guardians of the land and the cooking born of it. There is some truth in that, but it ignores the often fine foods that developed alongside industry and became staples of the working class, especially in the North of England, which has left a distinctive and underappreciated culinary legacy.

Take black pudding for example. The very best varieties of this gorgeous mixture of pig's blood, barley and oatmeal are to be found in the hills surrounding the beautiful medieval Tuscan hill town of Lucca... and in Lancashire towns such as Bury and Bolton. Though the latter cannot offer olive groves and Renaissance frescoes, its black puddings are miniature masterpieces, like those made by Jack and Richard Morris, and sold for a song in the local market on James Wallace's celebrated stall at Bury's thrice-weekly market. A slice of Bury black pudding finds a perfect partner in a glass of Chianti.

Not that Greater Manchester's industrial workers would have got their hands on the latter – more likely, a pint of mild. They needed cheap products, and oatmeal and blood fitted the bill. Black pudding, though, boasts a European heritage, having been introduced to England by monks who knew the dish as 'bloodwurst'. The key to great black pudding is the balance between the blood and the grain. Those of Bury, and Bolton too, remain wonderfully moist and soft inside, marbled with chunks of white pig fat, a true delicacy. Though many like to eat them as part of a traditional breakfast fry-up, try them with stewed apples for lunch, the slightly sour taste of the fruit a great partner to the soft, spicy sausage.

Equally famous as a northern dish is the much mythologised Lancashire hot pot, named, so it seems, after the brown or white pottery dish – the 'pipkin' – in which, traditionally, it was cooked.

In essence, it's a casserole, very similar to Irish stew, of mutton, onions and potatoes. The tendency these days is to use lamb, especially neck joints, but that was an unaffordable luxury for many in the past and, anyway, until well into the 19th century, it was wool rather than lamb that sheep were bred for. Mutton gives a greater depth of taste. One luxury – at least to our eyes – that was affordable was oysters, which, thrown in, gave the hot pot a warm tang (other modern luxuries, such as lobster and salmon, were food of the poor too, due to their abundance; only as they became scarce did the rich show interest).

The other great Lancastrian dish is potted shrimps, the ultimate comfort food and a favourite among the members of Pall Mall clubs. The finest brown shrimps, the *Crangon crangon*, come from Cartmel Wharf in the treacherous, vast, 'wet Sahara' of Morecambe Bay. Trawled for by men on half-submerged tractors – they once used horses – who are draped in oilskins against the relentless embrace of wind and water, the catch is boiled alive on the beach. Once cooked, the shrimps are taken to be smothered in vats of clarified butter spiced with mace, nutmeg and cayenne and placed not anymore in an earthenware pot but a plastic one. Spread on toast they are a marvel.

SIMPLE YET SUPERB
On the other side of northern England, the Northumbrian coast offers another highly traditional delicacy that is making a popular comeback, not least because its high levels of Vitamin D and rich oils offer protection against the prevalent life-threatening diseases of the 21st century, heart disease and cancer. The kippers made by Robsons, a fourth-generation family firm based in the picturesque fishing port of Craster, have a beautiful sheen of silver and gold to them; there are no additives, colourings or dyes used here. The method of splitting the plump herring, which gives

Kippers made by L Robson and Sons of Craster are renowned all over Britain – and beyond; Neil Robson is pictured on the previous page.

the kipper its distinctive flat appearance, was invented by local man John Woodger and perfected in Craster. When split, the herring is placed in brine and then, for 16 to 18 hours, is gently smoked over oak chips in the 130-year-old quarried stone smokehouse. Grilled or fried and accompanied by a cup of strong Ceylon tea, it surpasses even the traditional English breakfast as the best start to the day, the epitome of fine local food served simply.

Simplicity is a consistent feature of the food of the North East. Pan Haggerty, said to take its name from the French 'hacher', meaning to 'chop' or 'slice', is the region's most famous supper dish, made of multiple layers of onion, potatoes and cheese, cooked gently in a heavy frying pan, finished off with a good grilling and served in the pan. In Europe we would celebrate it as peasant food; in Britain we should celebrate it as a wonderful legacy of the ingenuity and resourcefulness of the industrial working class.

The same values inform the snacks, treats and desserts of the North. The griddle cakes called, evocatively, Singin' Hinnies, were a staple of the North East, a mixture of flour, lard and dried fruits that sizzles, or 'sings', on a griddle traditionally coated in mutton fat.

Eccles Cakes, mysteriously, have become closely associated with the eponymous Lancashire town -- mysterious because for centuries the word 'eccles' was synonymous with 'church', and the cakes became associated with religious festivals throughout the North. They are still hugely popular: the Lancashire Eccles Cakes Company makes up to three-quarters of a million of them each week. A mix of light, flaky pastry filled with dried fruit, they proved too delightful for the Puritans, who banned the people of Eccles from eating them in the 17th century. The embargo was ignored, an early victory for the forces of pleasure over those of privation. The struggle continues.

MARCUS WAREING

"Dad was a fruit and potato merchant on Merseyside," says Marcus Wareing, Head Chef at the Michelin-starred Savoy Grill, "supplying the food for school meals... when they were good. He gave me respect for food." Wareing went to catering college in Southport before getting a job, under Anton Edelmann, at the Savoy, one of London's most prestigious hotels, and also worked with the Roux brothers at Le Gavroche. In 1993 he formed a fruitful partnership with friend and mentor Gordon Ramsay, whom he had met at Le Gavroche, becoming his sous chef at Aubergine.

Wareing opened his first restaurant, L'Oranger, in 1996, and by the age of 30 he had gained his first Michelin star when he opened Pétrus. Another star soon followed. In 2003 he came full circle, returning to the Savoy Grill, where he "dissects classic British dishes", and is not afraid to challenge tradition: he ruffled some feathers when he got rid of the Savoy's legendary roast meat trolley, preferring the offerings to be as fresh as possible.

He has no doubt that the high profile of chefs has been to the benefit of British food culture. "It's slow, but our food culture is changing," he insists. "Cooking is becoming lighter and fresher. There's an understanding that a strong food culture protects our health. But, in the North, there's still a tendency to see eating out as a weekend activity. Mondays to Thursdays are a bit of a gap. We need to get people to think of eating out as an everyday activity, expand people's horizons."

MENU ONE
> Shellfish Tian with Wholemeal Toast
> Wild Sea Bass Glazed with a Pine Nut Crust, with Red Wine Shallots, Parsnip Purée and Baby Turnips
> Lancashire Hot Pot with Braised Red Cabbage
> Custard Tart with Garibaldi Biscuits

MENU TWO
> Field Mushroom Soup with Red Mullet
> Omelette Arnold Bennett
> Duck Tourte with Braised Root Vegetables and Mushroom Sauce
> Bread and Butter Pudding

SIMON RIMMER

In 1990, when Simon Rimmer teamed up with his business partner to take over a vegetarian café in Manchester, they could not afford to hire a chef. So, with the aid of a couple of second-hand books, Rimmer taught himself to cook vegetarian dishes, and Green's, the re-named restaurant, proved an enormous hit. Unlike many of Britain's leading chefs, Rimmer never trained in rigorous classic French technique, developing instead a highly eclectic style influenced in particular by the flavours of Thailand and wider South East Asia. "I had always been a fan of Asian food," says Rimmer, "and it offered a means of making exciting vegetarian food rather than the brown and stodgy version that was prevalent then."

Rimmer believes that concerns about BSE in 1992 proved a crucial factor in the success of Green's. "People began to take a greater interest in what they eat, and began to rethink their attitudes to food." Rimmer cites two recent developments in British food that he welcomes. "The introduction of vegetarian rennet by many cheesemakers has presented us with a whole new palate. I also welcome the world market. Though we do try to source a lot of ingredients locally, we've still benefitted from this explosion of new flavours."

Though he thinks Manchester still lacks "a really fantastic city centre restaurant", he's encouraged by the resurgence of high quality food production in the North West. "The success of new cheeses like Blacksticks Blue is incredibly exciting, as is the return of local cattle breeds."

MENU ONE
> Smoked Venison Loin with Pickles and Cumberland Sauce
> Indian Spiced Halibut with Southport Shrimp Biryani and Mini Bhajis
> Blacksticks Blue Roulade with Crispy Vegetarian Black Pudding and Onion Jam Dressing
> Sticky Toffee Bread and Butter Pudding

MENU TWO
> Poached Goosnargh Chicken Salad with Lentils
> Fillet of Trout with Girolle Mushrooms and Almonds
> Wild Boar Lancashire Hot Pot
> Lythe Valley Damson Cheesecake

SHELLFISH TIAN
WITH WHOLEMEAL TOAST

SERVES 4
120g picked white crab meat
50g peeled Southport brown shrimps
35g mayonnaise
½ bunch of chives, finely chopped
¼ bunch of chervil, finely chopped
pinch of mild paprika
juice of ¼ lemon
salt and pepper

GARNISH
1 hard-boiled egg, white and yolk separated and chopped
40 small capers, each cut in half
5 baby gherkins (cornichons), cut into rounds
1 shallot, finely diced
large sprig of parsley, chopped

TO FINISH
1 tbsp white wine vinegar
5 tbsp olive oil
small salad leaves
wholemeal toast and butter

1 In a cold mixing bowl combine the crab, shrimps, mayonnaise, herbs and paprika. When mixed, season with lemon juice, salt and pepper to taste.

2 Divide the crab mixture evenly among four 7.5cm metal rings set on a tray lined with cling film, filling the rings by about two-thirds. Press down with a spoon to compress, then refrigerate for at least 15 minutes.

3 Gently mix together the ingredients for the garnish.

4 Place a filled ring in the middle of each plate and gently push out the crab to form a tower. Neatly arrange the garnish in a circle around the crab.

5 To finish, whisk together the vinegar and oil, and season to taste. Lightly dress the salad leaves with this dressing, then arrange a small mound on the top of each of the crab tians. Serve immediately, with buttered wholemeal toast.

WILD SEA BASS
GLAZED WITH A PINE NUT CRUST
WITH RED WINE SHALLOTS
PARSNIP PURÉE AND BABY TURNIPS

SERVES 4
2 wild sea bass, 400–600g total weight,
    filleted and skinned
olive oil
salt and pepper

PINE NUT CRUST
100g toasted pine nuts
65g softened butter
1 tsp chopped chervil
½ garlic clove, chopped

RED WINE SHALLOTS
40g long shallots, finely diced
olive oil
30g caster sugar
30ml Cabernet Sauvignon vinegar
50ml Port
100ml red wine

PARSNIP PURÉE
75g butter
3 large parsnips, diced
1 tsp mild curry powder
50ml double cream

TURNIPS
8 or more leafy baby turnips
pinch of caster sugar
sprig of thyme
knob of butter

1 First make the pine nut crust. Roughly chop the pine nuts, then mix very well with all the other ingredients plus a pinch of salt. Place the mixture between two sheets of baking parchment on a tray and spread out evenly using a rolling pin until about 2mm thick. Place in the freezer. Once frozen, cut the crust to the same size as the sea bass fillets and return to the freezer.

2 Next prepare the red wine shallots. Fry the shallots in a little olive oil until slightly softened, without colouring them. Season with salt, then add the sugar and stir to dissolve. Add the vinegar and reduce until sticky. Add the Port and red wine, and reduce slowly. Before the sauce becomes thick, spoon out a little and reserve, then continue reducing the remainder until quite thick. Set aside.

3 To make the parsnip purée, melt the butter in a heavy-bottomed pan. When foaming add the parsnips and season with the curry powder and a little salt. Cook until very soft. If the parsnips look like they are becoming too dark or are sticking to the pan, add a little water from time to time. Add the cream, then purée in a food processor until very smooth. Correct the seasoning and set aside.

4 To prepare the turnips, take off the leaves, wash and reserve. Blanch the turnips in boiling salted water for 30 seconds, then cool in iced water. When cold, peel by

rubbing off the skin. Return to the pan, cover well with cold water and add the sugar, thyme and a pinch of salt. Bring to the boil and simmer until tender. Pour off most of the cooking liquid, then set aside.

5 When ready to serve, preheat the grill. Season the fish on both sides. Heat a little olive oil in a non-stick pan and fry the fish for 1 minute on each side. Transfer to a baking sheet and place the pine nut crust on top of the fish. Glaze under the grill until an even golden brown.

6 Meanwhile, warm the shallots. Add the butter to the turnips and warm through, then add the reserved turnip leaves and heat until wilted. Heat the parsnip purée in a small non-stick pot.

7 To serve, arrange the parsnip purée and shallots side by side on warm plates. Place the fish on the purée, and the turnips with their leaves around the fish. Drizzle round the reserved red wine sauce and a little olive oil.

Morecambe Bay is famous for wild sea bass, which thrive in its waters between May and October, reaching over 4kg in weight. It's a wonderfully adaptable fish, often at its best simply barbecued. Here it makes a brilliant though unlikely foil for the earthy, robust taste of turnip and parsnip.

50

LANCASHIRE HOT POT
WITH BRAISED RED CABBAGE

SERVES 4
1 middle neck of lamb, about 1kg
plain flour
vegetable oil
1 Spanish onion, thinly sliced
2 carrots, thinly sliced
1 garlic clove, thinly sliced
1 tbsp thyme leaves
1 tbsp chopped rosemary
3 Maris Piper potatoes, peeled
butter
salt and pepper

LAMB STOCK
1 large carrot, cut into 3 pieces
1 onion, cut into quarters

2 garlic cloves, peeled
sprig of rosemary
sprig of thyme
1 bay leaf
pinch of rock salt
1 tbsp tomato purée

BRAISED RED CABBAGE
1 small red cabbage, cored and sliced
1 red onion, diced
150g unsalted butter, diced
200ml red wine vinegar
50g clear honey
100g Demerara sugar
1 bay leaf
sprig of thyme

1 Preheat the oven to 200°C/gas 6. Remove the meat from the middle neck of lamb and set aside. To make the lamb stock, chop the bones and put them in a roasting tray. Roast until lightly browned.

2 Meanwhile, cook the carrot, onion and garlic in a little hot olive oil in a heavy-bottomed pot until lightly browned. Add the herbs and salt, then stir in the tomato purée and cook for a couple of minutes. Add the roasted bones and cover with 2 litres water. Bring to the boil, then turn down to a simmer and cook for 1 hour, skimming off any fat regularly. Pass the liquid through a fine sieve into a clean pan. Return to the heat and reduce until you have 1 litre of stock. Turn the oven to 150°C/gas 2.

3 To make the hot pot, cut the lamb into 2mm thick slices. Dust them with flour and quickly fry in hot oil until lightly coloured on both sides. Remove and set aside. In the same oil, quickly fry the onion, carrots and garlic until lightly browned.

4 Layer the lamb and vegetables in a heavy casserole dish, filling it to 1cm from the top. Season each layer with salt, pepper and herbs, and spoon liberal amounts of stock between each layer.

5 Evenly slice the potatoes about 1mm thick and arrange neatly all over the top of the dish. Put a few small knobs of butter on the potatoes, cover with a tight-fitting lid and cook in the oven for 1 1/2 hours. Remove the lid and cook for a further 45 minutes.

6 Meanwhile, make the red cabbage. Mix together all of the ingredients, seasoning well with salt. Put into a roasting tray and cover with foil. Place in the oven and cook for about 1 1/2 hours, stirring regularly, until most of the liquid has gone.

7 Serve the hot pot from the casserole on to warm plates with the cabbage.

CUSTARD TART
WITH GARIBALDI BISCUITS

SERVES 4

GARIBALDI BISCUITS
100g butter, melted
100g icing sugar, sifted
100g plain flour
100g egg whites
200g currants

PASTRY
225g plain flour
pinch of salt
grated zest of 1 lemon
150g butter
75g caster sugar
1 egg yolk and 1 whole egg,
    beaten together

CUSTARD FILLING
9 free range egg yolks
75g caster sugar
500ml whipping cream
freshly grated nutmeg

1 First, make the garibaldi biscuits. Mix together the butter, icing sugar and flour using a wooden spoon until the mixture is smooth. Slowly add the egg whites, stirring, until they are completely incorporated, then fold in the currants. Bring together into a ball, wrap in cling film and chill for at least 1 hour.

2 Roll out the dough on a lightly floured surface to 5mm thick. Cut into 3 x 7cm rectangles with a small sharp knife. Place on a baking tray lined with greaseproof paper, ensuring the biscuits are not touching each other. Put the tray into the fridge to rest for 30 minutes.

3 Preheat the oven to 180°C/gas 4. Bake the biscuits for 8–10 minutes or until golden brown. Remove and cool on a wire rack. Keep in an airtight tin.

4 To make the pastry, rub together the flour, salt, lemon zest and butter until the mixture resembles breadcrumbs. Add the sugar, then slowly add the eggs, mixing until the pastry forms a ball. Wrap tightly in cling film and refrigerate for 2 hours.

5 Preheat the oven to 170°C/gas 3.

6 Roll out the pastry on a lightly floured surface to 2mm thickness. Use to line an 18cm flan ring placed on a baking sheet. Line with greaseproof paper and fill with baking beans, then bake blind for about 10 minutes or until starting to turn golden brown. Remove the paper and beans and cool. Turn the oven down to 130°C/gas 1/2.

7 For the filling, whisk together the yolks and sugar. Add the cream and mix well. Pass the mixture through a fine sieve into a saucepan and warm to tepid.

8 Fill the pastry case with the custard, to within 5mm of the top. Carefully place in the middle of the oven and bake for 30–40 minutes or until the custard appears set but not too firm. Remove from the oven and cover the surface liberally with grated nutmeg. Allow to cool to room temperature.

9 Before serving, warm the biscuits through in the oven for 5 minutes. Cut the tart with a sharp knife and serve with the biscuits.

FIELD MUSHROOM SOUP
WITH RED MULLET

SERVES 4
1kg wide cap field mushrooms
150ml olive oil
3 large shallots, finely sliced
2 garlic cloves, crushed
juice of ½ lemon
1 litre hot vegetable or chicken stock
250ml cream
150g unsalted butter, diced (optional)
salt and pepper

GARNISH
100g mixed wild mushrooms
olive oil
4 small fillets of fresh red mullet,
  scaled

1 First make the soup. Remove the dark gills from the field mushrooms and discard.
Wash and dry the mushrooms, then slice 2mm thick.

2 Heat the oil in a large heavy-bottomed pan, add the shallots and cook until lightly
coloured. Add the garlic and cook until a little soft, then add the sliced mushrooms
and season with salt and a few turns of fresh black pepper. Cook for 5–8 minutes or
until lightly coloured. Add the lemon juice and reduce a little, then add the stock and
bring to a rapid simmer. Turn to a low heat and simmer for 15 minutes.

3 Check the seasoning is correct, then ladle the soup into a blender or food processor
and purée until smooth. Pass the soup through a fine sieve into a clean pan and stir
in the cream. Set aside. Before serving, heat the soup and stir in the optional butter
to make it really silky.

4 Heat some olive oil in a non-stick pan, add the wild mushrooms and quickly stir
fry until wilted. Season with salt, then remove the mushrooms from the pan and
reserve on kitchen paper.

5 Wipe out the pan, then heat some more olive oil in it. Season both sides of the
fish fillets with salt, then place gently in the pan, skin side down. Give the pan a little
shake to ensure that the fish doesn't stick. The fillets may curl up, but do not press
them down as this will zip back the skin; simply leave them and they should flatten
out naturally. Cook for about 1 ½ minutes, then turn over and cook for a further
1 minute. Take the fish out of the pan and drain briefly on kitchen paper.

6 To assemble, put a small mound of wild mushrooms in the middle of each warm,
wide-rimmed soup bowl, place the red mullet on top and pour the soup around. To
finish you can drizzle some nice olive oil in a ring on the soup. Serve immediately.

54

OMELETTE ARNOLD BENNETT

SERVES 4

250g naturally smoked haddock fillet,
    skinned
milk for poaching
6 large eggs
50g unsalted butter
small bunch of chives, chopped
40g mature Cheddar or Gruyère, grated
salt and pepper

HOLLANDAISE SAUCE

100ml white wine vinegar
a few herb stalks (parsley, tarragon)
1 shallot, finely sliced
2 egg yolks
250g butter, melted and clarified
juice of ½ lemon

GARNISH

chopped chives or sprigs of chervil

1 First make the hollandaise. Heat the vinegar, herb stalks and shallot in a small pan and reduce by half. Remove from the heat and leave to infuse for at least 4 hours. Strain through a sieve into a bowl. Discard the contents of the sieve.

2 Put the egg yolks and 50ml water into another bowl set over a pan of simmering water and whisk until thick ribbons will form. Gradually whisk in the vinegar reduction and carry on whisking until thick ribbons will form again.

3 Very slowly pour in the warm (not hot) clarified butter, whisking the whole time. When all of the butter has been incorporated, you should have a nice thick emulsion. Pass through a fine sieve to remove any bits of cooked egg. Season with the lemon juice and salt, then cover with cling film and keep in a warm place.

4 Gently poach the haddock in milk to cover for about 5 minutes. Drain and flake into large chunks, discarding any bones. Set aside in a warm place.

5 Preheat the grill to high.

6 Beat the eggs in a bowl and season with salt and freshly milled black pepper. Melt the butter in a large non-stick frying pan. When foaming add the eggs. Allow to set on the base, then mix with a fork until half cooked. Allow to set on the base again.

7 Put the fish, chives and cheese on to the omelette and fold the edges into the middle. Divide the omelette among four small dishes (ramekins or flat ovenproof bowls). This can be a bit messy, so clean the sides of the dishes before you cover the top of the omelettes with hollandaise sauce. Glaze under the grill.

8 Garnish each omelette with chives or a sprig of chervil and serve straight away.

DUCK TOURTE
WITH BRAISED ROOT VEGETABLES
AND MUSHROOM SAUCE

SERVES 4
2 sheets of puff pastry 4mm thick
500ml duck fat
4 duck legs
4 garlic cloves, peeled
1 bay leaf
large sprig of thyme
6 black peppercorns
pinch of rock salt
4 tbsp chopped parsley
2 egg yolks, beaten
1 egg, beaten

MUSHROOM SAUCE
500ml white wine
20g dried wild mushrooms

2 shallots, sliced
1 garlic clove, peeled
sprig of thyme
4 white peppercorns
pinch of rock salt
500ml chicken stock
400ml double cream
1 tsp lemon juice

BRAISED ROOT VEGETABLES
1 large swede
1 small celeriac
2 large carrots
100g unsalted butter
500ml chicken stock

1 First make the tourte. Cut each pastry sheet into a 20cm disc, place on trays and refrigerate while you prepare the filling. Put the duck fat and legs, garlic, bay leaf, thyme, peppercorns and salt into a deep heavy-bottomed pan and cook over a very low heat, or in the oven at 130°C/gas 1/2, for 3–4 hours or until the meat is falling off the bone. It is important not to cook the duck legs too fast or too hot, otherwise the meat will dry out.

2 Take the meat off the bones, discarding any fat, skin, sinew and small bones. Put it in a bowl and mix with the parsley and a few spoonfuls of the duck fat used for cooking. Check the seasoning. Form the meat mixture into a disc 15cm in diameter and 4cm high on a tray and put into the fridge to set.

3 Place the duck filling in the centre of one of the pastry discs. Brush the exposed pastry around the filling with the beaten egg yolks, right up to the duck, then carefully cover with the other pastry disc. Smooth down over the filling and press the pastry edges all around to seal well. Neaten up the edges with a sharp knife. Refrigerate for 30–45 minutes.

4 Next make the sauce. Put the white wine, mushrooms, shallots, garlic, thyme, peppercorns and salt into a pan and reduce by two-thirds. In another pan, reduce the stock by two-thirds. Add the stock to the wine mixture together with the cream and bring to a simmer. Pass through a sieve, then add the lemon juice and stir well. Set aside. Reheat for serving.

5 Preheat the oven to 180°C/gas 4.

56

6 Using the point of a small, sharp knife mark curved lines from the top centre of the pastry out to the edges. Make sure you only cut the pastry and not all the way through. Brush the surface of the tourte evenly with beaten whole egg. Allow to dry, then brush again. Place on a baking tray and bake for about 30 minutes or until well risen and a deep golden brown.

7 Meanwhile, to prepare the root vegetables, cut all of them into a 2cm dice. Divide the butter among three pans and heat until foaming. Add the diced vegetables to the pans, keeping them separate. Season, then cook until well coloured, stirring regularly. Add the chicken stock, equally divided, and cook until tender. Take care not to overcook or the vegetables will lose their shape. Remove the vegetables and reserve. Reduce any liquid to form a shiny emulsion. Before serving, reheat the vegetables in this emulsion.

8 This is a centre of the table dish. To serve, simply put the vegetables into a bowl and the sauce into a jug and cut the tourte into four. Then let everyone dive in.

BREAD AND BUTTER PUDDING

SERVES 4

1 loaf of crusty white bread, sliced
250g softened butter
4 whole eggs
2 egg yolks
250ml whole milk

500ml double cream
100g caster sugar
2 tsp ground cinnamon
150g mixed dried fruit
25g Demerara sugar
grated zest of 2 oranges

1 Lay out the sliced bread (with the crusts on or off, as you prefer) and leave overnight to dry out.

2 Preheat the oven to 150°C/gas 2.

3 Butter each slice of bread well. Whisk together the eggs and yolks, milk, cream, caster sugar and cinnamon. Layer the buttered bread in a deep baking dish, overlapping the slices slightly. Soak each layer with the custard mixture and sprinkle with dried fruit. Sprinkle the top with the Demerara sugar and orange zest.

4 Place the dish in a baking tray and add enough water to come one-quarter of the way up the side of the dish. Bake for about 45 minutes.

5 Serve on its own, or with ice cream or pouring cream.

BLACKSTICKS BLUE ROULADE
WITH CRISPY VEGETARIAN BLACK
PUDDING AND ONION JAM DRESSING

SERVES 4
65g butter
90g plain flour
400ml milk, warmed
7 eggs, separated
big handful of roughly chopped basil
100g Parmesan, freshly grated
400g ricotta
225g Blacksticks Blue cheese, crumbled
sprinkle of sun-blush tomatoes
salt and pepper

ONION JAM DRESSING
3 red onions, finely sliced
1 garlic clove, crushed
30g butter
125g sugar
100ml red wine vinegar
extra virgin olive oil

OTHER BITS
12 pieces of Ireland's vegetarian black pudding
vegetable oil
handful of baby spinach
30g butter

1 First make the onion jam dressing. Gently fry the onions and garlic in the butter until golden and caramelised. Add the sugar and vinegar and bring to the boil, then simmer for 40 minutes or until nice and thick, stirring from time to time. Season and thin with a little olive oil. Set aside.

2 Preheat the oven to 200°C/gas 6.

3 To make the roulade, melt the butter in a saucepan and stir in the flour. Cook for 3 minutes, then add the milk a little at a time, stirring constantly. Cook until thickened. Remove from the heat. Season well, then mix in the egg yolks.

4 In a bowl whisk the egg whites until stiff. Fold them gently and carefully into the yolk mixture, so you keep as much air as possible. Fold in the basil. Spread on a greased and lined 45 x 30cm baking tray. Sprinkle evenly with the Parmesan, then bake for 15 minutes or until springy and risen. Turn out on to a sheet of greaseproof paper or baking parchment and leave to cool.

5 Season the ricotta, then spread it evenly over the roulade base, leaving a gap at the top and bottom. Scatter over the crumbled cheese and tomatoes. Roll up and wrap in greaseproof and foil. If not eating straight away, chill for up to 2 hours.

6 When ready to serve, preheat the oven to 200°C/gas 6. Cut the roulade into eight pieces and heat through in the oven for 10 minutes. Then finish by glazing them under a hot grill.

7 Meanwhile, fry the black pudding in medium hot oil until crisp. Drain on kitchen paper. Quickly wilt the spinach in the butter and season well.

8 To serve, sit some wilted spinach in the centre of each warm plate and top with two pieces of roulade. Place three pieces of black pudding around and spoon some onion jam dressing in between.

STICKY TOFFEE
BREAD AND BUTTER PUDDING

SERVES 6

200g stoned Medjool dates
½ tsp bicarbonate of soda
6 slices of white bread, crusts off
75g softened butter
3 whole eggs
3 egg yolks
1 vanilla pod, split lengthways
75g caster sugar
500ml double cream
Demerara sugar
pouring cream to serve

SAUCE

100g butter
100g golden syrup
100g soft dark brown sugar
100ml double cream
100g stoned Medjool dates, finely
    chopped (optional)

1 Place the dates and bicarbonate of soda in a saucepan and just cover with water. Simmer gently until the dates break down.

2 Butter the bread, then cut each slice in half to make triangles or cut out rounds. Alternately layer the bread and dates in four buttered 150ml ramekins or a buttered 25 x 20cm baking dish, starting and finishing with a layer of bread.

3 Beat together the whole eggs, yolks, seeds scraped from the vanilla pod and caster sugar in a bowl. Heat the cream to scalding point, then pour on to the egg mixture, mixing well. Pour over the bread and dates. Leave to soak for at least 20 minutes.

4 Preheat the oven to 175°C/gas 4.

5 Set the ramekins or baking dish in a roasting tray of water. Bake for 16 minutes for the ramekins or 25 minutes for the large dish or until the custard has set.

6 To make the sauce, simply combine the butter, syrup and sugar in a saucepan and bring to the boil. When it's all smooth and dissolved, remove from the heat and stir in the cream and optional dates. Keep warm.

7 Sprinkle the top of the pudding evenly with Demerara sugar and caramelise under the grill. Serve a good portion of pudding with the sauce and pouring cream.

62

POACHED GOOSNARGH
CHICKEN SALAD WITH LENTILS

SERVES 4
2 chicken breasts, each 200g, skinned
1 tbsp parsley stalks
1 tbsp black peppercorns
4 spring onions
1 garlic clove, peeled
salt and pepper

LENTILS
200g Puy lentils, washed
1 red onion, finely chopped
1 red pepper, diced
olive oil for frying
50ml groundnut oil
50ml extra virgin olive oil
50ml sherry vinegar
juice of ½ lemon
1 tbsp chopped parsley

1 To shape the breasts into neat cylinders, wrap them individually in cling film. Put the chicken breasts, parsley stalks, 1 tsp salt, the peppercorns, onions and garlic in a pan. Cover with water and bring to the boil. Remove from the heat, cover and leave to poach in the residual heat for 2 hours.

2 Meanwhile, cook the lentils in water until al dente; drain. Gently fry the onion and red pepper in a little olive oil until soft. Tip into a bowl and add the lentils. Stir together, then allow to cool.

3 Make a dressing by whisking together the groundnut and extra virgin olive oils, vinegar and lemon juice. Season well. Toss the lentils in the dressing. Add the parsley just before serving.

4 Drain the chicken breasts. When they are cold, unwrap them and slice into neat medallions. Divide into four portions.

5 To serve, spoon the lentil salad on to plates and sit the chicken medallions on top.

FILLET OF TROUT
WITH GIROLLE MUSHROOMS AND ALMONDS

SERVES 4
4 trout fillets, each 100g
lemon juice
melted butter
salt and pepper

MUSHROOM AND ALMOND MIXTURE
1 shallot, finely chopped
50g butter
125g girolles
75g toasted flaked almonds
1 tbsp aged sherry vinegar
1 tsp chopped flat-leaf parsley
75g fresh brown breadcrumbs

1 Preheat the grill.
2 To make the mushroom and almond mixture, gently fry the shallot in the butter until soft but not coloured. Chuck in the mushrooms and crank up the heat, then cook for about 1 minute. Drop the heat right down and stir in the almonds, vinegar, parsley and seasoning. Finally, fold in the crumbs. Keep warm.
3 Season the fish, brush with a mix of lemon juice and butter and grill for a couple of minutes on each side.
4 Serve each fillet of trout on top of a spoonful of the delicious mushroom mix.

Grilled trout and mushrooms is a classic English combination, though the travel writer, novelist and special agent Elizabeth Ayrton insisted that the trout "should have been caught in the stream at the bottom of the field where the mushrooms were picked".

WILD BOAR
LANCASHIRE HOT POT

SERVES 4

900g boneless shoulder of wild boar, cubed
25g plain flour
vegetable oil for frying
2 onions, finely sliced
pinch of sugar
25g butter
2 carrots, sliced
2 celery sticks, peeled and chopped
300ml red wine
300ml beef stock
3 sprigs of thyme
2 bay leaves
splash of Worcestershire sauce
salt and pepper

TOPPING

450g Maris Piper potatoes, peeled
   and finely sliced
150g melted butter

1 Season the cubes of wild boar and toss in the flour, then brown all over in a little hot oil. Remove and set aside.

2 Add the onions and sugar to the same pan together with the butter and cook for 20 minutes or until the onions are golden. Stir in the carrots and celery and cook for a further 2 minutes.

3 Return the meat and stir in the remaining flour. Cook for 2 minutes. Now add the wine, stock, thyme, bay leaves and Worcestershire sauce. Bring to the boil, stirring all the time. Turn the heat right down and cook for 1 1/2 hours.

4 Preheat the oven to 200°C/gas 6.

5 Blanch the potatoes in boiling water for 1 minute. Drain and refresh.

6 Divide the wild boar mixture among four individual pie dishes. Top each dish with a good layer of potato slices and brush with lots of melted butter. Season. Bake for 10 minutes, then finish under a hot grill. Serve with braised red cabbage.

LYTHE VALLEY
DAMSON CHEESECAKE

SERVES 8
100g caster sugar
1 vanilla pod, split lengthways
250g damsons, stoned

CHEESECAKE
250g digestive biscuits, crushed
175g butter, melted
750g ricotta
500g cream cheese
150g caster sugar
6 eggs
1 vanilla pod, split lengthways

SAUCE
150g caster sugar
1 vanilla pod
200g damsons, stoned
100ml damson gin

TO SERVE
200g mascarpone
75g icing sugar, sifted
1 vanilla pod, split lengthways
sprigs of mint

1 Put the sugar, seeds from the vanilla pod and 100ml water in a saucepan and heat gently until the sugar has dissolved. Remove from the heat and add the damsons. Leave to poach for at least 20 minutes, then drain.

2 Preheat the oven to 180°C/gas 4.

3 To make the cheesecake, combine the biscuits and butter and press over the bottom of a 20cm spring-sided cake tin (or use individual moulds).

4 Put the ricotta and cream cheeses, sugar and eggs in a food processor. Scrape in the seeds from the vanilla pod and whiz until smooth. Stir in the drained damsons. Spoon on top of the biscuit base. Bake for about 1 hour.

5 Remove from the oven and allow to cool, then chill. Remove the cheesecake from the tin before serving.

6 To make the sauce, slowly bring the sugar, vanilla pod and 100ml water almost to the boil, then simmer until the sugar dissolves. Remove from the heat and stir in the fruit and gin. The sauce can be served warm or cool.

7 To serve, whisk the mascarpone with the icing sugar and seeds scraped from the vanilla pod. Place a slice of cheesecake on each plate and top with lashings of sauce, mascarpone and a sprig of mint.

CHAPTER THREE WALES
ANGELA HARTNETT & BRYN WILLIAMS

WALES

Wales is a land with more sheep than people. The remote family farms, long a mainstay of the nation's rural life, have bred the small, hardy, high-altitude breeds – the Speckled Face, the Welsh Mountain, the Beulah – for generations. It is an arduous, time-consuming task for which there are no short-cuts if the quality of produce is to be maintained. It is said that sheep have "a desire to die". The job of the shepherd is to stall their bleak ambition, checking on flocks often twice a day, traipsing across difficult terrain regardless of conditions. The heavy rainfall for which Wales is notorious has a beneficial effect on the flavour, nourishing the mountain grass and herbs on which the sheep graze.

Bob Kennard was a cattle rancher in Nigeria, Malawi and Swaziland who, on returning to Britain in the 1980s, was appalled by much of the meat on the market. From his base in the village of Dolau in Powys, on the Welsh side of Offa's Dyke, he has witnessed a food revolution, one in which he has played a significant role. His company, Graig Farm Organics, is a perfect example of the way technology, in the shape of the internet, has bolstered the best of traditional farming practice. By offering a wide range of fine Welsh produce from one easily accessible source, Kennard is satisfying customers way beyond the Principality. He works with around 200 different farmers, for whom the emphasis is on quality. "If people pay a premium, as they do for our produce, there has to be a real difference between what we sell and the rest."

Customers are increasingly adventurous in their tastes, rediscovering foods that seemed in terminal decline. Mutton is a case in point. Kennard is delighted by its revival: "Lamb, which is best around winter, is lovely tender meat, but if you want flavour nothing beats mutton."

Mutton, the meat of sheep over at least two years old, runs counter to the rhythms of our age. It requires slow, careful cooking, but the result is a deep and complex flavour and texture. As Kennard points out, Welsh mutton has been long admired: the travel writer George Borrow, who visited Wales during the middle of the 19th century, thought it the nation's hidden treasure. "The leg of mutton of Wales beats the leg of mutton in any other country," he wrote in *Wild Wales*. "Certainly, I shall never forget the first Welsh leg of mutton I ever tasted, rich but delicate, replete with juices derived from aromatic herbs."

THE LARDER OVERFLOWS

But the Welsh larder is crammed with more than Welsh lamb. Vegetables and fruit abound. "I must, of course, mention the leeks," says Kennard. This subtle, sweet relative of the onion was introduced to Wales by Phoenician traders in tin. By the late 16th century, it was recognised as the country's national symbol. The Elizabethan poet Michael Drayton wrote of its adoption by the Welsh at the battle of Heathfield in 633 AD, who wore it in their caps to distinguish them from their Anglo-Saxon enemies. Famous too are the early potatoes of Pembrokeshire, which arise in May thanks to the warming influence of the mild Atlantic breezes.

On the other side of the country, straddling the Welsh Marches, the hillsides blossom with fruit. There are around 7,000 varieties of apple in the world, but you wouldn't guess that from wandering around the average British supermarket. What we are missing can be seen in all their glory on Gellirhyd Farm, 36 hectares of woodland and meadow overlooking Sugar Loaf mountain. More than 500 different varieties of apple grow here: some sharp in taste, like Lane's Prince Albert, others sweet like Surecrop russets or Charles Ross, many more in between.

When Colin and Daphne Gardiner bought the land in 1991, "in a fit of mental aberration", they were horticultural novices, but a friend, botanist Ray

Woods, was astonished by the rare bounty found in this "unimproved land", and urged them to take the greatest care of it. In 1910, a hundred apple trees had been planted, many of them rare species. "I'm not the sort of man who can leave an apple on the ground," says Gardiner. But unimpressed by the money offered for his fallen apples by the big cider manufacturers, he and wife Daphne bought a hydraulic cold press and started making apple juice.

"We got people to taste the juices at farmers' markets," says Kennard. "Once they'd tasted them, they'd walk off with three bottles."

Gardiner had been told that it would prove too hard to grow apples 245m up on a north-facing slope. But his land has the perfect soil for it: light, free-draining sandstone, untouched, unlike most agricultural ground, by the addition of lime.

"The apples all ripen at different stages, and they all taste completely different," says Gardiner. Though his apples have won numerous awards, and have a loyal local following, he's not keen to expand. "We're proud of Wales, and we can sell all we make here locally. All Daphne and I want is a good quality of life and to make ends meet. And we do that." Gardiner is a genuinely local producer. "We've just turned down Harrods," he says with relish.

MINING A RICH SEAM

A great success of recent years has been the revival of real Caerphilly (as opposed to the crumbly, processed apology that bears the same name). It's one of the world's great cheeses, a fact confirmed when Gorwydd Caerphilly, made by brothers Todd and Maugan Trethowan just outside Llandewi Breffi in Cereidigion, West Wales, was recognised in the World Cheese Awards.

The style's origins, in the eponymous town and county of South Wales, are humble indeed. It was little more than a means of using up surplus milk, though by the 1830s its tangy, lemony taste was

Sheep graze on lush grass and herbs in the Welsh hills, which gives good flavour to the meat. David and Christine Pugh farm sheep in Powys.

attracting paying customers. It found special favour with Welsh miners who, because of the cheese's thick rind, could hold it with their dirty hands while underground. But when Cheddar became a privileged product due to rationing in the Second World War, Caerphilly, like many regional cheeses, declined.

The Trethowan's offerings, which adhere strictly to the original style, are things of beauty, housed within a thick rind that looks like roof slate. When cut, the interior is soft and spongy, and it has an unmistakeably fresh, citrus taste, born of the lush grass that feeds the herd of local Friesian cows with whom the whole process begins.

"It's an entirely hand-made cheese," says Maugan. "It's the handling that gives Caerphilly its texture. Handling curd ensures more of the whey remains with it. That and the two months of maturing account for the springy texture."

Despite Maugan's obvious relish for his cheese, it's not one to be precious about: most cheesemakers will tell you Caerphilly is the best cheese for that simplest of dishes, cheese on toast. And, as any Englishman will tell you, what else is Welsh Rarebit?

ANGELA HARTNETT

Though born in Kent and raised in Essex, Angela Hartnett comes from a long line of Northern Italian immigrants – the 'Bracchi' – who arrived in South Wales at the beginning of the 20th century and ran the fish bars and cafés within which the miners of the Rhondda Valley were introduced to the delights of 'frothy coffee'. "I really got into food at my grandad's fish and chip shop," Hartnett recalls, "and Mum said I should go to France to learn about cooking. But I wanted to get an education first. So I studied history in Cambridge."

As commis chef to Hans Schweitzer at Midsummer House, "the best restaurant in Cambridge", she was schooled in classic French techniques. After six months in Barbados, she got a job at Gordon Ramsay's Aubergine. "That was so exciting. Gordon was always in the kitchen; there was a real buzz about it." She also spent time in Tuscany, and cooked alongside Giorgio Locatelli, at Zafferano, and Marcus Wareing at Pétrus. After a stretch in Dubai, she's now in charge at the Connaught, offering cuisine influenced by the flavours of Italy and the wider Mediterranean.

"We're getting better in this country, but we're still behind Italy, France and Spain for everyday eating," she judges. "Food is still a middle class thing here – in Italy the working class eat as well as anyone. We need a push on seasonality, a boycott on ready meals, and some regulation to support local producers."

MENU ONE
> Leek and Potato Soup with Poached Oysters
> Salad of Sea Trout with Laver Bread
> Roasted Duck Breast with Red Cabbage and Home-made Mustard Fruits
> Welsh Cakes with Roasted Apricots and Welsh Cake Ice Cream

MENU TWO
> Leek and Wild Mushroom Tart with Hollandaise
> Salt Duck Salad
> Classic Fish and Chips
> Eve's Pudding

BRYN WILLIAMS

Bryn Williams, sous chef at the Orrery in London's Marylebone High Street, fell in love with food early on. Raised in Denbigh, North Wales, he was taken on a trip around a local bakery when he was 12. "To see the raw ingredients transformed into bread was fantastic. I was hooked," he recalls.

Bryn worked every Saturday, every hour that he could, making bread at Alwyn Thomas's bakery, and carried on full time after leaving school. At catering college in Llandudno, he was way ahead of the rest of his contemporaries, winning Student of the Year. Now, just 28, he's already worked under the wings of some of Britain's finest chefs: Marco Pierre White at the Criterion, and then at Le Gavroche, with the Roux Brothers. "With Marco, I learned about taste and quality. At Gavroche I began to understand why we cooked in a particular way," Williams says. "Michel Roux was a fantastic teacher."

Williams has ambitions to return to Wales, to make a difference in his own country, though he acknowledges that many Welsh chefs find it hard to go back. He is optimistic though. "Food culture in Wales is beginning to catch up with that of England," he believes. "Welsh produce has a fantastic reputation outside Wales: the lamb from the marshes and the mountains, Black Beef, with its wonderful red meat, mountain food like wild garlic. This is what I want to work with. And I think people in Wales are beginning to realise too just how good our produce is."

MENU ONE
> Glazed Goat's Cheese and Beetroot with a Salad of Welsh Herbs and Beetroot Dressing
> Pan-Fried Turbot with Cockles and Oxtail
> Roast Loin and Braised Shoulder of Salt-Marsh Lamb with Caper Jus
> Tost Wy of Bara Brith with Baked Plums and Yoghurt Ice Cream

MENU TWO
> Ham Hock Terrine, Pickled Mushrooms and Apple Compote
> Grilled and Smoked Mackerel with Citrus Fruits
> Welsh Black Beef, Caramelised Onions and Red Wine Sauce
> Buttermilk Pannacotta with Poached Strawberries and Welsh Shortbread Biscuit

LEEK AND POTATO SOUP
WITH POACHED OYSTERS

SERVES 4

25g butter
1 tbsp olive oil
1 small white onion, finely chopped
4 large leeks, about 300g total weight,
    finely sliced
2 large potatoes, peeled and cut into cubes
1 bouquet garni
8 small rock oysters
fish stock
snipped chives

CHICKEN STOCK

4 chickens, cut into portions
1 leek, roughly chopped
1 celery stick, roughly chopped
1 onion, roughly chopped
1 head of garlic, cut in half crossways
sprigs of thyme
1 bay leaf

1 First make the chicken stock. Place the chickens, chopped vegetables, garlic and herbs in a large pan, cover with cold water and bring to the boil. Skim off any fat that rises to the surface, then leave to simmer for 1 1/2–2 hours. Strain the stock through a colander set in a bowl, then pass through a sieve. You need 700ml stock for the soup; keep the remainder for another use.

2 Remove the 'oysters' from the chicken portions in the colander and leave to one side for use later as a garnish. Discard all the remaining contents of the colander.

3 Melt the butter with the olive oil in a saucepan. Add the onion and slowly cook without colouring. After a couple of minutes add the leeks, then sweat for about 5 minutes over a low heat. Do not allow the vegetables to colour.

4 Add the potatoes and bouquet garni and cook uncovered for 2 minutes, then pour in the hot chicken stock. Bring to the boil and cook until the potatoes are soft.

5 Remove the bouquet garni, then blitz the soup in a food processor or blender. Pour into a bowl and set over ice to cool. Chill in the fridge until ready to serve.

6 Remove the oysters from their shells and lightly poach in a touch of fish stock. Drain and allow to cool.

7 To serve, place the sea oysters and chicken 'oysters' in large soup bowls and ladle the soup on top. Finish with a sprinkling of chives.

SALAD OF SEA TROUT
WITH LAVER BREAD

SERVES 4
2 whole sea trout, filleted
8–12 baby violet artichokes
lemon juice
1 small carrot, diced
1 small bulb fennel, diced
1 garlic clove, crushed
olive oil

sprig of thyme
100ml white wine
rock salt and pepper

LAVER BREAD
100g laver bread
100g fine oatmeal
butter and vegetable oil

1 Remove any pin bones from the trout fillets, then score the skin. Set aside.

2 Prepare the artichokes by pulling off any large leaves, trimming and peeling them, then scooping out the chokes. As each one is prepared, drop immediately into a bowl of water and lemon juice to prevent discoloration.

3 Cook the carrot, fennel and garlic in a little olive oil with the thyme and a pinch of salt until lightly coloured. Add the artichokes and cover with the white wine and 100ml water. Cook for about 10 minutes or until the artichokes are tender (test with the tip of a sharp knife).

4 Meanwhile, mix together the laver bread and oatmeal with some salt and pepper and shape into four little cakes. Fry in butter with a touch of vegetable oil until golden brown on both sides. Remove from the pan and keep hot.

5 Pan-fry the trout fillets in a little hot olive oil, skin side down first, for about 2 minutes on each side.

6 To serve, place a laver bread cake in the centre of each plate and spoon the warm artichokes on top. Place the trout fillets on the vegetables.

Laver bread, or 'bara lawr' in Welsh, is an edible seaweed common to Wales's south west coast. Traditionally, it's boiled for up to 5 hours, reduced to a jelly and served with bacon.

ROASTED DUCK BREAST
WITH RED CABBAGE AND
HOME-MADE MUSTARD FRUITS

SERVES 4
2–4 duck breasts, depending on size
butter
rock salt and pepper

MUSTARD FRUITS
2kg small, firm pears such as William's
   or whatever is in season
400g sugar
mustard essence

DUCK SAUCE
500g duck bones, chopped
1 shallot, sliced
1 garlic clove, peeled
olive oil
sprigs of thyme
1 bay leaf
black peppercorns
50ml Madeira
150ml veal stock
150ml brown chicken stock

SPICE BAG
½ cinnamon stick, broken
3 juniper berries
3 cloves
2 star anise

BRAISED RED CABBAGE
1 red cabbage, finely shredded
100g brown sugar
250ml Port
500ml red wine
duck fat
1 onion, sliced
2 apples, peeled, quartered and
   sliced crossways
sprig of thyme
1 bay leaf
4 tbsp redcurrant jelly

LAYERED POTATOES
2 large Desiree potatoes
olive oil

1 First make the mustard fruits. Peel the pears and cut in half lengthways. Leave
the stalks and seeds. Place the pears in a container, add the sugar and stir to mix.
Cover and let sit at room temperature for 12 hours.

2 The pears will have begun to release their juices. Drain the juice into a pan and
bring to the boil. Simmer for 5 minutes.

3 Cover the pears with this syrup and leave for another 12 hours.

4 Once again, drain the syrup from the pears, bring it to the boil and simmer for
5 minutes. Pour back over the pears and leave for 12 hours.

5 Repeat this procedure two more times, then drain the syrup into a pan, bring
to the boil and reduce to one-third. Add the pears to the syrup and caramelise for
20 minutes. Allow to cool.

6 Add 10 drops of mustard essence to the pears, then seal in glass jars and leave
to mature for 2–3 weeks before using.

7 Next make the duck sauce. Preheat the oven to 180°C/gas 4, then roast the duck
bones until well browned. Meanwhile, sauté the shallot and garlic in a little olive
oil until golden brown. Add the herbs and peppercorns, and pour in the Madeira.

Bring to the boil and reduce to a glaze. Drain all the fat from the duck bones, then add them to the pan. Add the stocks and bring to the boil. Simmer, skimming regularly, until reduced to about 100ml. Pass through a muslin cloth and allow to cool. Keep in the fridge until needed; reheat before using.

8 For the red cabbage, first prepare the spice bag. Lightly toast the whole spices in a dry pan until fragrant. Allow to cool, then wrap in a piece of muslin. Put the red cabbage in a container with the sugar, Port, wine and spice bag, cover with cling film and place a heavy weight on top. Leave to marinate in a cool place for 24 hours.

9 Drain the cabbage in a sieve set over a bowl; reserve the liquid. Heat some duck fat and sweat the onion and apples with the thyme and bay leaf until soft. Add the cabbage and sweat down until tender. Add the reserved liquid and continue to cook until it evaporates to a glaze. Check the seasoning, then finish with the redcurrant jelly. Keep to one side, and reheat for serving.

10 Preheat the oven to 200°C/gas 6.

11 While the cabbage is cooking, prepare the potatoes. Peel them, then slice very thinly (1–2mm), preferably on a mandolin. Divide into four portions and 'tile' each portion evenly (lay the slices on top of each other, almost completely overlapping, so you end up with them resembling a deck of cards displayed in a cascade). Trim the edges of each cascade to make a neat rectangle roughly 15cm long, 7cm wide and 2cm thick. Season with salt and pepper on both sides.

12 Heat a little olive oil in a frying pan that can be put into the oven. Add the potatoes and colour a golden brown on both sides. At this point the potatoes will not be cooked through. Just before serving, add the hot duck sauce, cover with a buttered paper and finish cooking in the oven for 5 minutes or until the potatoes are tender.

13 Meanwhile, score the skin and fat on the duck breasts without cutting through into the meat. Heat a frying pan over a low heat and add the duck breasts, skin side down. Allow the fat to render down. Pour away the excess fat, then add the butter to the pan and cook for a further 3–4 minutes or until the duck is medium rare.

14 Remove the duck breasts from the pan and allow to rest for 4–5 minutes. Then place the duck breasts in the oven to finish cooking for 5 minutes.

15 To serve, spoon the cabbage on to the warm plates, place the potato and sliced duck on top and finish with some mustard fruits.

WELSH CAKES
WITH ROASTED APRICOTS
AND WELSH CAKE ICE CREAM

SERVES 4
12 apricots, halved and stoned
caster sugar
unsalted butter

WELSH CAKES
225g self-raising flour
½ tsp mixed spice
pinch of salt
85g caster sugar
115g butter or margarine
85g sultanas

1 large egg, beaten
milk if needed
lard for cooking

ICE CREAM
175g egg yolks
90g caster sugar
375ml whipping cream
125ml milk
1 vanilla pod, split lengthways
ground cinnamon
freshly grated nutmeg

1 First make the Welsh cakes. Sift the flour, spice and salt into a bowl and stir in the sugar, then rub in the butter until the mixture has a crumb-like texture. Add the sultanas and mix together, then mix in the egg using a fork. Gather into a dough. If too dry add a spot of milk.

2 Turn the dough on to a lightly floured board and roll out to about 5mm thick. Cut out four 8–10cm rounds and four 5cm rounds. Cut the remaining dough into rounds or other shapes of any size, re-rolling the trimmings as necessary (these cakes will be used for the ice cream).

3 Lightly grease a griddle with lard, then heat on a low heat. Start with a cake or two for the ice cream to test the heat of the griddle. Then lightly cook all the cakes for 20–30 seconds on each side or until golden brown. Leave to cool.

4 To make the ice cream, beat together the egg yolks and sugar in a bowl until pale. Pour the cream and milk into a saucepan and scrape in the seeds from the vanilla pod; add the pod too. Heat until the cream is just coming to the boil, then pour a little over the egg mix and whisk together. Pour this mixture into the rest of the hot cream mixture in the pan and cook, stirring, until thickened enough to coat the back of a wooden spoon. Take care not to let the custard boil. Remove from the pan and cool over ice, then strain.

5 Churn the custard in an ice cream machine. Just as it is ready, sprinkle in 300g crumbled Welsh cakes and finish with ground cinnamon and nutmeg to taste. Transfer to a container and freeze for about 2 hours to harden.

6 Roast the apricots in a frying pan with a touch of sugar and butter until soft.

7 To serve, spoon the warm apricots on top of the large Welsh cakes. Add the smaller Welsh cakes and top each serving with a scoop of ice cream.

LEEK AND WILD MUSHROOM TART
WITH HOLLANDAISE

SERVES 4
250g shortcrust pastry
2 leeks, finely sliced
butter
200g wild mushrooms
olive oil
finely chopped flat-leaf parsley
green salad to serve

HOLLANDAISE SAUCE
8 tbsp white wine vinegar
1 shallot, finely sliced
sprig of thyme
1 bay leaf
4 black peppercorns
3 egg yolks
150g unsalted butter, melted
1 tsp lemon juice

OPTIONAL ADDITIONS
fried quail's eggs
sliced fresh truffle

1 Preheat the oven to 180°C/gas 4. Roll out the pastry and use to line four 10cm tart rings placed on a baking tray. Line them with greaseproof paper and weight down with dried beans, then bake blind for 12–15 minutes or until golden brown. Leave to cool until needed. Remove from the rings before filling.

2 To make the hollandaise, put the vinegar, shallot, herbs and peppercorns in a pan and reduce by two-thirds. Strain the mixture into a bowl and whisk in the egg yolks. Set the bowl over another bowl of warm water and slowly add the butter, whisking well after each addition. When all the butter has all been incorporated add the lemon juice and 2 tsp water. Taste and season if necessary. Cover with cling film and set aside in a warm place.

3 Lightly sauté the leeks in butter until soft.

4 Meanwhile, sauté the mushrooms in olive oil, then toss with some parsley.

5 Fill the pastry cases with the leeks and mushrooms. To make them extra special you can add some fried quail's eggs or sliced truffle. Heat in the oven for 10 minutes.

6 Cover the tarts with the hollandaise, then flash under a hot grill to glaze. Serve with a crisp green salad.

SALT DUCK SALAD

SERVES 4
4 duck breasts
rock salt
1 carrot, roughly chopped
1 leek, roughly chopped
1 celery stick, roughly chopped
1 onion, roughly chopped
sprig of thyme
1 bay leaf
salt and pepper

VINAIGRETTE
100ml olive oil
10ml red wine vinegar
½ tsp honey

VEGETABLE SALAD
1 bulb fennel, finely sliced
2 celery sticks, finely sliced
6 radishes, finely sliced
bunch of watercress, stalks discarded

TO FINISH
toasted sesame seeds
flat-leaf parsley leaves, deep-fried
    until crisp

1 Rub the duck breasts all over with rock salt, then leave in the fridge for 3 days, turning them from time to time. Rinse to remove the salt.

2 Combine the carrot, leek, celery, onion, thyme and bay leaf in a large saucepan and cover with water. Add the duck breasts and bring to the boil. Reduce the heat and cook for 15 minutes at a simmer, skimming when necessary. Leave the duck breasts to cool in the liquid.

3 Mix together the vinaigrette ingredients with salt and pepper to taste.

4 Put all of the ingredients for the vegetable salad in a bowl and season with the vinaigrette, tossing to mix.

5 To serve, slice the duck thinly and arrange on plates with the salad. Finish with toasted sesame seeds and deep-fried parsley.

Illustrated overleaf

CLASSIC
FISH AND CHIPS

SERVES 4

4 large King Edward potatoes, peeled
   and cut into chips
vegetable oil for deep-frying
4 portions of haddock or cod fillet
seasoned flour
salt

BATTER

150g plain flour
75g cornflour
½ tsp caster sugar
1 tsp olive oil

1 Mix together all the ingredients for the batter with 225ml water and 1 tsp salt and leave to rest for about 20 minutes.

2 Heat a deep pan of oil to about 120°C. Blanch the chips in the oil, in batches if necessary, for 5–8 minutes or until soft but not coloured. Drain on kitchen paper.

3 Heat the pan of oil to 160–180°C. Dip the fish in seasoned flour to coat lightly, then dip into the batter. Shake off any excess batter, then fry in the hot oil until golden and crisp, and cooked in the centre. As the fish is cooked, remove and drain on kitchen paper, then keep warm in a low oven.

4 Add the blanched chips to the hot oil and fry until golden brown and crisp. Drain on kitchen paper and season with salt. Serve immediately with the fish, and Sarson's vinegar to sprinkle over.

EVE'S PUDDING

SERVES 4

6 large Bramley's apples, peeled, cored and sliced
100g sultanas
50g sugar
1 punnet of blackberries
whipped cream or custard to serve

SPONGE MIX

100g caster sugar
100g margarine
2 large eggs
100g self-raising flour

1 Preheat the oven to 220°C/gas 7.

2 Place the apples in a buttered baking dish. Scatter on the sultanas. Sprinkle with the sugar and then with the blackberries.

3 To make the sponge mix, cream together the sugar and margarine. Beat in the eggs, then fold in the flour.

4 Cover the fruit with the sponge mix. Bake for 30–40 minutes or until the sponge is golden brown and cooked through. Serve hot with whipped cream or custard.

Salt duck salad (recipe on page 81)

84

GLAZED
GOAT'S CHEESE AND BEETROOT
WITH A SALAD OF WELSH HERBS
AND BEETROOT DRESSING

SERVES 4

4 Welsh goat's cheeses, each 120g
sprigs of thyme
olive oil
120g sugar
3 large beetroots, cooked, peeled and roughly diced
2 tsp balsamic vinegar
12 or more raw baby beetroots
150g Snowdon mountain herbs, such as wood sorrel,
    hairy bittercress, pennywort or whatever is in season
20g toasted pine nuts
salt and pepper

1 Put the cheeses in a bowl with some thyme and olive oil to cover. Leave to marinate while you prepare the beetroot dressing.
2 Melt the sugar in a heavy-bottomed pan on a moderate heat, then cook until the sugar has turned golden brown. Add the cooked beetroot and cook for a further 3 minutes, stirring until the beetroot is completely coated with the caramel. Remove from the heat and add the balsamic vinegar. Transfer to a food processor and blend to a smooth consistency.
3 Pour the purée into a muslin-lined colander set in a bowl and allow the liquid to drain through. Season the liquid to taste and double the volume with olive oil to create a dressing. Season the purée. Set both dressing and purée aside.
4 Preheat the oven to 140°C/gas 1.
5 Wrap the baby beetroots in a foil envelope with some sprigs of thyme. Place in the oven and bake for 10–12 minutes. Peel the beetroots and leave to cool.
6 Remove the cheeses from the marinade and blot off any excess oil with kitchen paper. Glaze the tops of the cheeses using a blow torch (or under a hot grill) until golden brown.
7 Dress the Welsh herbs in the beetroot dressing.
8 To assemble, spread a tablespoon of beetroot purée on each plate. Add the dressed herbs and position the glazed cheeses on top. Drizzle round the remainder of the beetroot dressing, add the baby beetroots and sprinkle with toasted pine nuts. Serve with warm laver bread.

PAN-FRIED TURBOT
WITH COCKLES AND OXTAIL

SERVES 4
12oz sea beet, stalks removed
olive oil
freshly grated nutmeg
squeeze of lemon juice
4 pieces of skinned turbot fillet,
   each 120g
butter
salt and pepper

OXTAIL
1kg Welsh Black Beef oxtail, cut into pieces
1 litre red wine

1 large onion, chopped
1 large carrot, chopped
1 bay leaf
vegetable oil
seasoned flour
1 litre veal stock
2 litres chicken stock

COCKLES
400g cockles, cleaned
1 glass of white wine
2 tbsp crème fraîche

1 Put the oxtail in a bowl with the red wine, onion, carrot and bay leaf. Cover and leave to marinate in a cool place for 24 hours.
2 Preheat the oven to 140°C/gas 1.
3 Strain off the red wine from the oxtail and vegetables and place in a saucepan. Bring to the boil, skimming off any scum that rises to the surface. Meanwhile, heat some vegetable oil in a heavy-bottomed pan that can be put into the oven. Dust the oxtail in seasoned flour, then add to the pan and colour a golden brown on all sides. Remove from the pan and set aside. Add the marinated vegetables to the pan and cook until golden brown. Deglaze the pan with the hot red wine, then reduce by half.
4 Return the oxtail to the pan. Cover with the veal and chicken stocks and bring to the boil. Skim, then cover and place in the oven to cook for 2 1/2 hours.
5 Remove from the oven and leave to cool. When cooled, remove the oxtail and pick the meat from the bones, retaining the meat in large pieces; discard the bones. Strain the liquid into a saucepan and reduce by half. Keep the meat and sauce warm.
6 To cook the cockles place them in a warm pan with the white wine, cover and cook on a high heat for 1–2 minutes or until they open. Drain in a colander set in a bowl. Set the liquid to one side. Pick the cockles from their shells (leaving a few in shell).
7 Warm some olive oil in a deep pan and add the sea beet. Season with salt, pepper, nutmeg and lemon juice. Cook for 30 seconds to wilt. Keep hot.
8 Heat a little olive oil in a non-stick pan. Place the turbot in the pan and cook until the underside is brown. Turn the turbot pieces over and lower the heat. Cook for a further 2–3 minutes maximum. Add a knob of butter to finish.
9 To serve, place the sea beet on warm plates and arrange the cockles and picked oxtail around. Drizzle with the oxtail sauce. Position the turbot on the sea beet. Bring the cockle liquid to the boil, whisk in the crème fraîche and pour on to the plates.

ROAST LOIN AND BRAISED SHOULDER OF
SALT-MARSH LAMB
WITH CAPER JUS

SERVES 4

1 shoulder of salt-marsh lamb, about 2–3kg
vegetable oil
1 large onion, chopped
1 large carrot, chopped
2 sprigs of rosemary
250ml white wine
2 litres chicken stock
1 litre veal stock
2kg Desiree potatoes, peeled and finely sliced

1 best end of salt-marsh lamb, with 8 cutlets
salt and pepper

TO FINISH

selection of summer vegetables, such as
   baby carrots, broad beans and baby leeks
200g girolles or other wild mushrooms
   as available
olive oil
1 tsp capers

1 Preheat the oven to 140°C/gas 1.

2 Heat a little vegetable oil in a heavy-bottomed pan that can go into the oven. Sear the shoulder of lamb on all sides over a moderate heat. When coloured, remove the lamb from the pan and replace with the chopped onion and carrot and a sprig of rosemary. Cook for 4–5 minutes or until golden brown.

3 Add the white wine and reduce by half. Put the shoulder of lamb back in the pan on top of the vegetables and cover with the chicken and veal stocks. Bring to the boil. Cover the pan, then place in the oven and cook for 1 hour. Remove from the oven and leave to cool.

4 When cooled, pick the meat from the bone into small pieces. Strain the stock and discard the vegetables. Bring the stock back to the boil and skim.

5 Arrange some of the potato slices on the bottom of a 20 x 15cm square baking dish to create a thin layer. Season with salt, pepper and the remaining rosemary, chopped. Add a layer of picked lamb shoulder, then build up a further two layers of potato slices and lamb. Cover the layers with enough of the hot lamb stock to moisten. Place in the oven. Cook for 30 minutes or until the potatoes are tender and the liquid has been absorbed. Remove and keep hot. Turn the oven to 180°C/gas 4.

6 Season the best end of lamb, then sear, fat side down first, in a little vegetable oil in a heavy-bottomed pan. Turn to sear all over. Place in the oven and roast for 6–8 minutes. When cooked, leave to rest for 15 minutes.

7 Meanwhile, reduce 150ml of the lamb stock to a sauce consistency. Cook the summer vegetables in a little of the remaining lamb stock until tender; drain. Pan-fry the mushrooms in a little olive oil, then season.

8 To assemble, cut out four cylinders from the potato and lamb layers and place one on each warm plate. Carve the best end of lamb into cutlets and position to the side of the potato cylinder. Arrange the vegetables and mushrooms around the meat. Add the capers to the reduced lamb stock and pour over the dish. Serve immediately.

TOST WY OF BARA BRITH
WITH BAKED PLUMS AND
YOGHURT ICE CREAM

SERVES 4
9 plums, halved and stoned
1 tbsp honey
sprig of lemon thyme
1 vanilla pod, split lengthways

YOGHURT ICE CREAM
150ml milk
60g sugar
6 egg yolks
250g fresh plain yoghurt

PEPPER TUILES
150g unsalted butter
250g caster sugar
200ml canned coconut milk
1 tbsp cracked black pepper
100g plain flour

TOST WY
3 eggs
3 tbsp milk
4 slices of Bara Brith, cut 1cm thick, crusts removed
unsalted butter

1 First make the yoghurt ice cream. Combine the milk and sugar in a pan and bring to the boil. Pour the hot liquid onto the egg yolks and whisk. Return to the pan and put back on to the heat to thicken. When the custard coats the back of a spoon remove from the heat and leave to cool. When cold add the yoghurt and mix well. Churn in an ice cream machine, then keep in the freezer until needed.

2 Next make the pepper tuiles. Whisk together the butter, sugar and coconut milk until smooth, then mix in the pepper. Fold in the flour. Chill for 1 hour.

3 Preheat the oven to 180°C/gas 4.

4 Spread the tuile mixture very thinly (2–3mm) over a non-stick baking sheet. Bake for 8–10 minutes or until golden. Leave to cool on the sheet. When cold, remove and break into mouth-size pieces. (This will make more tuiles than you need for this recipe, but they will keep for a week.)

5 Create a foil envelope and in it place the plums, honey, lemon thyme and vanilla pod. Seal the package so it is airtight, then place on a baking tray in the oven and bake for 10–12 minutes. Remove from the oven, but do not open the bag, to ensure the contents keep warm.

6 To make the tost wy, whisk together the eggs and milk in a wide, shallow dish. Place the slices of Bara Brith in the mixture, turning them to coat, then fry them in a little bit of unsalted butter in a non-stick pan until the egg mixture has cooked and both sides are golden brown.

7 To serve, place a slice of tost wy on each plate and position some of the warm plums on top. Drizzle some of the plum juice over the plate. Place a scoop of yoghurt ice cream to the side and put some tuiles on it.

HAM HOCK TERRINE
PICKLED MUSHROOMS AND APPLE COMPOTE

SERVES 4
4 ham hocks
2 large carrots, chopped
2 large onions, chopped
4 sprigs of thyme
1 bulb garlic, cut in half crossways
large bunch of parsley, chopped
salt and pepper

PICKLED MUSHROOMS
4 shallots, finely chopped
100ml white wine vinegar
250g girolles, stalks scraped

APPLE COMPOTE
4 Cox's apples, peeled, cored and
    chopped
knob of butter

1 Put the ham hocks in a large pan and cover with water. Bring to the boil and skim. Add the carrots, onions, thyme and garlic and simmer for 3 hours or until the meat comes away from the bone. Remove from the heat and allow to cool.

2 Drain the hocks, reserving the liquid, and pick the meat from the bone. Place the meat in a large bowl and season with salt, pepper and chopped parsley.

3 Pass the liquid through a sieve into a saucepan and reduce it by one-third over a high heat. Add the liquid to the meat and mix together, then place in a 30cm long terrine mould lined with cling film. Put the terrine in the fridge to set.

4 To prepare the pickled mushrooms, cook the shallots in the vinegar and 100ml water for a few minutes, then pour the hot liquid on to the mushrooms in a bowl. Leave to cool.

5 Cook the apples with the butter until soft, then crush with a fork and season with salt and pepper.

6 To serve, cut the terrine into slices 1cm thick and place on the plates. Drain the mushrooms and sprinkle around the terrine. Finish with a quenelle of apple compote on top of the terrine.

Ham hock, the small joint at the lower portion of a pig's hind leg, is a traditional ingredient of cawl, a slow-cooked Welsh broth.

GRILLED AND SMOKED MACKEREL
WITH CITRUS FRUITS

SERVES 4
4 mackerel, each 350g
pinch of turmeric (optional)
olive oil
salt and pepper

SAUCE
1 carrot, chopped
1 onion, chopped
2 garlic cloves, crushed
1 lemon, sliced
6 black peppercorns
1 bay leaf
1 star anise
bunch of basil

100ml dry white wine
100ml olive oil
50g butter

CITRUS FRUITS
1 orange
1 pink grapefruit
100ml sugar
50ml white wine vinegar

GARNISH
12 Charlotte potatoes
50ml olive oil
2 celery sticks
1 small celeriac
butter

1 To make the sauce, put the carrot and onion in a large pan with garlic, lemon slices, peppercorns, bay leaf and star anise. Add water to cover and bring to the boil. Reduce the heat and simmer for 8 minutes. Add the basil stalks and cook for a further 2 minutes. Remove the pan from the heat. Add the white wine and leave to infuse until needed.

2 When ready to serve, strain the stock, bring back to the boil and whisk in the olive oil and julienned basil leaves. Finish by incorporating the butter.

3 To prepare the citrus fruits, thinly peel the zest from the orange and grapefruit and cut into julienne. Place in a small pan of water and bring to the boil, then drain and refresh. Repeat this blanching procedure three times. In another pan dissolve the sugar in 100ml water and bring to the boil. Add the zest and simmer for 40 minutes or until tender. Remove from the heat and add the vinegar to give a balance of sweet and sour flavours. Set aside.

4 Peel and segment the citrus fruits, keeping all the juices, and place to one side.

5 Prepare the mackerel by gutting and washing it. Dry with kitchen paper. For the optional garnish, cut off 6cm of the tail end, keeping it on the bone. (This is for the smoking part of the dish.) Fillet the fish. Remove all pin bones from the fillets, then wash the fillets and pat dry. Trim the edges to neaten and leave to one side.

6 If you are going to prepare the optional smoked fish garnish, score the tail skin, then mix the tails with half of the citrus juice and the turmeric. Leave for 30 minutes. Before serving, smoke on the stove for 4–5 minutes and keep warm.

7 For the garnish, 'turn' the potatoes (or just peel them and cut into neat shapes), then cook in boiling salted water until almost tender. When nearly ready drain them

and place in the remaining fruit juice with the olive oil. Leave to cool so they can take on the citrus flavours. Before serving bring the potatoes up to the boil in the juice and oil mixture.

8 Peel the celery and celeriac, then cut into equal-sized batons (12 of each). Cook in just enough seasoned water to cover with a knob of butter until just tender but not soft. Drain and keep hot.

9 Preheat the grill to high.

10 Place the mackerel fillets, skin side up, on an oiled baking tray. Brush the skin with oil and season. Place under the grill and cook for 3–4 minutes, without turning.

11 Meanwhile, make a bed of the hot batons of celery and celeriac on the warm plates. When the mackerel is ready place two fillets on each bed, skin side up. Place the warm mackerel tail standing up on top of the plate.

12 Add the hot potatoes to the side of the grilled mackerel and garnish the fish with segments of orange and pink grapefruit. Sprinkle the drained zest on the fish and spoon the sauce around the dish. Serve immediately.

WELSH BLACK BEEF
CARAMELISED ONIONS AND RED WINE SAUCE

SERVES 4
4 fillet steaks of Welsh Black Beef, each 180g
vegetable oil
20 baby onions, peeled
butter
2 leeks, finely chopped
100ml double cream
250g girolles, stalks scraped
olive oil
salt and pepper

RED WINE SAUCE
3 shallots, sliced
butter
sprig of thyme
300ml Port
300ml red wine
750ml veal stock

1 Preheat the oven to 180°C/gas 4.

2 First make the sauce. Sweat the shallots in a little butter with the thyme, then add the Port and red wine and bring to the boil. Reduce by one-third. Add the veal stock and reduce to a good sauce consistency. Check the seasoning.

3 Meanwhile, season the fillet steaks and sear on all sides in a little vegetable oil in a hot ovenproof pan. Place in the oven and roast for 7–9 minutes. When ready, leave to rest in a warm place.

4 While the fillets are cooking, roast the whole baby onions in a frying pan in some oil and butter until soft and golden brown.

5 Blanch the leeks in boiling salted water for 30 seconds, then drain. Bring the double cream to the boil and add the blanched leeks. Cook together for 4–5 minutes or until leeks are coated by the cream.

6 Pan-fry the mushrooms in olive oil with some salt and pepper.

7 To serve, position the creamed leeks in the centre of each warm plate and place a fillet of beef on top. Assemble the mushrooms and onions around the beef and pour on the red wine sauce.

BUTTERMILK PANNACOTTA
WITH POACHED STRAWBERRIES AND
WELSH SHORTBREAD BISCUIT

SERVES 4
350ml double cream
100g sugar
350ml buttermilk
3 gelatine leaves, soaked in cold water
   for at least 10 minutes

WELSH SHORTBREAD
200g unsalted butter

90g icing sugar, sifted
250g plain flour
pinch of salt

POACHED STRAWBERRIES
200g sugar
300ml white wine
500g strawberries, quartered

1 First make the shortbread. Mix the butter and icing sugar together, then gently mix in the flour and salt to make a dough. Roll into a cylinder, wrap in cling film and refrigerate for at least 2 hours.

2 Preheat the oven to 180°C/gas 4.

3 Cut the chilled shortbread dough into 5mm thick slices and place on a baking sheet. Bake for 10–12 minutes or until golden. Cool slightly on the baking sheet, then transfer to a wire rack to finish cooling. If you like, dust them with sugar.

4 Bring the double cream and sugar to the boil, stirring to dissolve the sugar, then pour on to the buttermilk. Gently squeeze the gelatine dry, add to the mixture and stir until completely melted. Pass through a sieve. Divide equally among four shot glasses and place in the fridge to set.

5 For the strawberries, dissolve the sugar in 200ml water and bring to the boil. Add the wine and bring back to the boil, then pour over the prepared strawberries. Cover with cling film and leave to cool.

6 To serve, put a shot glass of pannacotta on each plate with the shortbread to the side and add the strawberries with their juice.

CHAPTER FOUR

THE SOUTH WEST

JOHN BURTON RACE & MICHAEL CAINES

It's the wildness of the West the visitor remembers, the rugged moorlands of Dartmoor and Exmoor in the midst of 600km of craggy coast. And it's in these two distinctive environments that the best of the South West's produce is found: the lamb that roam the hills, the crabs that crawl the ocean floor, and the shoals – once, three-million strong – of Cornish pilchards, a thousand miles away from the mushy fish in tomato sauce that impoverished the name, and now again a food of world renown.

Wild it may be, but the West is warm too. Microclimates, which make the Dart estuary and the waters around Scilly attract swimmers as late as November, abound, and spring arrives earlier than anywhere else in Britain. The flat peatlands of Somerset and Avon, and the sandy lowland heaths of Dorset teem with vegetables from April on.

FIRST TASTE OF SUMMER

Asparagus is the ultimate seasonal food, wonderful in May and June, the first mouthful of summer. It puts a smile on the face for other reasons: it's long had a reputation as an aphrodisiac. Four centuries ago, the herbalist Nicholas Culpeper wrote that it "stirreth up bodily lust in man or woman". For whatever reason, John Burton Race is obsessed with it, creating 30 or more asparagus dishes for his Dartmouth restaurant, the New Angel. He gets his from Kingsbridge farmer Nigel Cuthburt.

For three decades Cuthburt was a 'pharmer', a researcher for one of the major drug companies. Now he's a real farmer, of asparagus, which thrives in the well-drained, sandy soils of his hectare plot on the edge of Dartmoor. "There's no clay here, that's the enemy of asparagus," he tells me. "Out in East Anglia, they grow it in not much more than sand, but I always beat them to the market. It's warmer out west, so I cut mine before they do."

He starts picking the purple-tinged tips of fibrous green at the end of April, harvesting twice a day if the weather's good. "When it's warm, asparagus can grow 15cm overnight."

Cuthburt grows a Dutch strain, gynlim, which is as robust as this delicate vegetable gets. "Hardly anyone knows what fresh asparagus tastes like. Even after a couple of days, it's not in perfect condition anymore. I suppose I'm one of the lucky few."

So what does really fresh asparagus taste like, cut from the ground and minutes later in a pan? "That's hard," pleads Cuthburt, struggling for description. "It's just so good. Nutty... crunchy... perfect."

THIS LOCAL THING

"There are more people buying local lamb now than at any time I can remember," says Stanley Wreyford, and he goes back a long way. All his life he's reared lamb on 80 hectares overlooking Blackawton, a place where tractors still outnumber SUVs, one of the last remaining working villages in the tourist haven of the South Hams.

"It's good, this local thing. People know where their meat comes from, and they like to buy stuff that's grown, reared and fed not far away."

Wreyford's sheep are mainly Poll Dorset ewes, crossed with a few black-faced Suffolk rams. He sells most of it to a local butcher – Luscombe – who has become a magnet for local chefs and foodies. "To be honest, I don't think most people have a clue what good meat should look like, but they know it when they taste it. So any butcher who sells good meat keeps his custom."

Good lamb, like all good meat, needs 'shape', muscle, and a little 'cover' – fat to you and me. "Sheep are fairly easy, 'cos they just roam, but you've got to take care of them, especially with what they eat. I give them a few pellets here and there, and lush grass. What you put in, you get out." Wreyford's lamb earns high praise from John Burton Race: "Even the French can't match it. It's simply second-to-none. Stunning."

Early every morning, Anthony Buscombe (pictured on the previous page) and his brother set out on their boat from Dartmouth to catch crab.

PILCHARD SHOALS

It is the coast that defines the South West, for holidaymakers, sailors, and the surfers who have made Newquay their own. Overlooking Towan Beach is a 14th-century Huer's Hut. The task of the huer (from the French 'huer' – to shout) was to alert the local fishermen of the arrival of the pilchard shoals, crying "Hevva, hevva". By the 1870s, like the tin mines, the industry was in decline. Now it's thriving again, the 'salacche inglesi' popular with northern Italians, and Britons in love with the anchovy-like taste and the healthy properties of Omega-3 oil.

"All these fish are swept in from the Bay of Biscay," John Burton Race tells me. "But the real glory round here is the crab."

CATCHING CRAB

Every morning, at 4.45am, Anthony Buscombe joins his brother on the quay at Dartmouth harbour to begin the 8km journey out to sea to catch crab. Dartmouth has long been home to crab-fishermen, ever since the trawlers departed when the fish market was set up in Brixham. Diners finishing lunch at John Burton Race's New Angel might snatch a sight of the Buscombes as they return around 3pm with, on a good day, a 600kg catch – as many as 800 crabs. The white meat from the claws of the cock crabs found here is said to be the sweetest anywhere. John Burton Race swears by it, but urges simplicity. "Eighty per cent of all Britain's crab comes from the Dartmouth and Salcombe coast, and it's the best there is. The delicate, sweet meat needs only a little butter and spice."

Some cock crabs can be 40 years old, every spare gap in their shell crammed with juicy flesh. August to mid-November is the high season, when the pots, which on a normal day will hold just a couple of crabs, will be crammed with ten or more, and the Buscombes make hay. "But it's an all year trade," says Anthony Buscombe. "In winter we get two or three times the price, so it evens itself out. And it's sustainable. Every immature crab goes back in the sea. People like to know the story of what they've eaten, and when they see the crabs, the mackerel, the herring being landed, they feel part of the story. They care about their health now, so the oily fish that were once unfashionable are in demand again."

JOHN BURTON RACE

"When I first moved here, I got in the car, drove around and was amazed at what I found. Fantastic fish, lamb, quail and duck, as good as anywhere." John Burton Race moved to Dartmouth four years ago, following the success of his television programme and book, *French Leave*, in which he took his substantial family over to France to get back to his culinary roots.

"In France I discovered simplicity. For years, I had been chasing Michelin stars, but France was a clean slate. I put the emphasis on the plate rather than the garnish. I call it progress."

His "progress" to a more simple culinary philosophy continues back on this side of the Channel, with the dishes he prepares at his highly rated Dartmouth restaurant, the New Angel, perfectly positioned to look out on to the picturesque harbour from where he gets much of his basic ingredients.

"I aim to cook with local produce, in season. That's my philosophy. It's all about taste. That can be difficult as there's no continuous supply. The area's not big enough. But there are just enough 'little nutcases' round here to make sure the produce never dries up. So far, so good. I am sure everyone says this about their own area, but I can honestly say, this region's got the lot."

MENU ONE
> Crown of English Asparagus
> Dartmouth Crab Plate
> Grilled Fillet of South Devon Beef with a Shallot and Tomato Sauce
> Tiverton Strawberry Shortcake with Basil Caramel

MENU TWO
> English Asparagus with a Warm Leek Purée, Puff Pastry Case, Hollandaise and Quail Reduction
> Blackened Fillet of Mackerel, Root Vegetables and Horseradish Cream
> Loin of Pork, Walnut Crust and Apple Juice Reduction
> Red Fruit Soup with Rosemary Syrup and Lemon Madeleine

MICHAEL CAINES

Adopted into a large family in Exeter, Michael Caines grew up surrounded by good food. "Mum was a good English cook who used fresh, seasonal ingredients and baked great cakes, while Dad cultivated vegetables and apples. Meals were always big family affairs."

At Exeter Catering College, Caines was Student of the Year, and a distinguished career beckoned. For three years he worked under Raymond Blanc at Le Manoir aux Quat'Saisons, before moving to France to work alongside legendary names such as Bernard Loiseau and Joël Robuchon. It was as Head Chef at Gidleigh Park, a country house hotel on the edge of Dartmoor, that he made his reputation, gaining two Michelin stars, despite an appalling car accident in which he lost his right arm. But he is keen to spread the gospel of good food beyond the trappings of haute cuisine, opening brasseries, bars and taverns in Exeter, Bristol and Glasgow.

"We're trying to make good food more accessible," he says. "People have more disposable income and are seeking a better quality of life. Michel Roux said that the key to improving the British diet would be through the pub, and I think he was right. The UK has a great larder, and the artisan approach to food should be encouraged. But we need more really good local restaurants, for a more relaxed experience that's real value for money. That's what we're trying to achieve."

MENU ONE
> Terrine of Capricorn Goat's Cheese, Apples and Celery and a Salad with Toasted Walnuts and Raisins
> Pan-fried Cornish Lobster with Young Summer Vegetables and Herbs in a Saffron Bisque
> Chicken Breast with St Enodoc Asparagus, Broad Beans, Wild Mushrooms and a Somerset Cider Brandy Cream Sauce
> Dartmoor Raspberry Mousse with its own jelly, with Devonshire Clotted Cream and Rice Pudding Ice Cream

MENU TWO
> Home-cured South Devon Beef with Wholegrain Mustard Vinaigrette
> Tian of Brixham Scallop and Crab Mousse with Lemongrass and Ginger Sauce
> Roast Best End of Lamb with Tomato Fondue, Fondant Potato and Onion Purée, with an Olive Sauce
> Caramelised Vanilla Egg Custard with Marinated Devon Summer Fruits and a Mint Broth

CROWN OF
ENGLISH ASPARAGUS

SERVES 4

28 asparagus spears
1 leek, white and pale green part only,
   halved lengthways and leaves separated
175g Vulscombe goat's cheese or other
   very soft, creamy goat's cheese
100ml single cream
1/4 garlic clove, crushed
cayenne pepper
2 gelatine leaves, soaked in cold water
   for at least 10 minutes
1 small raw beetroot
150ml cider vinegar
40g sugar
4 sprigs of chervil
salt

TARRAGON VINAIGRETTE

juice of 1/2 lemon
120ml white wine vinegar
pinch of caster sugar
500ml olive oil
2 garlic cloves, cut in half
3 sprigs of tarragon

1 First make the tarragon vinaigrette. Put the lemon juice, wine vinegar, sugar and a little salt and pepper in a bowl. Whisk in the olive oil. Using a small funnel, pour into a jar or bottle and add the garlic cloves and sprigs of tarragon. Put a lid or cork on the bottle or jar and set aside to infuse while you make the crowns. Shake the vinaigrette well before using. (This makes more vinaigrette than you need for this dish; keep it for salads and other preparations.)

2 For the crowns, you need four stainless steel rings, each 6cm wide and 3.5cm deep. Place the rings on a tray lined with cling film.

3 Peel the asparagus stalks and trim the ends so the spears will stand upright inside the rings with the tips above the rim. Plunge the asparagus into a pan of boiling salted water and cook for 1–2 minutes or until tender, then remove to iced water to refresh. Drain and set aside.

4 In the same water cook the leek leaves until tender, then refresh in iced water and drain. Dry on paper towels.

5 In a food processor work the goat's cheese until smooth. Add the cream, garlic, a tiny pinch of salt and a speck of cayenne pepper. Mix for 1 minute or until smooth.

6 Gently squeeze dry one of the gelatine leaves and melt it in a little warm liquid, then add to the cheese mixture and stir to mix thoroughly.

7 Place the cheese mixture in a piping bag and pipe a small amount into the bottom of each ring. Stand the asparagus in the cheese, seven spears to each ring. Pipe the rest of the cheese into the rings, filling them up and securing the asparagus. Place in the refrigerator to set.

8 Meanwhile, peel the beetroot, rinse it and grate on a coarse blade. Put in a saucepan, cover with the vinegar and 150ml water and add the sugar. Bring to the boil and simmer for 15 minutes.

9 Strain through a fine sieve into a clean pan, pressing well to extract all the juice. Discard the beetroot in the sieve. Bring the juice back to the boil and reduce by half. Squeeze dry the second gelatine leaf and add to the juice, stirring until it has completely melted. Set the pan over iced water to cool, stirring often, until a thick, oil-like consistency is achieved.

10 Remove the asparagus moulds from the fridge and carefully spoon the beetroot jelly on top. Return to the fridge to set.

11 To serve, lift off the rings from the asparagus moulds, using the warmth of your hands around the rings to loosen, if required. Wrap a leek leaf around each mould to look like a band. Carefully transfer the asparagus moulds to four plates. Sprinkle with tarragon vinaigrette and garnish with chervil.

No food is quite as delicate and fragile as asparagus. The sugar stored in its spears – which gives it its distinctive sweet and grassy flavour – begins to turn to starch as soon as the asparagus is plucked from the earth. Buying locally and seasonally is a must – do not even consider imported varieties.

102 DARTMOUTH CRAB PLATE

SERVES 4

SPIDER CRAB CONSOMMÉ

100ml olive oil
3 carrots, sliced
2 onions, sliced
1 bulb fennel, sliced
40g sea salt
15g black peppercorns
1 tsp coriander seeds
4 slivers of orange peel
5 garlic cloves
sprig of thyme
½ bay leaf
sprig of basil
6 tomatoes, halved and deseeded
20g fresh ginger
1 star anise
pinch of fennel seeds
1.5 litres fish stock
750ml dry white wine
50ml white wine vinegar
2 large or 3 small live spider crabs,
    2kg total weight, scrubbed clean

CLARIFICATION

50g diced celery
50g diced onions
50g diced leeks
25g diced carrots
225g white fish trimmings
50g tomato purée
5 egg whites

POTTED BROWN CRAB

1 live brown crab, about 1kg
court bouillon (or fish stock or very salty water)
1 tbsp mayonnaise
juice of 1 lemon
2 tbsp chopped parsley
4 hard-boiled eggs, yolks and whites separated
tarragon vinaigrette (see page xx)
4 tbsp clarified butter
freshly grated nutmeg
cayenne pepper
1 tsp brandy
2 tomatoes, skinned, deseeded and
    each cut into 4 'petals'
salt and pepper

GARNISH (OPTIONAL)

diced pickled cucumber or finely
    shredded lettuce

1 First make the consommé. Warm the oil in a large pan and gently sweat the sliced vegetables until soft, without colouring. Add the sea salt, peppercorns, coriander, orange, garlic, thyme, bay leaf, basil, tomatoes, ginger, star anise and fennel seeds. Cook for 10 minutes.

2 Pour in the fish stock and bring to the boil. Simmer for 20 minutes. Add the white wine and vinegar, and simmer for a further 10 minutes. Kill the crabs, then carefully add to the pan. Cook for 15 minutes. Leave to cool.

3 Mix together the ingredients for the clarification. Strain the cooled consommé into a clean pan. Add the clarification mixture. Bring to the boil, stirring often to prevent sticking. Once at boiling point, turn down the heat to simmer for 20 minutes. Finally, pass through a piece of clean muslin to trap any fine particles. Check the consommé for seasoning, then set aside.

4 For the potted brown crab you need four 5cm metal rings. Place them on a tray lined with cling film.

5 Cook the crab in court bouillon for 18 minutes. Remove and allow to cool. Pull off the large claws and legs. Break open the 'box' and scoop out the brown meat into a sieve; drain. Crack open the large claws and pick out the white meat into a bowl. Combine the white crab meat with the mayonnaise. Combine the brown meat with the parsley, 1 tsp lemon juice, salt and pepper.

6 Pass the egg whites and yolks separately through a sieve. Season with salt, pepper and tarragon vinaigrette.

7 Melt the clarified butter. Add the remaining lemon juice, a little nutmeg, a tiny pinch of cayenne pepper, salt and the brandy.

8 Dry the tomato petals on a cloth, then cut them to the size of the rings. Season with salt and pepper and place two petals in the bottom of each ring. Add a layer of white crab meat, then the sieved egg yolk, followed by the egg white. Top with the brown crab, then add another layer of white crab. Finish with the remaining tomato petals and seal with the spiced butter. Chill to set.

9 To serve, warm the spider crab consommé. Turn out the potted crab on to one end of four rectangular plates. Place a small soup cup of spider crab consommé opposite. In between you could garnish with a little pickled cucumber or finely shredded lettuce. Melba toast is a nice addition.

SERVES 4
4 fillet steaks of mature beef, each 150g
Maldon sea salt
2 tbsp groundnut oil
salt and pepper

SHALLOT AND TOMATO SAUCE
6 shallots, chopped
1 garlic clove, chopped
35g unsalted butter
8 tomatoes, deseeded and roughly chopped
sprig of tarragon
sprig of thyme
1 bay leaf
250ml white wine
200ml dry Madeira
100ml Port
200ml chicken stock

HERB BUTTER SAUCE
60g shallots, chopped
1/2 garlic clove, chopped
sprig of tarragon
2 tbsp white wine vinegar
3 tbsp dry white wine
1 tbsp double cream
200g cold unsalted butter, diced
lemon juice
cayenne pepper
2 tomatoes, skinned, deseeded and diced
1 tbsp chopped parsley
1 tbsp chopped chervil
1/2 tbsp chopped tarragon, blanched
1/2 tbsp chopped chives

1 First make the shallot and tomato sauce. Gently cook the shallots and garlic in 20g of the butter until very soft. Purée in a blender. Put the purée in a clean pan and add the tomatoes, tarragon, thyme and bay leaf. Cook gently for 5 minutes or until the tomatoes start to break down.

2 Add the white wine, bring to the boil and reduce by half. Pour in the Madeira and Port, boil and reduce by half. Add the chicken stock and bring to the boil. Skim and simmer for 30 minutes.

3 Pass through a fine sieve, then let the sauce drip through a clean piece of muslin, leaving quite a heavy residue behind; discard the residue. Pour into a clean pan, bring to the boil and cook for about 2 minutes or until the desired consistency is achieved. Whisk in the remaining butter and check seasoning. Set aside.

4 For the herb butter sauce, combine the shallots, garlic, tarragon sprig, vinegar and wine in a small heavy-bottomed saucepan. Boil until you have 1 tbsp syrupy liquid. Add the cream, then over a gentle heat whisk in the diced butter a little at a time. The finished sauce will be creamy and a delicate yellow. Do not allow to boil. Season with lemon juice, salt, cayenne and freshly ground pepper. Pass through a fine sieve into a bowl and set in a saucepan of hot water to keep warm.

5 Preheat the grill to high. Season the fillet steaks with sea salt. Heat the oil in a heavy-bottomed frying pan, then brown the fillets on all sides. Place under the hot

grill and cook to your taste: 5 minutes for medium rare, 6 minutes for medium etc. Remove from the heat and allow to rest for 5 minutes.

6 Meanwhile, warm the shallot and tomato sauce. Add the diced tomatoes and chopped herbs to the butter sauce.

7 To serve, place the fillets on warm plates. Pour a pool of shallot and tomato sauce close to each fillet, then carefully spoon the herb butter sauce over the top of the steaks. As an optional garnish, if serving this in the summer, add seasonal produce such as broad beans and new potatoes.

TIVERTON
STRAWBERRY SHORTCAKE
WITH BASIL CARAMEL

SERVES 6

SHORTBREAD
55g unsalted butter
45g icing sugar, sifted, plus extra for rolling
20g basil leaves, chopped
½ egg, beaten
100g plain flour
¾ tsp baking powder

BASIL AND LEMON MOUSSE
150g caster sugar
15g basil leaves, chopped
375ml double or whipping cream
1 ½ gelatine leaves, soaked in cold water
    for at least 10 minutes
juice of 2 ½ lemons

BASIL CARAMEL
100g glucose
150g fondant
handful of basil leaves

GARNISH
400g small strawberries
50ml strawberry coulis
10g icing sugar

1 First make the shortbread. Beat the butter with the icing sugar using an electric mixer until pale in colour. Add the basil and egg and mix well, then gradually add the flour and baking powder. When ready, the mixture will pull away from the sides of the bowl. Remove and chill for 2 hours before using.

2 Preheat the oven to 180°C/gas 4. Roll out the shortbread dough on a sugared surface to about 5mm thick. Cut out six oblong-shaped pieces, each 10cm long and 5cm wide. Place on greaseproof paper-lined baking trays and bake for 6–8 minutes or until golden brown. Remove from the oven. You may need to trim the edges to straighten the sides and make them equal, mainly for presentation. Leave to cool completely and reserve until needed.

3 Next make the mousse. Mix 50g of the sugar with 5 tbsp water in a pan. Bring to the boil and simmer for 10 minutes. Remove from the heat and add the basil. Cover with cling film and leave to cool.

4 Whip the cream until starting to thicken. Add the remaining sugar, then whip until thick but not stiff.

5 Gently squeeze the gelatine leaves dry, then melt in a little of the warmed basil stock. Add to the rest of the basil stock together with the whipped cream and lemon juice, mixing well. Pour into six oblong metal moulds, each 10cm long, 5cm wide and 5cm deep. Place in the freezer to set.

6 Make the basil caramel by heating the glucose and fondant to 168°C (a clear caramel). Add the basil, then pour on to two greaseproof paper-lined baking trays. When the caramel is completely cold and set, blitz to a fine powder in a food processor. Pass through a sieve, then spread out evenly on two baking trays. Re-cook the basil caramel in a 200°C/gas 6 oven until it melts together to form a thin, glass-like sheet. Leave to cool. Once cool break into irregular shapes.

7 To serve, place a shortbread biscuit in the centre of each of six plates. Turn out a mousse on to each biscuit. Glaze the strawberries by rolling them gently in the coulis and icing sugar, then arrange attractively on each mousse. Carefully place the basil caramel around to enclose the mousse and give an effect of stained glass.

Though Scottish shortbread is the most famous variety, there are many regional variations on this light, rich and crisp biscuit. Summer makes a welcome appearance when shortbread is combined with the strawberries for which Devon is renowned.

ENGLISH ASPARAGUS
WITH A WARM LEEK PURÉE, PUFF PASTRY CASE, HOLLANDAISE AND QUAIL REDUCTION

SERVES 4
400g puff pastry
12 asparagus spears, peeled and trimmed
8 quail's eggs
butter
4 sprigs of chervil
50ml truffle oil (optional)
salt and pepper

LEEK PURÉE
50g unsalted butter
4 medium leeks, cut into 1cm dice
1 bouquet garni
500ml chicken stock

QUAIL REDUCTION
400g quail bones, chopped
200g chicken wings, chopped
40ml vegetable oil
40ml white wine vinegar
300ml white wine
1 litre chicken stock
sprig of thyme
¼ bay leaf
1 shallot, chopped

½ carrot, chopped
1 celery stick, chopped
1 medium leek, chopped
2 garlic cloves, chopped
35g dried morels, powdered

HOLLANDAISE SAUCE
25g unsalted butter
1 shallot, finely chopped
1 garlic clove, finely chopped
½ tsp crushed black peppercorns
sprig of tarragon
sprig of thyme
½ bay leaf
1 parsley stalk
25ml white wine vinegar
25ml dry white wine
2 egg yolks
75ml warm clarified butter
pinch of cayenne pepper
juice of ½ lemon

1 First make the puff pastry boxes. Preheat the oven to 200°C/gas 6. Roll out the pastry 1cm thick and cut out four 8 x 5cm rectangles. Place on a baking tray. Bake for 20 minutes or until golden brown. Remove the lid and scoop out the soft centre. Set the boxes and lids aside.

2 Blanch the asparagus spears in boiling, slightly salted water for 3 minutes. Refresh in iced water, drain and set aside.

3 Add a cap of white wine vinegar to a wide pan of boiling, slightly salted water and poach the quail's eggs for 2 minutes or until softly poached. Refresh immediately in iced water. Drain and reserve until needed.

4 To make the leek purée, melt the butter in a saucepan over a moderate heat, add the leeks and bouquet garni and sweat for 6–8 minutes to start the release of their flavour. Do not allow them to colour at all, as this will discolour the finished purée. Cover with the chicken stock, bring to the boil and skim. Simmer for 20 minutes or until the leeks are very tender.

5 Discard the bouquet garni, then blitz the leeks in a blender until smooth and velvety. Pass through a fine chinois, then season with salt and pepper and set aside.

6 Next make the quail reduction. Preheat the oven to 200°C/gas 6. Put the quail bones and chicken wings in a roasting tray with half the vegetable oil. Place in the oven and roast until golden in colour. Remove the bones and wings to a saucepan and reserve. Discard the excess fat.

7 Add the white wine vinegar to the roasting tray, bring to the boil and stir to deglaze. Over a moderate heat reduce down to a syrup. Add the white wine and reduce by half. Pour into the saucepan with the bones. Cover with the stock, bring to the boil and skim. Reduce the heat slightly, add the herbs and leave to simmer.

8 Meanwhile, heat the rest of the vegetable oil and brown the vegetables and garlic until evenly caramelised. Drain thoroughly and add to the quail stock. Stir in the morel powder and reduce the liquid by two-thirds. Strain through a fine chinois and reduce down again until syrupy in consistency. Keep warm.

9 Next make the hollandaise sauce. Melt the butter in a saucepan, then add the shallot, garlic, peppercorns and herbs. Cook over a moderate heat for 5 minutes, without colouring. Pour the vinegar into the pan and boil until it has completely evaporated. Add the wine and boil until reduced to a syrup. Take the pan off the heat, remove the herbs and discard.

10 Put the egg yolks and 2 tsp cold water in a stainless steel bowl set over a saucepan of almost boiling water. Whisk the yolks until they thicken and form soft peaks. Gradually add the warm clarified butter, whisking rapidly until the sauce becomes smooth. Add the wine and shallot reduction and continue whisking vigorously. Season with the cayenne, a little salt and the lemon juice. Remove from the heat but leave over the pan of water to keep hot.

11 Heat the puff pastry cases in the oven for 3–4 minutes. Reheat the leek purée and check seasoning. Reheat the asparagus spears in a little butter and season to taste. Reheat the quail's eggs in boiling water for 30 seconds, then drain on kitchen paper.

12 To assemble, place a pastry box on each of four warmed plates and fill with a spoonful of leek purée. Place three asparagus spears in each box and top with two quail's eggs. Spoon the hollandaise over the quail's eggs and replace the pastry lids on a slant. Dress the plates with the quail reduction, garnish with sprigs of chervil, drizzle over a little truffle oil to intensify the flavours and serve immediately.

BLACKENED
FILLET OF MACKEREL
ROOT VEGETABLES AND HORSERADISH CREAM

SERVES 4

1 tsp black peppercorns, crushed

pinch of cayenne pepper

1 tsp cumin seeds, toasted and crushed

1/2 tsp fennel seeds, crushed

1 tsp coriander seeds, crushed

4 large fillets of mackerel, all tiny bones
removed

50ml olive oil

salt and pepper

ROOT VEGETABLES

100g diced cooked celeriac

60g diced cooked beetroot

10g coriander leaves, chopped

50ml tarragon vinaigrette (see page 100)

2 tsp lime juice

5g caster sugar

HORSERADISH CREAM

200ml whipping cream

55g freshly grated horseradish

1/2 bunch of chives, chopped

TO FINISH

25ml balsamic vinegar

salad leaves tossed in a little vinaigrette

juice of 1 lemon

1 Mix together the peppercorns and spices on a plate. Place the mackerel fillets, skin side down, in the spice mixture. Set aside.

2 Combine the celeriac and beetroot in a bowl. Add the remaining ingredients for the root vegetables, with 1/3 tsp salt and pepper to taste.

3 Make the horseradish cream by combining the cream with the horseradish, chives and seasoning to taste, passing through a sieve and then whipping until thick.

4 On four plates, make lines of horseradish cream alternating with lines of balsamic vinegar. Dress each plate with a bouquet of salad leaves tossed in vinaigrette.

5 Heat the oil in a heavy-bottomed frying pan until it is smoking. Carefully place the mackerel fillets in the pan, skin side down. Reduce the heat slightly and cook for 2 minutes on each side.

6 Spoon the root vegetables on to the warm plates in a mound.

7 Flip the mackerel fillets and cook for a further 1 minute. Sprinkle with lemon juice, then carefully place the fillets over the vegetable dice. Serve at once.

LOIN OF PORK
WALNUT CRUST AND APPLE JUICE REDUCTION

SERVES 4

240g walnut bread
60g walnut halves
1 garlic clove, crushed
20ml walnut oil
4 small potatoes, peeled
250ml chicken stock
1 garlic clove, crushed
sprig of thyme
1 bay leaf
melted butter
75cl bottle Heron Valley apple juice
4 noisettes of pork cut from the boned loin,
    each 100g, excess fat trimmed
vegetable oil
sprigs of watercress to garnish
salt and pepper

BONED, SPICED AND BRAISED PORK BELLY

1.5kg pork belly, boned and skinned
20g crushed mixed spices (coriander
    seeds, cinnamon stick, cloves, juniper
    and allspice berries)
100g unsalted butter
50ml olive oil

1 large carrot, chopped
1 large onion, chopped
2 celery sticks, chopped
1 apple, cored and chopped
2 garlic cloves, crushed
2 sprigs of thyme
1 bay leaf
2 litres chicken stock

APPLE PURÉE

1 Granny Smith apple, peeled,
    cored and chopped
1 tsp apple juice
sprig of tarragon, blanched and chopped
sugar to taste

CHOUCROUTE OF SAVOY CABBAGE

450g Savoy cabbage, outer leaves and
    core removed, the rest shredded
4 shallots, diced
1 garlic clove, crushed
1 tsp white wine vinegar
120ml sweet white wine
60g unsalted butter
120g smoked bacon, diced and blanched
60g parsley, chopped

1 Preheat the oven to 180°C/gas 4.

2 First prepare the pork belly. Season the inside of the pork with salt and pepper and sprinkle evenly with the spices. Roll the pork into a sausage and secure tightly with string. Melt the butter with the oil in a deep roasting tray until just smoking. Add the pork belly and colour golden brown on all sides. Remove the belly and reserve.

3 Add the vegetables to the tray and cook until golden brown. Add the apple, garlic and herbs. Put the belly back into the tray and pour in the stock. Cover with foil and transfer to the oven to cook for 1 hour.

4 Remove the foil and continue to cook for 1–1 1/2 hours, turning and basting regularly, until the pork is soft to the touch. Remove from the oven and leave to cool for at least 1 hour. Then lift the belly from the liquid and reserve. Pass the liquid through a fine sieve into a saucepan and reduce by one-third. Check seasoning. Set the belly and sauce aside. Before serving, slice the belly into four equal portions (remember to remove the string).

5 Blitz the walnut bread in a food processor until fine crumbs are obtained. Add the walnut halves, garlic, walnut oil, and some salt and pepper. Whiz again to make fine moist crumbs. Reserve.

6 To make the apple purée, cook the apple gently with the apple juice until tender. Crush with a fork to a coarse purée. Add the tarragon and sugar to taste. Set aside.

7 Put the potatoes in a small, shallow baking pan, half cover with the stock and add the garlic, thyme and bay leaf. Brush the tops with a little butter. Bring to the boil, then transfer to the oven and cook until the potatoes are golden and tender.

8 Meanwhile, reduce the bottle of apple juice by half by boiling rapidly, and make the choucroute. Add the cabbage to a saucepan of boiling salted water and cover with a lid. When the water starts to boil again, remove from the heat and drain in a colander. Refresh under cold running water, then drain on a kitchen cloth. Set aside.

9 Combine the shallots, garlic and vinegar in a shallow sauté pan and reduce down on a high heat until syrupy. Add the wine and reduce by two-thirds. Add the butter and, when it has melted and blended in, add the bacon. Fry the mixture until velvety and syrupy. Now add the cabbage and carry on cooking for a further 2 minutes, stirring constantly. Sprinkle with the chopped parsley and keep hot.

10 While the choucroute is being cooked, place the pork belly in a roasting tray, cover with the reduced sauce and gently heat through in the oven for 5–10 minutes. Keep basting to give a beautiful glossy and sticky texture.

11 Season the pork noisettes, then sear on both sides in a little vegetable oil in a hot pan that can be put into the oven. Sprinkle the pork with the walnut crust and cook in the oven for 5 minutes.

12 To serve, on each plate place a spoonful of choucroute and next to it a piece of pork belly. Spoon a little apple purée on the belly. Place a potato between the cabbage and belly. Carefully position the pork on the cabbage. Garnish with a sprig of watercress and serve with a jug of hot apple juice.

A nice addition is a beetroot-cider vinegar reduction: simmer 2 large grated raw beetroots with 500ml cider vinegar, 500ml water and 160g sugar for 20 minutes. Pass through a fine sieve, then reduce until syrupy. Spoon this randomly around each plate before serving.

RED FRUIT SOUP
WITH ROSEMARY SYRUP
AND LEMON MADELEINE

SERVES 4
600g red fruits (strawberries, raspberries,
    redcurrants)
50g icing sugar, sifted
25ml crème de framboise

ROSEMARY SYRUP
50g brown sugar
75g clear honey
200g white wine
25g powdered pectin
1 tsp chopped rosemary

LEMON MADELEINES
125g egg yolks
100g caster sugar
grated zest of 1 lemon
100g plain flour
5g baking powder
125g butter, melted

1 Mix together the red fruits, icing sugar and framboise. Cover with cling film and
leave to macerate for at least 3 hours, to extract as much juice and flavour as possible.
2 For the rosemary syrup combine all the ingredients with 150ml water in a
saucepan and bring to the boil. Skim off any scum and reduce by half. Pour into
a bowl, then allow to cool. Chill to set to a jelly.
3 Next make the mixture for the madeleines. Beat the egg yolks and sugar together
until pale in colour. Add the lemon zest. Gradually add the flour and baking powder
and mix well. Slowly add the melted butter, mixing until incorporated. Leave to rest
for 30 minutes.
4 Meanwhile, blitz the red fruits in a blender or food processor. Pass through a sieve
and check the soup for sweetness; it may need a little extra icing sugar. Reserve.
5 Preheat the oven to 190°C/gas 5.
6 Spoon the madeleine mixture into a large madeleine tin with eight depressions.
Bake for 10 minutes or until lightly golden. Remove from the oven and keep warm.
7 To serve, ladle the soup into four chilled soup bowls. Place a spoonful of the
rosemary jelly in the centre of each bowl and serve the madeleines on a side plate.

TERRINE OF CAPRICORN
GOAT'S CHEESE, APPLES AND CELERY
AND A SALAD WITH TOASTED WALNUTS
AND RAISINS

SERVES 4

TERRINE OF GOAT'S CHEESE
300g Capricorn goat's cheese, or other mild
    but mature goat's cheese that isn't too soft
200g plain Greek yoghurt
200ml whipping or double cream
4 gelatine leaves, soaked in cold water for
    at least 10 minutes
60g finely diced celery
60g finely diced apple
100g goat's cheese log (plain, not covered
    with ash or herbs), cut into lengths
salt and white pepper

MARINATED RAISINS
40g raisins
100ml Down St Mary sparkling wine,
    or other sparkling or still wine

WALNUT VINAIGRETTE
100ml walnut oil
75ml groundnut oil
50ml Champagne or white wine vinegar

TO SERVE
80g walnut halves
milk
1 Cox's apple
mixed salad leaves

1 First put the raisins to soak in the wine for 24 hours.
2 To make the terrine, place the 300g goat's cheese in a food processor and blend until a smooth purée. Blend in the Greek yoghurt, then remove from the food processor and place in a bowl.
3 Heat the cream until hot but not boiling. Gently squeeze the softened gelatine dry, then add to the hot cream and stir until completely melted. Cool slightly, then whisk this into the yoghurt and goat's cheese purée. Add the diced celery and apple, and season with a little salt and pepper.
4 Line a terrine mould or small loaf tin with cling film (or you can use individual moulds), then fill halfway with the cheese and yoghurt mixture, spreading it evenly into the corners. Place the goat's cheese lengths down the middle. Top with the remaining cheese and yoghurt mixture, smoothing the surface flat. Tap the terrine on the work surface to ensure there are no air pockets. Cover and leave to set in the refrigerator for 1 hour.
5 Mix all the ingredients for the vinaigrette together, with salt and pepper to taste, and place in a bottle or plastic pourer. Before using the vinaigrette, shake it well.
6 To prepare the walnuts, put them in a small pan and cover with a mixture of half water and half milk. Bring to the boil, then remove from the heat and leave to soak

for a few minutes. Drain and peel off the thin brown skins, using a small paring knife. This is a bit fiddly, but takes away any bitterness in the nuts. Toast the walnuts in a dry pan, or in the oven, then set aside.

7 When ready to serve, drain some of the raisins from the wine and place in a bowl with some of the walnuts. Add a little vinaigrette and toss to coat. Slice the Cox's apple finely, then cut into thin batons. Toss with some vinaigrette.

8 Combine the salad leaves with the remaining drained raisins and toasted walnuts in another bowl and dress with vinaigrette.

9 Turn the terrine out of the mould and slice using a hot knife.

10 To assemble, place the terrine at one end of each plate (ideally use long or oval plates). Pile the salad at the other end of the plate. Put the raisins and walnuts into the middle and place the apple batons on top, or sprinkle them around the terrine.

PAN-FRIED CORNISH LOBSTER
WITH YOUNG SUMMER VEGETABLES
AND HERBS IN A SAFFRON BISQUE

SERVES 4

4 live Cornish lobsters, each 500g
12 baby carrots
12 bulbs baby fennel
12 asparagus tips
4 small leaves spring cabbage, cut into
    small batons
50g shelled broad beans
50g shelled peas
olive oil
chopped tarragon
salt and pepper
picked tarragon, chervil and chives
    to garnish

SAFFRON BISQUE

500ml extra virgin olive oil
50ml Cognac
100g carrots, finely chopped
100g onion, finely chopped
100g fennel, finely chopped
1/2 garlic clove, chopped
1 tsp white peppercorns
1 tsp coriander seeds, crushed
1 tsp cumin seeds, crushed
1 tsp cardamom seeds, crushed
good pinch of saffron strands
1 star anise, crushed
1 bay leaf
5 sprigs of thyme
30g tomato purée
250g plum tomatoes, chopped
100g unsalted butter
a little lemon juice

1 Kill the lobsters, then pull off the claws and separate the tail from the body and head section. Drop the tails into boiling water and cook for 30 seconds only, then place in iced water. Bring the water back up to the boil and add the lobster claws. When boiling again, cook for 3 minutes. Place in the iced water.

2 Remove the meat from the lobster tails in one piece. Crack the claws to remove the meat, keeping it as whole as possible. Place the lobster meat on a tray for later use.

3 Next make the bisque using the lobster carcasses (tail shells and body and head sections). Preheat the oven to 200°C/gas 6. Pour 400ml of the olive oil into a roasting tray and place in the oven to heat, then add the lobster carcasses. Roast for 30 minutes (do not let the shells burn). Remove from the oven and deglaze the roasting tray with the Cognac.

4 While the lobster carcasses are roasting, sweat the carrots, onions, fennel and garlic in the remaining olive oil in a stainless steel saucepan for 10 minutes without colouring. Add the spices and herbs and sweat for a further 5 minutes. Now add the tomato purée, fresh tomatoes and 200ml water, and cook for 10 minutes.

5 Add the roasted lobster carcasses and the juices from the tray. Pour in enough water almost to cover the lobster carcasses and bring to the boil. Simmer for 20 minutes. Pour into a colander set in a bowl and leave to drain, then pass the resulting liquid through a fine sieve. Add 5g salt, then taste and adjust seasoning. Put 200ml of the bisque in a saucepan with the butter and set aside, ready to reheat. (This recipe makes more bisque than you need; serve the remainder as a soup.)

6 When ready to serve, preheat the oven to 200°C/gas 6. Cook all the vegetables separately in boiling salted water, or in a steamer, until just tender; drain and refresh. Peel the broad beans to remove the tough skins. Set aside.

7 Heat some olive oil in two non-stick frying pans (one for the lobster tails and the other for the claw meat). Carefully add the lobster, then place in the oven to heat for 2 minutes. Turn the lobster meat over, add some chopped tarragon and heat for a further 2 minutes.

8 Meanwhile, heat the lobster bisque. Reheat the vegetables in a steamer.

9 Slice each lobster tail into six pieces and arrange around the warm bowls or plates. Place the claw meat in the middle and scatter the vegetables around.

10 Froth the bisque using a hand blender and season with salt, pepper and a drop of lemon juice. Spoon around the dish. Drizzle some of the cooking oil from the lobsters around and sprinkle over the picked herbs to finish.

CHICKEN BREAST
WITH ST ENODOC ASPARAGUS, BROAD BEANS WILD MUSHROOMS AND A SOMERSET CIDER BRANDY CREAM SAUCE

SERVES 4

4 free range 'Ark' chicken breasts, each 200g
12 asparagus tips
100g shelled broad beans
unsalted butter
200g mixed wild mushrooms
200g baby spinach leaves
salt and pepper

SOMERSET CIDER BRANDY SAUCE

25g shallots, sliced
2 garlic cloves, peeled
200g unsalted butter
5 sprigs of thyme
1 bay leaf
50ml Somerset cider brandy
500ml home-made chicken stock
50ml double cream

1 First make the sauce. Sweat the shallots and garlic in 20g of the butter, without colouring. Add the thyme and bay leaf and sweat for a further 2 minutes, then add the brandy and reduce down to nothing. Add the chicken stock and reduce by half, then add the cream. Whisk in the remaining butter in small pieces. Season the sauce with salt and pepper and set aside.

2 Season the chicken breasts, then wrap them individually in cling film to keep the shape tight. Heat a saucepan of water to 90°C and poach the chicken breasts for 12–15 minutes or until cooked. Remove and leave to rest for 10 minutes.

3 While the chicken is poaching, cook the asparagus and broad beans separately in boiling salted water until tender; drain and refresh in iced water. Cut the asparagus tips to the same length and peel the broad beans to remove their tough skins.

4 Unwrap the chicken breasts. Heat a knob of butter in a frying pan, add the chicken and slowly colour the skin until golden and crisp.

5 Meanwhile, pan-fry the mushrooms in a little butter with salt and pepper. Add the mushrooms to the sauce together with the asparagus and broad beans and reheat. Quickly pan-fry the spinach with a little butter, salt and pepper, then drain on a tray lined with kitchen paper.

6 To serve, slice each chicken breast into five rounds and arrange around the warm plates. Place the spinach in the middle. Add three asparagus tips to each plate, then spoon around the mushrooms and broad beans with some sauce.

120

DARTMOOR RASPBERRY MOUSSE
WITH ITS OWN JELLY
WITH DEVONSHIRE CLOTTED CREAM
AND RICE PUDDING ICE CREAM

SERVES 4

RASPBERRY MOUSSE
200g caster sugar
4 egg whites
200g raspberries
3 gelatine leaves, soaked in cold water for
   at least 10 minutes
200ml whipping cream, whipped until thick

RASPBERRY JELLY
200g raspberries
40g sugar
juice of ½ lemon
2 gelatine leaves

RICE PUDDING
200g pudding rice
200g caster sugar
50g desiccated coconut
1 litre milk
1 vanilla pod, split lengthways

CLOTTED CREAM CURD
3 eggs
6 egg yolks
100g caster sugar
200ml milk
200g clotted cream

TO SERVE
120g raspberries
raspberry coulis

1 To make the mousse, dissolve the sugar in 75ml water, then boil to the soft ball stage (120°C on a sugar thermometer). Whisk the egg whites until they form soft peaks. Slowly pour the sugar syrup on to the whites while whisking. Continue whisking the meringue until cold.

2 Purée the raspberries in a food processor, then pass through a sieve. Warm some of the purée. Gently squeeze dry the gelatine, add to the warm purée and stir until completely melted. Add to the rest of the purée. Leave in the refrigerator until starting to set, then fold in the meringue followed by the whipped cream. Pipe the mousse into four 6 x 6cm rings set on a tray lined with baking parchment and leave to set in the refrigerator.

3 To make the jelly, place the raspberries, sugar and lemon juice in a saucepan with 100ml water. Cover with cling film or a tight-fitting lid and bring to the boil, then remove from the heat. Drain in a sieve lined with a muslin cloth set over a bowl. Gather up the cloth and leave to hang over the bowl for about 2 hours so the clear juice filters through. Reserve the cooked raspberries.

4 Soak the gelatine in cold water for about 10 minutes, then gently squeeze dry. Warm a little of the juice, add the gelatine and stir to melt completely. Put the cooked raspberries in the bottom of four shot glasses. Fill up the glasses with the juice mixture and leave to set in the refrigerator.

5 Next make the rice pudding for the ice cream. Blanch the rice in boiling water for 2–3 minutes, then drain and refresh in running cold water. Put back into the saucepan and add the sugar, coconut and milk. Scrape in the seeds from the vanilla pod, then add the pod too. Bring to the boil, then cook for 30 minutes, stirring from time to time. The mixture should be boiling to reduce the cooking liquid. Tip the rice into a colander and leave to drain.

6 For the clotted cream curd, cream together the eggs, egg yolks and sugar. Bring the milk to the boil, then stir into the creamed mixture. Pour back into the saucepan and cook out well until very thick.

7 Put the clotted cream in a blender and add the curd. Blend well until smooth, then place in a bowl and allow to cool. Combine with the rice pudding (remove the vanilla pod first) and churn in an ice cream machine (do this just before serving, so as not to freeze the rice hard).

8 To serve, turn out each mousse at the end of an oval plate and dress the top with fresh raspberries. Place a shot glass at the other end of each plate and top the jelly with a ball of ice cream. Decorate the plate with a few raspberries and coulis.

Clotted cream is, along with jam and scones, an essential ingredient of afternoon tea. Very much a speciality of the South West, it's made by scalding milk with boiling water, then leaving it to cool overnight. By morning, it's crusty, creamy and sweet. Combine with fruit to counter its artery-clogging qualities.

HOME-CURED
SOUTH DEVON BEEF
WITH WHOLEGRAIN MUSTARD VINAIGRETTE

SERVES 4
600g salt
150g sugar
2 litres red wine (Cabernet Sauvignon)
25g whole black peppercorns
1 heaped tsp juniper berries
15g thyme leaves
15g rosemary
1 beef topside or silverside joint, about 800g

WHOLEGRAIN MUSTARD VINAIGRETTE
75g wholegrain mustard
50ml white wine vinegar
200ml olive oil
salt and white pepper

TO SERVE
olive oil
young mixed salad leaves
picked mixed herbs (chive flowers, chervil,
    baby purple basil and mustard cress)

1 Combine the salt, sugar and 2 litres water in a saucepan and bring to the boil, stirring until dissolved. Remove from the heat and allow to cool.

2 In another pan, bring the wine to the boil. Flambé to burn off the alcohol completely. Once there are no more flames, remove from the heat and allow to cool slightly, then add the peppercorns, juniper berries and herbs. Cool completely.

3 Combine the two mixtures in a bowl and put in the beef. Cover and leave to marinate in the fridge for 10 days.

4 Remove the beef from the marinade (discard the marinade) and wrap it in a muslin cloth. Hang in a cool, airy place for 4–8 days, depending on the environment and humidity. When ready, the surface of the meat will be dry.

5 Unwrap the beef and cut away the dry meat. Wrap the joint in cling film and put it into the freezer. The beef is best kept frozen to prevent it from discolouring; the meat will discolour if left in the freezer for longer than 3 months.

6 To make the vinaigrette, place the mustard in a bowl and whisk in the vinegar and 50ml water, then the olive oil. Season with salt and pepper. Emulsify using a whisk or a hand blender. (This vinaigrette will keep well in the fridge.)

7 To serve, slice the beef from frozen and arrange on the plates. Brush lightly with olive oil to prevent the beef from oxidising, then leave until the beef is at room temperature At the last minute brush with the mustard vinaigrette. Toss the mixed salad leaves with vinaigrette and use with the herbs to dress the beef.

TIAN OF BRIXHAM
SCALLOP AND CRAB MOUSSE
WITH LEMONGRASS AND GINGER SAUCE

SERVES 4
150g shelled scallops
50g brown crab meat
1 egg yolk
250ml whipping cream
150g white crab meat
10g fresh ginger, finely diced
pinch of cayenne pepper
juice of 1 lemon
2 large courgettes, sliced lengthways
salt and pepper

LEMONGRASS AND GINGER SAUCE
75g shallots, chopped
25g fresh ginger, chopped
50g fresh lemongrass, chopped
175g unsalted butter
5g white peppercorns
5g coriander seeds
75g brown crab meat
250g crab carcasses
250ml fish stock
chopped fresh coriander (optional)

GARNISH (OPTIONAL)
grapefruit segments
batons of fresh ginger

1 First prepare the sauce. In a stainless steel saucepan sweat the shallots, ginger and lemongrass in 75g of the butter for 5 minutes, without colouring. Add the peppercorns and coriander seeds and sweat for a further 2 minutes. Add the brown crabmeat and crab carcasses and sweat for 5 minutes longer. Pour in the fish stock, bring to the boil and cook for 20 minutes. Pass through a colander set over a bowl and then through a fine sieve. Reserve in a saucepan for later use.

2 To make the mousse, combine the scallops, brown crab meat, egg yolk and cream in a blender or food processor and blend until very fine and smooth. Remove from the blender and place in a bowl. Set over ice and mix in the white crab meat and ginger, then season with salt, pepper, cayenne and a dash of lemon juice. Set aside.

3 Preheat the oven to 180°C/gas 4.

4 Warm six 6cm diameter metal rings, then wrap cling film tightly around the bottom half. Allow the rings to cool, then butter the insides with softened butter.

5 Blanch the courgettes in boiling water, then drain and pat dry on a cloth. Line the sides of the metal rings with the courgette ribbons. Set them in a baking tray. Fill the moulds with the mousse.

6 Pour some hot water into the baking tray (no higher than the cling film wrapping) and cook in the oven for 8–10 minutes.

7 Meanwhile, to finish the sauce, warm it through, then whisk in the remaining butter and season with salt, pepper and a drop of lemon juice. Add the coriander.

8 To serve, turn out the mousses into the centre of the warm plates, garnish with grapefruit segments and batons of ginger, if using, and drizzle the sauce around.

124

ROAST BEST END OF LAMB
WITH TOMATO FONDUE, FONDANT POTATO AND ONION PURÉE, WITH AN OLIVE SAUCE

SERVES 4
1 best end of lamb (8 cutlets minimum)
vegetable oil
200g spinach
unsalted butter
salt and pepper

OLIVE SAUCE
1kg lamb bones, chopped small
75g diced onion
75g diced leek
75g diced carrot
½ head of garlic
50ml olive oil
5g thyme
5g rosemary
150g ripe plum tomatoes
40g tomato purée
700ml chicken stock
200ml veal glace
1 tsp black olive tapenade or to taste

TOMATO FONDUE
400g plum tomatoes
30g chopped onion
1 tsp finely chopped garlic
40ml olive oil plus extra for brushing
1 tsp finely chopped thyme

ONION PURÉE
4 large onions, each cut into 4
sprig of thyme
1 bay leaf
50g white breadcrumbs
30g butter
pinch of chopped thyme

FONDANT POTATOES
2 large baking potatoes
50g butter
1 garlic clove, crushed
sprig of thyme

1 First make the olive sauce. Preheat the oven to 180°C/gas 4. Roast the bones lightly for 20–30 minutes.

2 Meanwhile, sweat the onion, leek, carrot and garlic in the olive oil, without colouring. Add the thyme and rosemary and sweat for a further 5 minutes. Stir in the tomatoes and tomato purée and cook for 10 minutes.

3 Transfer the roasted bones to a saucepan and add the sweated vegetables, stock, veal glace and 300ml water. Bring to the boil, then reduce to a simmer and cook for 30 minutes. Pass through a colander set in a bowl and then through a fine sieve into a clean saucepan. Reduce to a sauce consistency and pass through muslin. To finish, whisk in tapenade to taste and pass through a fine sieve. Reserve for later use.

4 Next prepare the tomato fondue. Cut the tomatoes in half and squeeze out the seeds. In a thick-bottomed copper pan sweat the onion and garlic in the olive oil, without colouring. Add the thyme and then the tomatoes halves. Season lightly and stir together. Place the pan in the oven and cook for 10 minutes, then stir again. Replace in the oven and cook for a further 10 minutes. Repeat the process until the tomato fondue is dry. Leave to cool, then put to one side and reheat when needed.

5 Turn the oven up to 200°C/gas 6. For the onion purée, put the onions in a saucepan, cover with water and add the thyme sprig and bay leaf. Bring to the boil, then reduce to a simmer and cook until the onions are completely soft. Drain well in a colander. Discard the herbs, then place the onions in a blender or food processor and blend until a fine purée.

6 Measure 200g of the onion purée and place in a thick-bottomed pan. Add the breadcrumbs and butter and cook gently for 15 minutes. Stir in the chopped thyme and some salt and pepper. Adjust the texture if necessary, adding a little liquid if the purée is too thick or cooking longer to thicken. Put into a piping bag and keep in a warm place until needed.

7 While the onion purée is cooking, season the best end with salt and pepper. Sear it all over in a little vegetable oil in small roasting tray on top of the cooker, then turn it fat side down and place in the oven. Roast for 5 minutes, then turn it over and roast for a further 4 minutes. Remove from the pan and leave to rest for 15 minutes. Reheat in the oven for 5 minutes before serving.

8 Prepare the fondant potatoes while the lamb is in the oven. Peel the potatoes and cut each one in half. Using a 4cm round cutter, cut out a cylinder from each half and block them off to an even height.

9 When the lamb has finished roasting, turn the oven down to 170°C/gas 3. Melt the butter in a small thick-bottomed pan (preferably copper) and add the potatoes, garlic, thyme and a seasoning of salt and pepper. Colour the base of each potato cylinder well before turning them over. Add a splash of water and cover the pan with a buttered paper. Place the pan in the oven and cook for 15 minutes or until the potatoes are soft in the middle.

10 Meanwhile, stir fry the spinach with a little butter, salt and pepper, and reheat the tomato fondue and olive sauce.

11 To serve, pipe the onion purée in a square around each warm plate. With the 4cm cutter used to cut the potatoes, dress the spinach in the middle of the plate, then place the fondant potatoes on top and on this put the tomato fondue. Slice the best end into eight cutlets and place two on each plate, on either side of the fondant potato. Spoon the sauce around, but within the onion purée.

CARAMELISED
VANILLA EGG CUSTARD
WITH MARINATED DEVON SUMMER
FRUITS AND A MINT BROTH

SERVES 4
5 egg yolks
50g caster sugar
850ml milk
3 vanilla pods, split lengthways
500ml whipping cream
Demerara sugar

MARINATED SUMMER FRUITS
100g each strawberries, raspberries, redcurrants,
  blackcurrants and blackberries
caster sugar
chopped mint

MINT BROTH
300ml milk
30ml crème de menthe

1 First make the custard mixture. Cream the egg yolks with the sugar. Pour the milk into a saucepan and scrape in the seeds from the vanilla pods; add the pods too. Bring just to the boil. Add the hot milk to the creamed eggs and sugar, stirring. Then add the cold cream. Pour into a bowl, cover and leave in the refrigerator for 12 hours to infuse. Then lift out the vanilla pods.

2 Preheat the oven to 100°C/gas low. Warm four 6 x 4cm metal rings, then wrap a double layer of cling film around the bottom half. Place the rings in a baking tray and fill them three-quarters full with the custard. Pour hot water into the tray around the rings (no higher than the cling film). Cook in the oven for 45 minutes or until the custard has set. Remove from the oven and leave to cool.

3 For the marinated fruits, remove the stalks and hulls from the fruits and cut the strawberries into four. Rinse the fruit in cold water and drain well in a colander. Put 100g of the fruit in a mixing bowl and, using a fork, mash well with some caster sugar. Add the rest of the fruit and some freshly chopped mint and leave to stand for 5 minutes. Taste and add a little more sugar if the fruit is too sharp.

4 While the fruit is marinating, put the milk and crème de menthe in a small saucepan and warm to 80°C.

5 Sprinkle the top of the custards with a thin, even layer of Demerara sugar. Peel off the cling film from the bottoms, then place a custard on each plate and remove the ring. Quickly melt and caramelise the sugar using a blow torch.

6 Dress the marinated fruit on the plates around the custards. Froth the mint broth using a hand blender to create a cappuccino effect, then spoon over the fruit and around the plate. Serve immediately.

CHAPTER FIVE **NORTHERN IRELAND**

PAUL RANKIN & RICHARD CORRIGAN

NORTHERN IRELAND
PAUL RANKIN & RICHARD CORRIGAN

"The bread that's made in Northern Ireland bears comparison with the best of France." That's the view of Robert Ditty, whose bakery in Castledawson, a town of 3,000 people nestled between the bountiful Loughs of Neagh and Beg and the beauty of the Sperrin mountains, baulks the trend towards processed bread that's taken hold in the rest of the UK. "In Northern Ireland," Ditty says, "baking still has its roots in domestic life, because traditionally we don't bake with yeast. We use bicarbonate of soda as a raising agent for our soda bread and potato bread. It makes the whole process much quicker. We just make the domestic commercial."

Northern Ireland is undergoing not so much a revolution as a reaffirmation of its culinary traditions. The Province still has around 150 village bakeries. Ditty's has teamed up with six others to launch a collective brand, to market their products in mainland Britain and beyond. His products have already made the shelves of Fortnum and Mason, and Terence Conran is a fan.

"Bakers in Northern Ireland were tempted by commercialisation," Ditty admits, "but we caught ourselves in time. Many of us have gone back to basics, using traditional methods of sifting flour, for example, skills that were slipping away."

Sourcing quality wheat has proved a problem. "Many modern millers, who are more concerned with quantity than quality, use too much heat in the process. The wheat gets damaged as a result, and so they add glutens and chemicals to repair the damage." So Ditty gets his ingredients from small Scottish mills. "It's just better for you," he claims. "There's more bran and wheat in it."

"Britain has the cheapest bread in the world. It's no more than a commodity," Ditty says with regret. "Here baking is part of the community, it's part of a slower lifestyle. Northern Ireland is sometimes seen as backward, but for food that can be a good thing. This emphasis on retro-experience is very welcome."

FRESH IS THE WORD

One of the reasons Ditty's bread tastes so good is that it is made with organic buttermilk, produced by Glen Huey on his Castlederg farm. "It's a top class raw product, 99 per cent of which goes to local bakeries," says Huey, born into a family of dairy farmers whose land sits in a perfect vale of rolling pasture. The soil has just the right mix of nutrients to produce lush grass and clover – aided by Northern Ireland's considerable rainfall – for his dairy cattle, a Friesian-Jersey cross. "The milk they produce," says Huey, "has a very high solid content, which gives it a very 'fresh' taste. That's the word people use time and time again to describe our milk, 'fresh'. And that's what gives the bread its special taste too."

DEAD SIMPLE

In Irish, Oisín (pronounced 'osh-een') means 'young deer'. It's the name given to the venison produced by Denis Lynn on his Finnebrogue estate near Downpatrick. He claims it's the best venison in the world, and he's not alone in that opinion. Chefs such as Paul Rankin and Rick Stein agree, and Lynn supplies many of the finest restaurants in Britain and Ireland, as well as Marks and Spencer. So why did a former beef farmer switch to rearing venison?

"That's dead simple," Lynn says. "I wanted to get out of subsidised agriculture. The problem was, I only had six deer on my land. So I bought 750 hind. It was around the start of BSE, and people were looking for alternative meats. In 1996, I started producing venison. I wanted to produce the best possible meat, whatever the animal. The principles are pretty much universal."

They are: that you need happy animals, which are killed young in stress-free environments. Lynn even goes to the lengths of testing his deer's pH levels, which are an accurate indicator of stress. "Anything above 6pH and the animals are stressed, and the meat will be tough."

At Finnebrogue, Denis Lynn (pictured on the previous page) produces superb venison, presenting a blueprint for modern animal husbandry.

Lynn chose to call his product Oisín because he felt venison was just too broad a word. "We don't talk about sheep," he says, "we talk about 'lamb' or 'mutton', specific terms. So we use 'Oisín' to describe our animals, which are all pure-bred red deer, killed between nine and 21 months. It's lean and tender meat, full of iron and Omega-3, and it's more consistent in flavour and texture than a purely 'wild' product." Though they roam Lynn's 242-hectare estate, the deer are housed occasionally in bad weather, and he is reluctant to describe them as free range. "I think some people think our venison is a bit too consistent. But they're a small minority."

WILD FOOD

Lower Lough Erne, a beautiful stretch of coves, inlets and islands in gentle, rolling Co Fermanagh, is renowned for its wild brown trout. Lean and healthy, fresh grilled trout is a superb example of wild food,

available to anyone with a facility with rod and fly. Michael Shortt, who's fished Lough Erne for years, and is one of Northern Ireland's foremost angling authorities, links the quality of the trout to that of the wider environment. "There's a saying they have here," he tells me. "If you see fat cattle, you'll see fat trout." The same foundation of limestone that gives rise to the Province's lush pasture, also nurtures Lough Erne's nutritious alkaline waters, teeming with the tiny invertebrates on which the trout flourish. It's a treat for twitchers too, with snipe, redshanks and curlews common.

It's hardly surprising then that, with the demise of the Troubles and the growth of political stability in the Province, more and more people are coming to cast fly on Northern Ireland's accessible public waters. Many will take a catch to their cottage for supper. As Michael Shortt puts it, "If you kill a fish and don't eat it, you want shooting."

PAUL RANKIN

A native of Ballywater, Co Down, Paul Rankin gained Northern Ireland's first ever Michelin star at his original Roscoff restaurant in Belfast city centre. He had fallen in love with cooking while travelling the world with his Canadian wife Jeanne. On returning to Europe, they both worked for three years under Albert Roux at Le Gavroche before heading for California's Napa Valley, which, Rankin recalls, "was like a Garden of Eden", where small producers provided him with baby greens, wild mushrooms, ten different types of tuna and line-caught wild salmon. "There was a freedom to mix things up." When he opened Roscoff in Belfast in 1989 he put culinary skills on display. Seeking a more casual "funky, fusion" experience, he refitted Roscoff as Cayenne (though he's found a new home for Roscoff in Belfast's Linenhall Street).

Rankin is a keen advocate of the best Northern Irish produce. "Where you win or lose in this game is in the shopping. We've got quality food here. There's been terrific progress over the past 15 years. But we still need more artisanal small producers. I think of Parmesan cheese as the model: fine food produced on a large scale to a high standard, a balance between quality and the market."

MENU ONE

> Prawn and Avocado 'Cocktail'
> Wild Trout with Asparagus, Peas and a Citrus Butter Vinaigrette
> New Season Lamb with a Herb and Mustard Crust and Scallion Crushed Potatoes
> Buttermilk Cream with Rhubarb and Rose Petals

MENU TWO

> Smoked Salmon and Wheaten Bread 'Sandwich'
> Roast Turbot with a Lobster, Tomato and Tarragon Vinaigrette
> Finnebrogue Venison with Colcannon Pie and Wild Mushrooms
> Lemon Cream Tart with Fresh Strawberries

RICHARD CORRIGAN

Raised on a farm in County Meath in the Irish Midlands, one of a family of seven, Richard Corrigan was surrounded by an abundance of food from the beginning. Disillusioned with school, he began his professional career earlier than most. At 14 he was working in the restaurant of the local Kirwin Hotel with his father's friend and formative influence Ray Vaughan. Moving to London at the age of 21, he worked under Michel Lorrain at the Meridian in Piccadilly, and at the Irish restaurant Mulligans, where he expressed frustration with "twiddly, intellectual food". He made a considerable impression cooking at Searcy's, the restaurant at the Barbican Centre, previously something of a culinary desert. But he made his reputation at his own Lindsay House Restaurant in Soho, producing food born of a "whole carnal culture", and gaining his first Michelin star in 1999. It has remained a perennial favourite of food critics.

He's now revived the fortunes of the iconic London fish restaurant Bentley's, which, on opening in October 2005, met with considerable acclaim. Passionate and committed, with an intense natural flair, Corrigan is now firmly established as one of the most remarkable chefs of his generation.

MENU ONE
> Smoked Salmon with Blinis and Woodland Sorrel and Wild Cress
> Poached Turbot with Oysters and Seaweed Salad
> Venison Wellington with Pickled Cabbage
> Rhubarb Compote with Mango, Vanilla Ice Cream with Nutmeg

MENU TWO
> Ulster Vegetable Soup with Bacon Dumplings
> Poached Salmon with Fennel Purée and Almond and Shrimp Butter
> Reggie Johnson's Chicken with Summer Leeks and Morels
> Spice Cake with Summer Fruits

PRAWN AND AVOCADO
'COCKTAIL'

SERVES 4
12–16 live Strangford prawns (langoustines)
4 tbsp home-made mayonnaise
2 tbsp chopped basil
salt and white pepper

AVOCADO LAYER
1 ripe avocado, peeled and diced
1 tsp finely chopped shallot
1 tsp finely snipped chives
1 tbsp lemon juice

CHERRY TOMATO VINAIGRETTE
2 tbsp sherry vinegar
½ tsp smooth Dijon mustard
pinch of caster sugar
120ml extra virgin olive oil
8 cherry tomatoes, very finely diced
1 tsp very finely chopped shallot

GARNISH
6 quail's eggs, boiled for 2 ½ minutes,
    peeled and quartered
mixed salad leaves
4 strips of home-made potato chips
    (optional)

1 Bring a large pot of water to the boil and season heavily with salt: it should taste like the sea. Add the langoustines, bring back to the boil and boil for 1 minute. Remove the langoustines and allow to cool. When they are cool enough to handle, peel them.

2 Cut each langoustine into two or three, then combine with the mayonnaise, basil and a little salt and pepper. Toss gently together, and set aside.

3 Mix the diced avocado with the shallot, chives and lemon juice and season with salt and pepper. Set aside.

4 To make the vinaigrette, whisk the sherry vinegar with the Dijon mustard, sugar and a pinch each of salt and pepper until dissolved. Stir in the oil. Reserve 2 tbsp vinaigrette, then toss the tomatoes and shallot into the rest. Taste for seasoning.

5 To assemble, place a 4–5cm metal ring in the centre of each plate. Put about 2 tbsp of the avocado mixture in each ring and push down well. Top with the langoustine mayonnaise, again pushing down well. Surround each ring with a few tablespoons of cherry tomato vinaigrette and set three quail's egg quarters on top of the tomatoes. Remove the rings.

6 Toss the salad leaves with the reserved vinaigrette, and carefully set a few leaves on the langoustines. Top each with a strip of potato chip and serve.

WILD TROUT
WITH ASPARAGUS, PEAS AND
A CITRUS BUTTER VINAIGRETTE

SERVES 4

1 large fillet of wild trout, about 500g
2 tbsp light olive oil
125g shelled fresh peas
8 asparagus spears, peeled and cut into
   1cm dice
1 leek, cut into 1cm slices
handful of pea shoots (optional)
salt and white pepper

CITRUS BUTTER VINAIGRETTE

2 tbsp finely chopped shallots
150ml dry white wine
1 tsp grated lemon zest
150g butter

1 Check the fish for bones and carefully scale the skin side with a blunt serrated knife. Rinse and pat dry. Cut into four portions and carefully make four or five shallow incisions in the skin of each portion using a very sharp knife. Brush with the olive oil and season, then place skin side up on a baking sheet. Set aside.

2 To make the vinaigrette, boil the shallots with the white wine in a small saucepan until reduced by half. Remove from the heat. Add the lemon zest and allow to infuse while you clarify the butter.

3 Melt the butter in another saucepan, bring to the boil and boil for 3–4 minutes. Remove from the heat and allow to settle, then skim off any foam or scum from the top. Pour the clear butter into the shallot reduction, leaving any milky residue behind in the pan (discard the milky residue). Season the vinaigrette and set aside. Warm through for serving.

4 Preheat the grill to high.

5 Place the trout fillets under the grill. Cook, without turning, until the skin is nicely crisp and the fish is just cooked. This should take 5–8 minutes, depending on the heat of the grill and the thickness of the fillets.

6 While the fish is grilling, cook the vegetables. Drop the peas and diced asparagus into a pan of boiling salted water and cook for 3 minutes, then add the leeks and cook for a further 2 minutes or until just tender. Drain thoroughly, then toss with the optional pea shoots.

7 To serve, spoon the hot vegetables into the centre of each warmed plate. Spoon over the warm citrus butter vinaigrette and top with the fillets of fish.

NEW SEASON LAMB
WITH A HERB AND MUSTARD CRUST
AND SCALLION CRUSHED POTATOES

SERVES 4
4 boneless loins of lamb, each 150g
4 tbsp light olive oil
6 tbsp fresh breadcrumbs
1 tsp roughly chopped thyme
1 tbsp chopped parsley
1 tbsp smooth strong Dijon mustard
1 tbsp wholegrain Dijon mustard
salt and pepper

SAUCE
300ml good brown lamb stock,
    made from bones and trimmings

pinch of thyme leaves
1 tsp chopped parsley
1 tsp wholegrain Dijon mustard
15g butter

SCALLION CRUSHED POTATOES
700g new potatoes, peeled
85g butter
4 spring onions (called scallions in
    Ireland), finely chopped

GARNISH
seasonal vegetables, such as new carrots,
    braised lettuce and broad beans

1 Preheat the oven to 200°C/gas 6.

2 Season the lamb with salt and pepper. In a heavy frying pan, heat 3 tbsp of the olive oil until it is nearly smoking. Add the lamb and cook over high heat until well browned all over. This should take about 5 minutes; the loins should still be rare inside. Place on a wire rack and allow to cool to room temperature.

3 Pour the breadcrumbs on to a baking sheet and drizzle with the remaining olive oil. Mix gently with your fingers. Put into the oven and toast until lightly browned, stirring two or three times. When browned, allow to cool, then add the herbs.

4 For the sauce, reduce the lamb stock until it has a light sauce consistency.

5 To prepare the scallion crushed potatoes, cook the new potatoes in boiling salted water until tender, then drain. Melt the butter in a saucepan over a moderate heat, add the spring onions and a little salt and cook gently for 1 minute. Add the potatoes and crush gently with a fork. Keep warm.

6 While the potatoes are cooking, finish the lamb. Mix the two mustards together and brush over the top of each loin. Dip the mustard-coated part of the loin into the breadcrumbs and gently press the crumbs on to the mustard. Set the loins on a baking sheet, crumb side up. Place in the top of the oven and roast for 4–5 minutes for medium rare, or 8 minutes for medium well done. Remove from the oven and allow to rest in a warm place while you cook the vegetables and finish the sauce.

7 Bring the sauce to the boil, then remove from the heat and stir in the herbs, mustard and butter. Check for seasoning.

8 To serve, spoon the vegetable garnishes and scallion crushed potatoes on to the warmed plates. Slice each loin into three thick slices and place on the potatoes. Spoon the sauce over or around.

BUTTERMILK CREAM
WITH RHUBARB AND ROSE PETALS

SERVES 8

600ml double cream

2 vanilla pods, split lengthways

200ml condensed milk

4 gelatine leaves, soaked in cold water
for at least 10 minutes

700ml buttermilk, at room temperature

CRYSTALLISED ROSE PETALS

30 organic rose petals

3 pasteurised egg whites, lightly whisked

sifted caster sugar

HAZELNUT SHORTBREAD

300g plain flour

100g caster sugar

75g hazelnuts, toasted and ground

225g unsalted butter, chilled and diced

RHUBARB

500g tender young rhubarb

200g sugar

200ml grenadine syrup

3 tbsp rose water

1 First prepare the crystallised rose petals. Brush the petals lightly with the egg white, then dust generously with sugar. Place on a tray and allow to dry overnight.

2 Next make the hazelnut shortbread. Place all the ingredients in a chilled food processor and process until it just comes together. (Over-processing will cause the butter to start to melt.) Tip out on to a clean work surface and, using the heel of your hand, quickly press together to make sure that all the ingredients are well mixed. Pat into a round, wrap tightly in cling film and chill for at least 1 hour.

3 Roll out the chilled dough to a round or rectangle just under 1cm thick. If round, cut into pie-shaped wedges; if a rectangle, cut into squares or other shapes as desired. Transfer to a baking sheet and chill again for at least 30 minutes.

4 Preheat the oven to 150°C/gas 2. Bake the shortbread for 25–30 minutes. Allow to cool and set slightly before removing to a wire rack to finish cooling.

5 For the buttermilk creams, heat the double cream with the split vanilla pods. As soon as it comes to the boil, remove from the heat and add the condensed milk. Gently squeeze dry the gelatine leaves, add to the hot cream and stir until melted.

6 When the cream mixture has cooled to near body temperature add the buttermilk. Strain through a fine sieve. Scrape the seeds from the vanilla pods and stir into the cream mixture. Carefully pour into eight 8–10cm ramekins or other moulds. Allow to set in the fridge for at least 4 hours.

7 Cut the rhubarb on a sharp angle into 2mm slices. In a wide pan, bring the sugar, 400ml water, grenadine syrup and rose water to the boil. Add the rhubarb and cook gently at a simmer for 2–3 minutes. Remove from the heat and allow to cool.

8 To serve, dip the moulds into hot water for a few seconds, then gently turn out a buttermilk cream on to the centre of each cold plate. Surround with a spoonful of rhubarb and its gorgeous sauce. Place two or three rose petals on top of the buttermilk cream and serve with the hazelnut shortbread.

SMOKED SALMON
AND WHEATEN BREAD 'SANDWICH'

SERVES 4
100g cream cheese
4 tbsp crème fraîche
1 tsp freshly grated horseradish,
    or 2 tsp prepared horseradish
4 tbsp peeled and deseeded cucumber,
    diced into 1cm cubes
1–2 tbsp very finely chopped red onion
2 tbsp finely snipped chives

2 tbsp capers, rinsed and roughly chopped
lemon juice
4 slices brown Irish soda bread
120g smoked salmon, finely sliced
salt and white pepper
GARNISH
1–2 radishes, finely sliced
½ bunch of mustard cress

1 Mix together the cream cheese, crème fraîche, horseradish, cucumber, red onion, chives, capers and some salt and pepper. Taste for seasoning, and add some lemon juice if desired.

2 With a 5cm metal ring, cut a disc from each slice of soda bread. Set the 5cm ring in the centre of a plate and insert a disc of bread, pressing it down to the bottom of the ring. Top with 2 tbsp of the cream cheese mixture and push it down on to the bread. Top generously with smoked salmon. Remove the ring, and repeat with the remaining plates.

3 Garnish each 'sandwich' with two slices of radish and a little mustard cress.

In Northern Ireland, the brown soda bread is called 'wheaten bread' and is made, often at home, from a coarse wheatmeal flour. It's wonderful with smoked fish and hard cheese, and is the best bread to use with smoked salmon.

ROAST TURBOT
WITH A LOBSTER, TOMATO AND TARRAGON VINAIGRETTE

SERVES 4

1 live lobster, about 500g
4 skinned fillets of turbot, each 120g
1 tbsp light olive oil
15g butter
salt and white pepper

LOBSTER CREAM SAUCE

1 tbsp light olive oil
1 tbsp each chopped carrot and onion
1 garlic clove, crushed
½ tbsp tomato paste
1 tbsp brandy
75ml white wine
150ml double cream

TOMATO AND TARRAGON VINAIGRETTE

½ tsp Dijon mustard
1 ½ tbsp white wine vinegar
90ml extra virgin olive oil
½ tsp crushed garlic
1 tsp chopped tarragon
½ tbsp chopped parsley
½ tbsp snipped chives
1 plum tomato, skinned, halved,
    deseeded and cut into 5mm dice

GARNISH

a few sprigs of tarragon and chervil

1 Bring a large pan of salted water to a vigorous boil. Kill the lobster, then put into the boiling water. Cook for 12 minutes. Lift it out and plunge into a sink or bowl of cold water to stop the cooking process.

2 When cool enough to handle, pull off the claws, crack them and remove the meat. Pull the head and body section from the lobster tail, then cut the tail in half along the length. Discard the intestinal tract. Remove the tail meat and slice it up neatly, along with the claw meat. Set the meat aside.

3 To make the sauce, heat the oil in a very large pot until smoking. Roughly chop the lobster shells and head and body section, toss into the pot and sauté over a high heat for 3 minutes. Add the vegetables and garlic and cook for a further 2 minutes. Add the tomato paste, brandy and white wine. Allow the wine to reduce by half. Add 1 litre of water, reduce the heat and simmer for 20 minutes.

4 Strain the lobster stock through a fine sieve into a clean pan, then reduce to about 250ml. Add the cream and boil until thick and creamy. Set aside. Reheat for serving.

5 For the vinaigrette, whisk together the mustard, vinegar and some seasoning. Whisk in the oil, then the garlic and herbs. Stir in the tomato dice. Transfer to a pan.

6 Season the turbot with salt and pepper. Heat the oil in a large, heavy frying pan until it is almost smoking. Add the butter and, as it begins to foam, put the fillets in the pan. Sauté for about 3 minutes on each side. Test for doneness by pressing the fillets. If they want to flake apart, they are cooked and ready.

7 While the fish is cooking, gently heat the lobster in the vinaigrette.

8 To serve, spoon the lobster and vinaigrette on to warmed plates and drizzle round the lobster sauce. Place a fillet in the middle and garnish with tarragon and chervil.

WITH COLCANNON PIE AND WILD MUSHROOMS

SERVES 6-8
1 haunch of venison, about 2.5kg
30g butter
1 tbsp olive oil
salt, cracked black pepper and white pepper

COLCANNON PIE
300g puff pastry
2 medium potatoes, about 300g, peeled
    and very thinly sliced
1 large parsnip, very thinly sliced
1 large Savoy cabbage, finely sliced, blanched
    and well drained
egg wash (1 yolk beaten with a little cream)
100ml whipping cream
1 egg yolk

SAUCE
200ml red wine
2 tbsp sherry vinegar
200ml venison or brown chicken stock
½ tsp thyme leaves
2 tsp redcurrant jelly
½ tsp cracked black pepper
45g butter

GARNISH
wild mushrooms, such as chanterelles,
    ceps, horn of plenty (trompettes),
    shiitake and oyster
Savoy cabbage, shredded or chopped
butter

1 Preheat the oven to 190°C/gas 5. To make the colcannon pie, roll out two-thirds of the pastry and use to line a 24cm ovenproof frying pan or round baking dish.

2 In a large bowl, toss the potatoes, parsnip and cabbage together and season well with salt and pepper. Fill the pastry case with the potato mixture. Brush the edges of the pastry with egg wash, then top with the remaining pastry and press to seal. Brush the lid with egg wash and cut a 1cm hole in the centre. Bake the pie for 55 minutes.

3 Mix together the cream and egg yolk. Carefully pour into the hole in the lid. Bake for a further 5 minutes. Allow to cool slightly before cutting into wedges for serving.

4 While the pie is baking, prepare the venison. Trim the outside of the haunch to remove any sinew and fat. Work carefully to be sure you don't remove too much of the meat. Separate each large muscle one at a time and place them to one side. Reserve the trimmings and the very small muscles for stock, or another use.

5 Season the large muscles generously with salt and cracked black pepper. Heat the butter and oil in a large ovenproof frying pan or heavy roasting tray and fry the pieces of venison until they have a nice colour on all sides. Place in the oven and roast for 5 minutes for medium rare, or 8 minutes for medium to well done. Remove from the pan and allow to rest in a warm place while you make the sauce.

6 Pour off excess fat from the pan, then add the wine and vinegar. Bring to the boil, scraping the bottom of the pan to release any delicious juices and sediment. Reduce the liquid by two-thirds. Add the stock and boil until reduced and concentrated, but still a fairly light sauce consistency. Remove from the heat and whisk in the thyme, redcurrant jelly, pepper and butter. Add a little salt if necessary.

142

7 While you are reducing the sauce, sauté the mushrooms and cabbage, separately, in a little butter.

8 To serve, slice the venison. Spoon some of the sautéed cabbage and mushrooms on to each warm plate and top with a few slices of venison. Arrange a wedge of colcannon pie behind the meat and spoon a little sauce around.

LEMON CREAM TART
WITH FRESH STRAWBERRIES

SERVES 6-8

225g sweet shortcrust pastry
beaten egg yolk

LEMON CUSTARD FILLING
750ml whipping cream
grated zest and juice of 2 unwaxed lemons
½ vanilla pod, split lengthways
9 egg yolks
125g caster sugar

STRAWBERRY SAUCE
640g fresh strawberries
60g caster sugar
1 tbsp lemon juice

GARNISH
sifted icing sugar
mint sprigs

1 Roll out the pastry to about 5mm thick and use to line a 23cm flan ring set on a baking tray. Chill for at least 30 minutes.

2 Preheat the oven to 180°C/gas 4. Line the pastry case with greaseproof paper and fill with dried beans. Bake for 12–14 minutes or until golden brown. Remove the paper and beans, and bake for a further 1–2 minutes, just to allow any moisture left in the bottom to cook out. Remove from oven, brush the pastry lightly with egg yolk to seal and allow to cool.

3 To make the custard filling, place the cream, lemon zest and vanilla pod in a pan and bring just to the boil. Remove from the heat and leave to infuse for 30 minutes.

4 Add the lemon juice to the cream. Whisk together the egg yolks and sugar in a bowl. Strain the cream mixture over, whisking constantly.

5 Turn the oven to 160°C/gas 3. Pour the custard filling into the pastry case and place in the oven. Bake for about 30 minutes. Remove when the centre is still slightly wobbly, like a crème brûlée. Allow to cool to room temperature.

6 For the sauce, purée about 200g of the strawberries in a blender with the caster sugar and lemon juice, then pass through a sieve. Toss the remaining strawberries into the sauce.

7 To serve, slice the tart into wedges. If you want to brûlée the tart, sprinkle with icing sugar and use a blow torch to achieve a golden caramelised surface. Place a slice of tart in the centre of each plate and add a generous spoonful of strawberries and a drizzle of sauce. Decorate with a sprig of mint and a sprinkle of icing sugar.

144
SMOKED SALMON WITH BLINIS
AND WOODLAND SORREL AND WILD CRESS

SERVES 4
50g woodland sorrel
50g wild cress
25ml olive oil
juice of ½ lemon
500g smoked wild salmon
salt and pepper

IRISH SODA BREAD
100g wholemeal flour
100g self-raising flour
1 tbsp bicarbonate of soda
50g jumbo oatmeal
25g wheat germ
25g wheat bran
10g salt
75g runny honey
25g black treacle
400ml buttermilk

BLINIS
85g plain flour
pinch of freshly grated nutmeg
1 whole egg
1 egg yolk
150ml milk
115g warm mashed potato
knob of butter

TO SERVE
St Killian cheese or other
    soft creamy cheese
a few snipped chives

1 Preheat the oven to 150°C/gas 2.

2 First make the soda bread. Put all the ingredients into a large bowl and mix by hand to make a soft dough.

3 Using floured hands, shape the dough into two oval shapes and place on a floured non-stick baking tray. Bake for 45 minutes or until the breads sound hollow when tapped on the base.

4 Meanwhile, make the blini batter. Put the flour in a bowl with 1 tsp salt and the nutmeg and stir in the egg and egg yolk. Whisk in the milk, then fold in the cooked warm potato. Cover and leave to rest in the fridge until ready to cook.

5 Pick the woodland sorrel and wild cress by removing just the soiled end and washing in a little salted water. Leave to dry on kitchen paper, then place in a bowl. Just before serving, dress with the olive oil, lemon juice and some seasoning.

6 To cook the blinis, heat a little butter in a non-stick frying pan. Add spoonfuls of the blini batter and fry for 1–2 minutes on each side or until golden brown. This will make eight blinis.

7 To serve, cut the smoked salmon into 2cm slices and arrange three slices on each serving plate. Add two blinis to each and a quenelle of cheese. Dress the plates with the sorrel and cress and garnish with some chives. Remove the bread from the oven and serve alongside.

POACHED TURBOT
WITH OYSTERS AND SEAWEED SALAD

SERVES 4

1 leek, finely shredded

unsalted butter

1 fillet of turbot, about 600g, cut into 4 portions

8 rock oysters from Loch Leagh

splash of soy sauce

25g shallots, chopped

20g chives, chopped

salt and pepper

SEAWEED SALAD

500g mixed dried and wet seaweed

2 tsp olive oil

1 tsp white wine vinegar

25g shallots, finely chopped

COURT BOUILLON

knob of unsalted butter

2 carrots, diced

3 celery sticks, diced

2 leeks, diced

2 onions, diced

1 bay leaf

sprig of thyme

1 tsp coriander seeds

1 tsp fennels seeds

100ml white wine

50ml white wine vinegar

1 The night before, soak the dried seaweed for the salad in water to cover, to rehydrate. Next morning, drain and rinse well in cold water. Set aside.

2 To make the court bouillon, heat the butter in a large pan and sauté the carrots, celery, leeks and onions for a few minutes. Add the bay leaf with the thyme and stir in the coriander and fennel seeds. Pour in the white wine and vinegar and cook down for few minutes. Cover with water and bring to the boil, then simmer for 30 minutes. Strain into a clean pan and leave to simmer gently until required.

3 Place the leek in a buttered flameproof dish. Season the turbot fillets with salt and pepper, then place on the leek. Spoon over some of the court bouillon and cook for 3–4 minutes. Remove the fish using a slotted spoon and keep hot. (You can keep the court bouillon in the fridge or freezer to use for poaching other fish.)

4 Open the oysters, retaining the juices. Place the oysters in a sieve set in a bowl and drain, reserving the juices. Heat the oyster juices in a pan, add the oysters and poach for 1 minute. Add the soy sauce, a knob of butter and the shallots, then stir in the chopped chives. Heat for a further 2–3 minutes.

5 Meanwhile, make the seaweed salad. Whisk the olive oil and vinegar in a bowl and add the shallots. Place the seaweed in a separate bowl and add the vinaigrette. Toss together to coat.

6 To serve, place the turbot on the warm plates, arrange the dressed seaweed alongside and place the drained oysters on top.

VENISON WELLINGTON
WITH PICKLED CABBAGE

SERVES 4

1 venison fillet, about 650g

3 tbsp mixed crushed juniper berries and
    crushed black peppercorns

olive oil

500g shallots, chopped

2 garlic cloves, chopped

⅓ bunch of thyme, leaves picked

1kg button mushrooms, chopped

200g foie gras, diced (optional)

handful of flat-leaf parsley, chopped

2–4 leaves of Savoy cabbage, stalk removed

1 sheet of ready-rolled puff pastry,
    about 500g

1 egg, beaten

PICKLED RED CABBAGE

500g red cabbage, cored and finely shredded

20g coarse rock salt

300ml red wine

100ml red wine vinegar

100ml Cabernet Sauvignon vinegar

20g sugar

1 star anise

¼ cinnamon stick

2 cardamom pods

3 black peppercorns, crushed

1 tsp crushed coriander seeds

1 tsp crushed fennel seeds

1 tsp crushed juniper berries

1 tsp freshly grated nutmeg

sprig of thyme

½ bay leaf

1 garlic clove, crushed

VENISON SAUCE

250g venison bones, chopped

10ml vegetable oil

25g chopped carrots

25g chopped parsnips

1 celery stick, chopped

2 shallots, chopped

25g chopped leek

3 sprigs of thyme

1 bay leaf

2 garlic cloves, crushed

4 juniper berries, crushed

100ml red wine

50ml ruby Port

300ml veal stock

1 First make the pickled red cabbage. Toss the cabbage with the rock salt in a large bowl. Cover with cling film and keep overnight in the fridge. Next morning, rinse well and drain.

2 To make the marinade, put the wine, vinegars and sugar in a heavy pan and bring to the boil, stirring occasionally to dissolve the sugar. Tie all the remaining ingredients in a piece of muslin and add to the pan. Add the cabbage and stir, then leave to simmer gently for 30 minutes.

3 Remove from the heat and leave to cool. When it is cold, place the cabbage in a container, cover and keep in the fridge until needed.

4 Preheat the oven to 160°C/gas 3.

5 To make the venison sauce, roast the venison bones for 15–20 minutes, then leave to cool. Meanwhile, heat the oil in a heavy pan and caramelise all the vegetables with the thyme, bay leaf and garlic. Add the crushed juniper berries and roasted venison

bones. Add the red wine, bring to the boil and reduce by half. Add the Port and reduce by half again. Add the veal stock and season, then leave to cook slowly at a slight simmer for 1 hour.

6 Pass the sauce through a fine sieve into a clean pan. Using a ladle, skim any fat or scum from the sauce. Place back on the heat and reduce by half. Then set the sauce aside until needed.

7 Season the venison fillet with the crushed juniper berries and peppercorns.

8 Heat a little olive oil in a non-stick frying pan until hot. Add the venison fillet to the pan and sear for 1 minute on each side, to colour. Remove from the pan and leave to rest for 15 minutes.

9 Meanwhile, heat 1 tbsp olive oil in a separate pan and sauté the shallots and garlic with the thyme for 1–2 minutes, to soften. Add the chopped mushrooms and fry for 2–3 minutes. Cook until excess liquid has evaporated. Add the diced foie gras and parsley and heat until the foie gras is cooked through. Set aside to cool.

10 Bring a saucepan of salted water to the boil and blanch the cabbage leaves for 1–2 minutes. Remove the leaves and refresh in iced water. Drain on kitchen paper to remove the excess water.

11 Place a large sheet of cling film on a flat surface. Arrange the cabbage leaves on the film to make a layer that is the same length as the venison fillet and about twice the width. Spread the mushroom mixture over the cabbage and set the venison on top. Wrap the cabbage and mushroom mixture around the venison, with the help of the cling film. Roll up tightly in the film to form a cylinder shape and secure, then place in the freezer to set for 20 minutes.

12 Roll out the puff pastry to two 10 x 20–25cm rectangles. Remove the cling film from the wrapped fillet and place it on one of the puff pastry rectangles. Lay the second pastry rectangle over the venison and press the edges together to seal. Place on a greased baking tray. Brush the pastry with beaten egg and leave to rest in the fridge for 20 minutes.

13 Preheat the oven to 180°C/gas 4.

14 Place the venison parcel in the oven and roast for 15–20 minutes.

15 While the venison is in the oven, reheat the pickled cabbage. Also warm enough sauce for four servings. If you want a more juniper flavour, add 2 crushed berries to infuse in the sauce for 10 minutes, then pass the sauce through a sieve.

16 To serve, slice the venison Wellington into four pieces and place on warm plates. Drizzle over the sauce and serve with the pickled cabbage.

RHUBARB COMPOTE
WITH MANGO, VANILLA ICE CREAM WITH NUTMEG

SERVES 4
300g sugar
sprig of rosemary
300g rhubarb, cut into batons
splash of grenadine
3 Alfonso mangos, peeled, stoned and sliced
freshly grated nutmeg to finish

SABLÉ BISCUITS
125g icing sugar, sifted
125g unsalted butter
2 vanilla pods, split lengthways
250g plain flour

pinch of salt
2 eggs
100ml double cream

VANILLA ICE CREAM
600ml double cream
300ml milk
2 vanilla pods, split lengthways
4 egg yolks
175g caster sugar
pinch of freshly grated nutmeg

1 First make the paste for the sablé biscuits. Place the icing sugar, butter, seeds scraped from the vanilla pods, flour and salt in a bowl and rub together using your fingertips. Add the eggs and stir in the cream. Cover with cling film and put to chill in the fridge.

2 Meanwhile, make the vanilla ice cream. Put the cream and milk in a pan and scrape in the seeds from the vanilla pods. Add the pods too. Bring to a gentle simmer. In a bowl set over a pan of boiling water, whisk the egg yolks with the sugar until pale and fluffy. Pour the hot cream mixture over the egg mixture, whisking constantly. Pass the mixture through a sieve into a bowl set over iced water to cool. Once cooled, add the grated nutmeg, then churn in an ice cream machine.

3 Preheat the oven to 120°C/gas 1/4.

4 Roll out the sablé biscuit paste on a floured surface and cut into 9–10cm rounds using a metal ring. Place on a baking tray lined with non-stick silicone paper and bake for 12–14 minutes or until golden. Remove and allow to cool on a wire rack. (You will make more biscuits than you need for 4 servings; the rest can be kept in an airtight tin for 2–3 days.)

5 Make a stock syrup by heating the sugar and 300ml water, stirring to dissolve the sugar. Add the rosemary and cook for 8–10 minutes or until syrupy. Add the rhubarb pieces and grenadine and cook over a low heat for 5–6 minutes or until just tender. Remove from the heat and leave to cool.

6 To serve, place a sablé biscuit on each serving plate. Place the metal ring used to cut the biscuits on top and spoon the drained rhubarb inside. Arrange the mango slices on the rhubarb in a circular pattern, then remove the cutter and top with quenelles or scoops of ice cream. Dust with grated nutmeg.

ULSTER VEGETABLE SOUP
WITH BACON DUMPLINGS

SERVES 4
600ml vegetable stock
small bunch of fresh thyme
olive oil
50g onion, chopped
1 ½ garlic cloves, chopped
2 carrots, neatly chopped
1 celery stick, neatly chopped
1 courgette, neatly chopped
1 small leek, neatly chopped
pepper
freshly grated Parmesan to serve

DUMPLINGS
4 rashers of good unsmoked bacon
olive oil
50g finely chopped onion
1 large garlic clove, chopped
25g parsley, chopped
25g tarragon, chopped

1 First make the dumplings. Cut the rind off the bacon rashers; reserve the rinds for the soup. Mince the bacon very finely in a food processor – if the bacon is minced too coarsely it will not roll into dumplings and bind properly and the dumplings will break up. Transfer to a bowl.

2 Heat a little olive oil in a frying pan, add the onion and garlic and sweat over a low heat until soft but not coloured. Remove from the heat and stir in the parsley and tarragon. Leave to cool, then add to the minced bacon. Season to taste with pepper. Roll the mixture into walnut-sized dumplings, pressing firmly together. Keep covered in the fridge until ready to use.

3 For the soup, put the vegetable stock in a saucepan and add the bacon rinds and thyme. Bring to the boil and simmer for 15 minutes. Strain.

4 Heat a little olive oil in the saucepan, add the onion and garlic and sauté over a moderate heat for about 2 minutes, stirring frequently. Add the carrots and sauté for 2 minutes. Add the celery and courgette and sauté for another 2 minutes. Finally, add the leek and sauté for 2 more minutes. Pour the stock into the pan and bring to the boil. Simmer for 7–8 minutes or until the vegetables are just tender but still a little crunchy.

5 Remove the pan from the heat and add the dumplings. Return to the heat and bring the soup almost to the boil. Simmer gently for 7 minutes.

6 Check the seasoning, then serve, sprinkled with Parmesan.

POACHED SALMON
WITH FENNEL PURÉE AND ALMOND
AND SHRIMP BUTTER

SERVES 4
1 whole fillet of salmon
court bouillon (see page 145)
salt and pepper

ALMOND AND SHRIMP BUTTER
50g chopped shallots
100g unsalted butter, softened
70g blanched almonds, sliced
250g peeled brown shrimps
20g dill, chopped
20g chives, chopped
10ml Pernod
juice of ½ lemon

FENNEL PUREE
2 bulbs fennel, finely sliced on
   a mandolin
75g chopped shallots
10g unsalted butter
5g fennel seeds
5g coriander seeds
150ml chicken stock
50ml double cream
20ml Pernod
100g fennel tops, chopped

1 First make the almond and shrimp butter. Sweat the shallots in a little of the butter, to soften. Transfer to a bowl and add the remaining softened butter. Mix in the almonds, shrimps, dill, chives, Pernod, lemon juice and salt and pepper to taste. Place the butter mixture in the centre of a piece of cling film and wrap up tightly to form a neat cylinder shape. Secure the ends and place in the fridge (or in the freezer) to harden.

2 To make the fennel purée, sauté the sliced fennel and shallots in the butter with the fennel and coriander seeds for 12–15 minutes, to soften. Add the stock and reduce by half.

3 Pour in the cream and add the Pernod, fennel tops and salt and pepper to taste. Transfer the mixture to a food processor and blend until smooth. If not serving straight away, pour the purée into a bowl set over a bowl of iced water, to cool (this will preserve the colour); reheat for serving.

4 Cut the salmon fillet into four pieces. Poach in the court bouillon for 6 minutes. Remove from the bouillon and allow to rest for 2–3 minutes.

5 To serve, spoon the warm fennel purée on to the plates and place the poached salmon on top. Remove the almond and shrimp butter from the cling film and cut into discs. Place on top of the salmon.

152

REGGIE JOHNSON'S CHICKEN
WITH SUMMER LEEKS AND MORELS

SERVES 4

1 organic chicken, about 1.5kg
olive oil
4 shallots, chopped
2 garlic cloves, chopped
100g small button mushrooms
sprig of thyme
1 bay leaf
splash of Pedro Eminent sherry
handful of tarragon
2 bunches of young English leeks,
    about 250g total weight
200g fresh morels
200g crème fraîche

100ml double cream
chervil to garnish

CHICKEN STOCK

olive oil
2 carrots, diced
3 celery sticks, diced
2 leeks, diced
2 onions, diced
knob of unsalted butter
1 bay leaf
sprig of thyme
1 tsp coriander seeds
1 tsp fennel seeds
50g dried morels, rehydrated in water

1 Joint the chicken and set aside the legs, thighs and breasts. Use the remainder of the chicken carcass to make the stock.

2 Roast off the chicken carcass and trimmings in a little oil in a hot pan until golden. Meanwhile, sweat the carrots, celery, leeks and onions in the butter in a saucepan until soft and coloured. Add the bay leaf, thyme and coriander and fennel seeds. Add the chicken carcass and pour in enough water to cover. Bring to the boil, then reduce the heat and simmer for 1 hour.

3 Strain the stock into a clean pan. Add the dried morels and continue to simmer gently until required.

4 Heat 2 tbsp oil in a large pan and fry the chicken pieces until coloured on all sides. Remove and set aside. Add half the shallots, the garlic and button mushrooms to the pan and cook for a few minutes to soften. Stir in the thyme and bay leaf, then add the sherry. Pour in 300ml of the chicken and morel stock and add half the tarragon leaves. Bring to the boil. Return the chicken pieces to the pan and cook for a further 10 minutes or until the chicken is tender.

5 Meanwhile, blanch the leeks in boiling water for 2 minutes. Drain.

6 Heat 1 tbsp oil in a pan and sauté the fresh morels with the remaining shallots for 2–3 minutes, to soften. Stir in the crème fraîche and cream and heat gently for a further few minutes.

7 Add the leeks and morels in cream to the chicken. Season with salt and pepper and add the remaining tarragon leaves. Warm through.

8 To serve, transfer the chicken, leeks and morels to four warm serving bowls and garnish with chervil. Serve with a glass of Pedro Eminent.

SPICE CAKE
WITH SUMMER FRUITS

SERVES 4
100g strawberries
100g raspberries
100g blueberries
50g caster sugar
sifted icing sugar

SPICE CAKES
500g caster sugar
200g plain flour
150g ground almonds
25g liquorice powder
25g ground cinnamon
25g ground star anise
25g ground ginger
25g ground cardamom
1 tsp bicarbonate of soda
500g unsalted butter, melted and heated
   to a light nut brown
100g honey
8 egg whites

LEMON CURD
75ml lemon juice
50g caster sugar
2 eggs
50g unsalted butter

1 For the spice cakes, mix together all the dry ingredients in a bowl. Add the butter and honey and mix well, then add the egg whites and mix again, to combine. Cover and leave in the fridge to chill for at least 1 hour.

2 Place half the strawberries, raspberries and blueberries in a pan with the caster sugar and cook on a gentle heat until the sugar has dissolved, stirring occasionally. Pass the fruit through a sieve and leave to cool. Once cool, gently stir in the remaining whole fruits. Set aside.

3 For the lemon curd, combine the lemon juice, sugar, eggs and butter in a bowl set over a pan of simmering water. Whisk until you reach the ribbon stage. Remove from the heat and allow to cool.

4 Preheat the oven to 180°C/gas 4.

5 Grease 8–9cm rings with butter or oil and place on a non-stick baking tray. Fill the rings with the spice cake mixture and bake for 9–11 minutes or until a cake will spring back when lightly pressed in the middle. Remove from the oven and allow to cool. Remove from the rings before serving. (This makes more than four cakes; the rest will keep in an airtight tin for up to a week.)

6 To serve, spoon the lemon curd on each plate and set a spice cake on top. Arrange the summer fruits alongside and dust the cake with icing sugar.

CHAPTER SIX

THE MIDLANDS & EAST ANGLIA
ANTONY WORRALL THOMPSON & GALTON BLACKISTON

The north Norfolk coast feels as remote as anywhere in England, its barely populated flintstone villages seeming to be all that stand between the salt marsh and the sea. But once this was the most prosperous part of the realm, closer to the continent than London, and so the beneficiary of the great medieval wool trade that linked England and Flanders and proclaimed Norwich England's second city. Look around and marvel at the 'wool churches', such as St Margaret's in Cley-next-the-sea, founded by rich merchants concerned for their soul, whose congregations diminished as Britain's early industrial revolution called them to the towns and cities of the Midlands.

Yet before industrialisation, East Anglia had undergone its own revolution, in agriculture. Refugees from the Low Countries, fleeing persecution from their Spanish Catholic rulers, found in East Anglia a mirror of the landscape they had been forced to abandon: flat, fertile, perfect for market gardening. Their pioneering efforts, regarded with suspicion at the time (though not when the fruits of their labour stalled famine in London), have not necessarily proved beneficial to the landscape – East Anglia is very much the home of Britain's great agro-industrial concerns, most evident in the vast, heavily subsidised fields of sickly coloured rape all too common here. But there are still many farmers in East Anglia whose careful methods result in fine produce that would find favour with their hardworking Calvinist forebears.

A LABOUR OF LOVE

Desmond McCarthy grows "cracking fruit and vegetables", according to Galton Blackiston, whose Michelin-starred restaurant, Morston Hall, he supplies. McCarthy is a modest man who, when he isn't selling his produce to one of the best chefs in the country, sells it to the public from his stall on the Coast Road near Holt. "We produce small quantities of redcurrants, strawberries, gooseberries, and vegetables like artichokes and beans," he tells me. "We take a lot of trouble, there's much hoeing and it's all very labour intensive. Ultimately, it's all down to luck and a bit of judgement and common sense." McCarthy follows the seasons, one of the reasons why Blackiston's set menu changes every day.

Another Norfolk man who bucks the trend towards industrial agriculture is Willie Weston. Most mornings he traipses the bleak and blustery beach at Blakeney Point, raking for the Stiffkey (pronounced 'stookey') cockles that, from September onwards, are all but bursting out of their shell. Mussels too are another of his winter harvests, recalling a line from *The Vision of Piers Plowman*, William Langland's 14th-century epic: "A farthing's worth of mussels or a farthing's worth of cockles were a feast for them on a Friday." Too many people turn their nose up at shellfish, but, it is claimed, they were the reason the Romans invaded England.

Weston is a lobster man too, supplying Blackiston with his best catches – "those with the hardest shells, crammed with meat, you can tell that by how heavy they are. The ones with lighter shells are fine, but I send them off to Spain. They can't get enough of our English lobsters." He disagrees with Blackiston on one point though: "I like to eat lobster meat straight out of the shell, not with all those concoctions over it. I leave that to Galton."

You don't need to be an expert to make the most of Norfolk's bounty. Pheasant, that exotic import from the Far East, is shot on the sprawling royal estate at Sandringham. Throughout the summer there are easy pickings for passers-by on the quiet country roads, where wild plums and sloes grow, as well as elderflowers and the asparagus-like alexander, horseradish, and wild petals to adorn a salad. Returning to the seashore, there is samphire, or glasswort, eaten in lightly boiled bundles with a little butter, though it can also be eaten raw.

MULTICULTURAL DELIGHTS

To many the Midlands means industry, but its food traditions are many and varied, stretching from the fruit vales of Hereford and Worcester, a landscape celebrated in the quintessentially English music of Elgar and Vaughan Williams and the poetry of Housman, to the nearby foodie haven of Ludlow, over to the hunt country of Leicestershire and to the flatlands and fens of Lincolnshire, noted for its eponymous sausages. Even much maligned Birmingham draws food lovers to its southern suburbs – notably Sparkbrook and Sparkhill – where they delight in that fixture of the Brummies' night out, a balti. It's the gift to the sprawling metropolis of its Kashmiri immigrants: chunks of lamb, chicken or vegetables fast-cooked in the wok-like balti, spiced up with coriander, cloves, cumin, cardamom, some cassia bark and ginger, and scooped up with chapatis. Yet as ethnic cuisine has boomed, the Black Country has witnessed the decline of the once ubiquitous 'faggots and peas' (pronounced 'pays' in the local dialect): pork meatballs made of sausage meat and liver (very Italian in flavour) served with mushy, almost lurid green peas, a dish surely due a comeback.

PROTECTING QUALITY

Other traditions continue to flourish. Further east, in Leicestershire, a battle with important repercussions for Britain's artisanal food producers is being fought. The Melton Mowbray pork pie is one of the glories of British cuisine – though not one to clear the arteries – absolutely nothing like the grey, pasty affairs that the words 'pork pie' have come to mean for many. The Melton Mowbray version, made in the town since 1851 by the local firm of Dickinson and Morris, has a distinctive bow-walled shape, as it is made without a tin or hoop; the high animal fat content that keeps it moist also gives the pastry firm support. Within, the pork is

At Blakeney in Norfolk, Willie Weston, a maverick and food hero if ever there was one, catches lobster and rakes for cockles on the beach.

a bright pink, as the meat is, distinctively, uncured – and though the recipe is closely guarded, anchovy essence appears to be a key ingredient.

It deserves the kind of protection thought worthy of Parma ham or Parmesan cheese, or any other of Europe's great artisanal foods, and that is what its makers demand: that, according to law, it must be produced in a certain way in a certain area, like that other delicacy of the East Midlands, Colston Bassett Stilton cheese, to distinguish it from the bland offerings all too prevalent on our supermarket shelves. According to Matthew O'Callaghan of the Melton Mowbray Pork Pie Association: "It is important for the protection of traditional regional foods that applications like ours should not be defeated merely by the threat of legal action from large manufacturers."

The sausage makers of Cumberland and Lincolnshire, the crafters of Bury black pudding, the growers of Yorkshire rhubarb see in the pie-makers' claims an opportunity to protect their produce too from the modern drive to mass-produced mediocrity. It is a small but important step in the battle for Britain's food.

ANTONY WORRALL THOMPSON

One of the most familiar chefs on British television, Antony Worrall Thompson was born in Stratford-upon-Avon to two Royal Shakespeare Company actors who, romantically, were performing in *Romeo and Juliet* at the time. After swimming the Channel at the age of 16, he turned his attention to cooking, and has been involved in a roster of celebrated London restaurants: Ménage à Trois (a favourite of Princess Diana), One Ninety Queen's Gate, dell'Ugo, Zoe, Atrium, Palio, Drones, De Cecco. Today, he runs Notting Grill in Holland Park, and its sister Kew Grill, which specialise in organic meat, fish and vegetables, cooked simply, and according to the seasons. "We must get back to basics," he says. "We need local food for local people. People get used to soils around a particular region, and the fact that food is now imported from all over the place has led, I believe, to a rise in diseases such as psoriasis."

Worrall Thompson is especially concerned with the increase in diabetes and obesity among children, and is currently writing a children's cookbook. "There's a feeling that we've mucked about too much with our food. That's why I'm keen that we buy the best British produce, especially organic food." Worrall Thompson puts his preaching into practice, running a small organic garden where he rears Middle White pigs and grows herbs and vegetables for his Grills and another interest, the Angel Coaching Inn at Heytesbury in Wiltshire. He also owns an avocado farm in Spain.

MENU ONE
> Chilled Potato Soup with Watercress Pesto and Goat's Cheese Cream Crostini
> Pan-fried Wild Salmon with Spiced Shellfish Butter
> Slow-cooked Hereford Oxtail with Stout and Prunes, Horseradish Mash
> Baked Egg Custard with Summer Fruits

MENU TWO
> Cured Duck, Duck Liver Loaf and Pickled Pears with Grilled Walnut Bread
> Trout and Leek Pie with Sorrel Hollandaise
> Poached Fillet of Hereford Beef with Baby Vegetables, Wild Mushroom Broth and Herb Sauce
> Cooked Cream with a Compote of Gooseberries and Elderflower

GALTON BLACKISTON

"I was a bit of a rebel without a cause at school," admits Galton Blackiston, Head Chef at Morston Hall, near Blakeney on the north Norfolk coast. "But I was useful with a bat." So he put all his youthful energies into becoming a professional cricketer. It was at Kent County Cricket Club that another talent emerged. His home-made fruitcakes proved a hit in the club house, so he put them on sale at Rye market. Demand was so high, he was regularly baking until six o'clock in the morning. Hooked on cooking, an opportunity to become a professional chef arose in the Lake District: chef John Tovey needed a hand with the pastry at the Miller Howe Hotel at Windermere, and Blackiston got the job. He stayed there ten years, meeting wife Tracy, and eventually becoming head chef.

After travelling through the US and South Africa, they scrimped and scraped together the money to buy Morston Hall, an 18th-century near-derelict manor house that was spotted by his mother. Fourteen years on, it's a big success, not least because Galton and Tracy "eat, sleep and drink the place". The four-course set dinner menu changes every day, but lobster, mussels, duck and venison make regular appearances, demonstrating Galton's fundamental philosophy of food, which seeks a return to "real cooking". "I'm spoilt for produce here," he says. "I just ask local producers 'what are we going to cook today?' I never want for anything."

MENU ONE
> Pastry Layers with Wild Mushrooms and Norfolk Asparagus, Blue Cheese Dressing and Salad Leaves
> Lasagne of Morston Lobster with Gruyère Cream Sauce
> Roast Norfolk Duckling with Orange served with Bubble and Squeak
> Steamed Treacle Sponge Pudding with Clotted Cream Ice Cream

MENU TWO
> Soup of Jerusalem Artichokes with Norfolk Pheasant
> Morston Hall Crab Cakes and Tartare Sauce
> Casserole of Norfolk Sausages with Mash
> Hot Rhubarb Soufflé with Custard and Ginger Ice Cream

162

CHILLED POTATO SOUP
WITH WATERCRESS PESTO AND GOAT'S CHEESE CREAM CROSTINI

SERVES 4-6

2 tbsp olive oil

2 leeks, white and pale green parts only, sliced

2 onions, finely chopped

2 garlic cloves, finely chopped

½ tsp soft thyme leaves

4 King Edward potatoes, peeled and cubed

1 bay leaf

2 litres chicken or vegetable stock

pinch of freshly grated nutmeg

300ml double cream

3 tbsp snipped chives

salt and white pepper

GOAT'S CHEESE CREAM CROSTINI

1 baguette

3 tbsp extra virgin olive oil

1 garlic clove, peeled

125g very soft, young goat's cheese

3 tbsp double cream

WATERCRESS PESTO

4 garlic cloves

1 tsp Maldon sea salt

1 bag or large bunch of watercress, chopped

5 tbsp olive oil

4 tbsp freshly grated Parmesan

lemon juice to taste

1 Heat the olive oil in a saucepan, add the leeks, onions, garlic and thyme, and cook over a moderate heat for 15 minutes or until the vegetables are soft but not coloured.

2 Add the potatoes and bay leaf and cook until the potatoes start to stick to the bottom of the pan. Add the stock and nutmeg and stir. Bring to the boil, then reduce the heat and simmer for 15–20 minutes or until the potatoes are cooked.

3 Purée the soup in a blender until smooth, then pass through a fine sieve into a clean saucepan. Season to taste. Thin down with more stock, if necessary. Allow the soup to cool, then chill in the fridge.

4 For the crostini, preheat the oven to 160°C/gas 3. Slice the baguette on the diagonal into 5–10mm slices. Use 2 tbsp of the olive oil to brush over the slices, then place them on a baking tray and bake until crispy and golden, turning halfway through the time. Remove from the oven and rub each slice with the garlic clove to flavour. Set aside.

5 Place the goat's cheese in a bowl with the double cream and remaining olive oil. Mash to combine, then season with salt and pepper. Keep in the refrigerator until half an hour before use.

6 To make the pesto, crush the garlic cloves with the sea salt in a mini food processor until you have a fine paste. Add a little of the watercress and work together vigorously, then stir in the olive oil, Parmesan and remaining watercress. Add lemon juice and seasoning to taste.

7 To serve, stir the double cream into the soup, then fold in the chives and top with the watercress pesto. Spread the goat's cheese cream on the crostini.

164 PAN-FRIED WILD SALMON
WITH SPICED SHELLFISH BUTTER

SERVES 4

150ml dry white wine
2 shallots, finely chopped
1 garlic clove, finely chopped
½ tsp soft thyme leaves
350g each small mussels and cockles
   or small clams
1 tsp olive oil
4 fillets of wild salmon, each about 175g,
   skinned
25g unsalted butter
1 tbsp reduced tomato passata or
   thinned tomato purée
115g peeled cooked brown shrimps, peeled
2 large diver-caught scallops, diced
8 Ratte or Pink Fir Apple potatoes, steamed
   until tender and peeled
salt and pepper

CAFÉ DE PARIS BUTTER

35ml tomato ketchup
25g English mustard
25g capers
2 shallots, finely chopped
handful of parsley, finely chopped
1 tbsp snipped chives
½ tsp chopped marjoram
½ tsp thyme leaves
6 tarragon leaves, finely chopped
½ tsp chopped rosemary
1 garlic clove, finely chopped
6 anchovy fillets, finely chopped
1 tbsp brandy
1 tbsp Madeira
½ tsp Worcestershire sauce
1 tbsp paprika
½ tsp curry powder
½ tsp cayenne
grated zest and juice of 1 lemon
grated zest of 1 orange
450g butter, at room temperature,
   cut into small cubes

1 First make the Café de Paris butter. Combine all the ingredients, except the butter, and add 1 tsp salt. Set aside for 4 hours. Beat the butter until fluffy, then mix in the other ingredients. Transfer to a sheet of cling film and shape into a neat log about 2.5cm in diameter. Wrap in the film and chill. (This will make more butter than you need for this recipe, but it can be kept in the freezer for up to 6 months; it is good on steaks, chicken and fish.)

2 Heat the wine with the shallots, garlic and thyme in a large saucepan over a low heat for 3 minutes. Increase the heat and add the mussels and cockles. Cover with a lid and give the pan a good shake, then cook for about 3 minutes or until all the shells have just opened. Discard any that don't open.

3 Tip into a sieve or colander set over a bowl so you can retain the juices. When cool enough to handle, remove the mussels and cockles from their shells and set aside. Retain a few in shell for garnish.

4 Return the juices to the pan and reduce over a high heat until you have 4 tbsp left. Remove from the heat and keep warm.

5 Heat a large frying pan until very hot. Add 1 tbsp of the Café de Paris butter and the oil. Season the salmon and place in the pan. Cook for 2–3 minutes on each side, depending on the thickness; remove and keep warm in a low oven.

6 Pour the shellfish juices into the hot fish pan and stir to combine with the pan juices. Add 2 tbsp Café de Paris butter, the unsalted butter and the reduced passata and cook until emulsified. Check the seasoning. Add the shelled mussels and cockles, shrimps and scallops to the shellfish butter and warm through.

7 To serve, place the salmon fillets on four warmed plates and spoon the shellfish and shellfish butter mixture over the fish. Garnish with the mussels and cockles in shell and the steamed potatoes.

Wild salmon, now rare, was once abundant in the Wye and Severn. One 19th-century chef at London's Reform Club had his salmon sent from Shrewsbury to London in time for that evening's dinner. In the Middle Ages, wild salmon was so common that apprentices insisted they should be fed it no more than three times a week.

166

SLOW-COOKED
HEREFORD OXTAIL
WITH STOUT AND PRUNES
HORSERADISH MASH

SERVES 4

6 pieces of oxtail, each 5cm, about 1.5kg
   total weight
2 tbsp olive oil
85g unsalted butter
3 onions, finely sliced
½ tbsp chopped sage
10 pitted prunes
6 canned anchovies, cut in half lengthways
500ml Young's luxury double chocolate stout
   or equivalent local beer
450ml chicken stock
4 pickled walnuts, quartered
4 sheets of caul fat

MARINADE

4 tsp coarsely ground black peppercorns
2 tsp Maldon sea salt
2 tsp dried oregano
1 tsp thyme leaves
4 garlic cloves
6 tbsp soft brown sugar
2 tbsp olive oil
2 tbsp wine vinegar

ROAST VEGETABLES

12 baby onions, peeled
12 baby carrots, trimmed
12 button mushrooms
12 garlic cloves, unpeeled
1 tbsp olive oil
40g unsalted butter
2 tsp aged vinegar
2 tbsp chopped parsley

HORSERADISH MASH

1kg floury potatoes, peeled and chopped
115g unsalted butter
6 tbsp strong horseradish cream
225ml hot milk

1 For the marinade, blend the peppercorns, salt, herbs, garlic and sugar in a food processor, then gradually add the oil and vinegar.

2 Rub the oxtail with the marinade, then leave to marinate in a cool place for at least 3 hours or, ideally, overnight.

3 Preheat the oven to 150°C/gas 2.

4 Wipe off the marinade and retain. Fry the oxtail in half of the oil and butter in a flameproof casserole until browned on both sides; remove and set aside.

5 Add the remaining oil and butter to the casserole and heat gently until foaming, then add the onions and chopped sage. Allow the onions to cook over a gentle heat until they are caramelised. This will take about 20 minutes. Add six of the prunes and the anchovies.

6 Place the oxtail back on top of the onions in the casserole. Add the reserved marinade, the stout and chicken stock and bring to the boil. Cover the casserole and transfer to the oven to cook for about 3 hours or until the meat is very tender and almost falling off the bone. Allow to cool.

7 Remove the oxtail from the pot and set aside. Pour all the pan juices with the onions and prunes into a food processor and blend until smooth. Pour into a clean saucepan and add the pickled walnuts; cook until the sauce has reached a coating consistency. Remove 4 tbsp of sauce to a large bowl and allow to cool. Set the pan of remaining sauce aside, to reheat for serving.

8 Remove the oxtail meat from the bone, shred it with two forks and place in the bowl with the 4 tbsp sauce. Season the mixture and divide into four 'burgers'. Lay the four sheets of caul fat on a work surface and place an oxtail burger in the centre of each one. Make an indentation in each burger and push in a prune, enclosing it in the oxtail, then wrap the burgers neatly in the caul fat. Pan fry the parcels until they are lightly golden all over.

9 Place the oxtail parcels in a roasting tray. Add the baby onions and carrots, mushrooms and garlic with the oil and butter. Set over a moderate heat and shake the pan to brown the vegetables all over. Increase the oven heat to 200°C/gas 6 and pop the roasting tray into the oven. Roast for 30 minutes.

10 Meanwhile, make the horseradish mash. Cook the potatoes in boiling salted water until tender. Drain and pass through a potato ricer or food mill into a medium bowl. Add the butter, horseradish cream and half the milk and stir to combine. Add the remaining milk if the mash is too stiff. Season to taste. Keep hot.

11 Remove the oxtail parcels and keep hot. Add the vinegar and parsley to the roast vegetables and season with salt and pepper to taste. Serve the oxtail with the roast vegetables, a little sauce and the horseradish mash.

BAKED EGG CUSTARD
WITH SUMMER FRUITS

SERVES 4
400ml double cream
175ml full fat milk
6 free range egg yolks
6 tbsp runny honey
freshly grated nutmeg
mint to garnish (optional)

RASPBERRY SAUCE
450g ripe, undamaged raspberries
juice of 2 lemons
juice of 1 orange
175g caster sugar
1 bottle red wine

RED FRUIT COMPOTE
450g raspberries
55g redcurrants, picked
55g blackcurrants, picked
85ml crème de framboise

1 Preheat the oven to 160°C/gas 3.

2 Heat the cream and milk together until almost boiling, then remove from the heat. Beat the egg yolks and half the honey together, then pour in the hot cream mixture. Strain into a jug.

3 Drizzle the remaining honey into four non-stick dariole moulds. Grate a little nutmeg on top of the honey, then pour in the custard. Sprinkle the top with a little more grated nutmeg.

4 Place the dariole moulds in a baking tray and pour in hot water to come halfway up the sides of the moulds. Place in the oven and bake for 50–60 minutes or until just set. Remove the moulds from the water and allow to cool. Keep in the refrigerator until half an hour before serving.

5 For the sauce, purée the raspberries with the two citrus juices in a blender until smooth. Pass through a fine sieve into a non-reactive saucepan. Discard the pips. Add the sugar and red wine and bring to the boil over a moderate heat. Reduce the heat and simmer until reduced to about 300ml. Skim off any scum that may come to the surface and discard.

6 Add the fruit and cook for 3 minutes. Remove from the heat and allow to cool, then add the framboise. Using a slotted spoon, spoon the fruit into four dariole moulds lined with cling film. Cover with the overhanging cling film, then weigh down with a light weight to compress the fruit. Leave overnight. Reserve the sauce in a cool place.

7 Turn the custards out on to four plates. Turn out the fruit compotes beside the custard, then add a swirl of the raspberry sauce.

CURED DUCK, DUCK LIVER LOAF
AND PICKLED PEARS WITH
GRILLED WALNUT BREAD

SERVES 4

PICKLED PEARS

1cm piece fresh ginger

½ tsp whole cloves

½ tsp allspice berries

2 sticks cinnamon

thinly peeled rind of ½ lemon

350ml red wine vinegar

350ml red wine

375g soft brown sugar

1kg Conference pears, peeled, cored
  and each cut into 6 lengthways

CURED DUCK

1 tsp crushed toasted white peppercorns

1 tsp crushed toasted coriander seeds

½ tsp bay leaf powder

½ tsp crushed toasted cumin seeds

85g Maldon sea salt

85g caster sugar

2 large duck breasts

300ml light chicken stock

DUCK LIVER 'LOAF'

450g duck livers, trimmed of any white
  skin and bile stains

2 garlic cloves, crushed to a paste with salt

1 shallot, finely chopped and sweated
  in a little butter until soft

3 tbsp Port

1 tbsp brandy

225g unsalted butter, melted

salt and white pepper

1 First prepare the pickled pears. Bruise the ginger with a rolling pin, and crush the cloves and allspice with the back of a firm knife. Tie the ginger, cloves, allspice, cinnamon and lemon rind in a piece of muslin. Put the red wine vinegar, red wine and sugar in a non-reactive saucepan and add the spice bag. Bring to the boil, stirring to dissolve the sugar, then simmer gently for 10 minutes.

2 Add the pears and continue simmering very gently for 10–15 minutes. With a slotted spoon remove the pears to two warm, clean 1 litre kilner jars. Allow the syrup to cool, then remove and discard the spice bag. Pour the cold syrup over the pears and seal the jars. Leave in a cool, dark place for at least 1 month before using. The pears can be kept for up to a year.

3 Next prepare the cured duck. Mix together all the ingredients except the duck breasts and stock. Scatter half the cure mixture in a shallow tray lined with overhanging cling film. Place the duck breasts, flesh side down, in the tray and cover with the remaining cure. Wrap up in the cling film, place a weight on top and refrigerate for 24 hours, turning the duck parcel over from time to time.

4 Once the duck breasts are in the fridge, make the duck liver loaf. Preheat the oven to 120°C/gas ¹/₂. Place the duck livers, 1 tsp salt, ¹/₄ tsp white pepper, the garlic, shallot and its butter, Port and brandy in a liquidiser and blend for 1 minute or until smooth. Pulse in the melted butter, then pass the mixture twice through a fine drum sieve into a bowl.

5 Line a small terrine mould with cling film. Spoon in the liver mixture and cover with oiled cling film. Set the mould in a roasting tray and add nearly boiling water to come three-quarters of the way up the sides of the mould. Place in the oven and cook for 45 minutes to 1 ¹/₂ hours or until firm.

6 Remove the mould from the roasting tray and allow to cool, then remove the oiled cling film. Re-cover with fresh cling film to keep out the air. Chill overnight.

7 Rinse the cure from the duck breasts, then place them skin side down in a non-stick frying pan. Cook over a low heat for about 10 minutes to release some fat; remove and allow to cool.

8 Preheat the oven to 160°C/gas 3. Place the duck breasts in a snug-fitting roasting tray and add the stock. Cook them in the oven for 15–20 minutes or until the internal temperature of the duck reaches 60°C (use a meat probe or instant-read thermometer to check). Remove from the roasting tray and allow to cool.

9 To assemble, cut the duck breasts lengthways on the diagonal into thin slices. Arrange two or three slices to one side of each of four cold plates. Slice the duck liver loaf and place one slice almost opposite the sliced duck. Create a food triangle on the plate by adding the pear pickle. Put a little Maldon salt and crushed white pepper on the duck liver loaf. Serve with grilled walnut bread.

Pickled pears are traditionally served as a Boxing Day treat with leftover turkey or capon. Rich, spicy and with a complex texture, they are the perfect foil for cold meats.

172

TROUT AND LEEK PIE
WITH SORREL HOLLANDAISE

SERVES 4

4 fillets of brown trout, each about 125g,
   pin bones removed
4 discs of puff pastry, each 9cm diameter
4 discs of puff pastry, each 14.5cm diameter
beaten egg yolk
salt and pepper
rocket and sorrel leaves to serve

LEEK FILLING

55g unsalted butter
900g leeks, white and pale green parts only,
   thinly sliced
1 garlic clove, crushed to a paste with
   Maldon sea salt

1 tsp soft thyme leaves
1 bay leaf
3 tbsp vegetable stock
150g cream cheese
1 tbsp anchovy essence
4 tbsp double cream

QUICK SORREL HOLLANDAISE SAUCE

2 large free range egg yolks
juice of ½ lemon
250g unsalted butter, melted
pinch of cayenne pepper
25g unsalted butter
2 handfuls of sorrel leaves

1 First make the filling. Melt the butter in a non-stick saucepan, add the leeks, garlic, thyme, bay leaf and stock, and cook over a gentle heat for 15–20 minutes or until all the liquid has evaporated and the leeks are soft and tender. Allow to cool, then beat in the cream cheese, anchovy essence and cream. Season to taste.

2 Preheat the oven to 200°C/gas 6.

3 Cut each trout fillet into three equal pieces. Poach them in boiling salted water for 2 minutes; drain and cool.

4 Lay the four smaller pastry discs on a work surface and prick them with a fork. Arrange some of the leek filling on the pastry, leaving a 2cm border. Add three pieces of trout to each, then cover with the rest of the leek mixture. Lay the larger pastry discs on top. Crimp the edges, brush the dome with egg yolk and trim the border. Use the point of a knife to make a light crescent-shaped indentation on the dome of each pastry. Bake for 30 minutes or until golden brown and crusty.

5 Meanwhile, make the hollandaise. Put the egg yolks in a food processor and add the lemon juice and 1 tbsp cold water. With the motor running, gradually add the melted butter through the feed tube. Add cayenne pepper and salt to taste. You may want to add a little more lemon juice. Keep warm over a pan of hot water.

6 Melt the 25g butter in a shallow pan. When it is hot and foaming add the sorrel leaves and gently heat until the leaves have wilted. Stir the wilted sorrel into the hollandaise sauce.

7 Serve the pies with the sorrel hollandaise and a small salad of rocket and sorrel.

174

POACHED
FILLET OF HEREFORD BEEF
WITH BABY VEGETABLES
WILD MUSHROOM BROTH AND HERB SAUCE

SERVES 4

2 pieces of beef fillet, centre cut, each 325g,
   fat removed and tied
8 French beans, blanched
8 strips of peeled roasted red pepper
6 long strips of canned anchovy
1 tbsp olive oil
salt and pepper

WILD MUSHROOM BROTH

85g dried ceps (porcini), soaked in boiling
   water for 30 minutes
450g leeks
225g carrots, peeled
225g turnips, peeled
½ head celery, cut in half lengthways
1 head garlic, cut in half crossways
¼ Savoy cabbage
450g tomatoes, skinned, quartered and deseeded
2 onions, 1 stuck with 2 bay leaves and 2 cloves
3 sprigs of thyme
½ bunch of chervil
2 bay leaves
15g Maldon sea salt
12 white peppercorns
3 litres beef stock or water
1 bottle red wine

BABY VEGETABLES

4 baby leeks
4 asparagus tips
4 baby turnips, scraped, leaving 2.5cm
   of green top
4 baby carrots, scraped, leaving 2.5cm
   of green top
4 baby Jersey Royal potatoes, scraped
8 sugar snaps
8 French beans
4 broccoli florets
4 best quality, small fresh ceps, lightly
   pan fried in butter
4 cherry tomatoes, peeled
55g unsalted butter

HERB SAUCE

2 handfuls of flat-leaf parsley leaves
2 pickled cucumbers, roughly chopped
3 garlic cloves, roughly chopped
2 tbsp capers, rinsed
4 canned anchovy fillets, rinsed
1 tbsp red wine vinegar
1 tbsp lemon juice
8 tbsp good extra virgin olive oil
1 tbsp Dijon mustard

1 First prepare the broth. Drain the dried ceps, reserving the soaking liquid, and put them in a saucepan with the remaining broth ingredients. Simmer very gently for 1 ½ hours. Strain the broth and pour into a clean, wide saucepan. Add the mushroom soaking liquid and simmer gently for 30 minutes.

2 While the broth is cooking, prepare the baby vegetables (excluding the ceps and tomatoes). Bring a pan of salted water to the boil and cook each vegetable separately, removing when cooked, plunging into iced water and draining.

3 Next make the herb sauce. Chop together the parsley, cucumbers, garlic, capers and anchovies until medium coarse. Or, pulse in a food processor, although you get a better product if you hand chop this salsa. Transfer to a non-reactive bowl and slowly whisk in the remaining ingredients. Season with salt and pepper. Set aside.

4 Lard each beef fillet with four French beans, four strips of roasted pepper and three anchovy strips by threading the ingredients through the beef with a larding needle. Heat the oil in a large frying pan. Season the beef and sear all over until golden brown. Place the meat into the simmering broth. Cook for 12 minutes (do not allow the liquid to boil) for a wonderfully rosy interior. When the meat is cooked to your satisfaction, remove and set aside to rest for 10 minutes.

5 Meanwhile, make the vegetable parcels by dividing all the vegetables (including the ceps and tomatoes) equally among four sheets of cling film. Season with salt and pepper and dot with the butter. About 5 minutes before serving place the vegetable parcels in a steamer to reheat.

6 To serve, carve each fillet into four slices. Place the vegetables in the bottom of four large bowls, top with a little broth and then add two slices of steak, pink side up. Serve the herb sauce separately or drizzle a little over the steaks.

COOKED CREAM
WITH A COMPOTE OF GOOSEBERRIES
AND ELDERFLOWER

SERVES 4
600ml double cream
55g caster sugar
1 vanilla pod, split lengthways
2–3 gelatine leaves, soaked in
    4 tbsp water for 10 minutes

GOOSEBERRY AND ELDERFLOWER COMPOTE
225g caster sugar
grated zest and juice of 1 lemon
2 tbsp elderflower cordial
2 heads of elderflowers, washed
450g gooseberries, trimmed

1 Place the cream, sugar and vanilla in a pan and bring to a near simmer. Once the sugar has dissolved, add the gelatine and its soaking water and stir until melted. Strain through a fine sieve, then pour into four individual glasses. Chill for 3 hours.

2 To make the compote, place the sugar, lemon zest and juice, cordial, 600ml water and the elderflowers in a saucepan and simmer gently for 20 minutes. Strain and return to the saucepan. Bring back to a simmer, then add the gooseberries and cook for about 10 minutes or until they are tender but still hold their shape. Remove the gooseberries to a sieve set over a bowl and return any juices to the pan.

3 Return the pan to the heat and simmer gently to reduce the liquid until you have a viscose syrup. Skim from time to time. Allow to cool, then spoon the gooseberries gently into the syrup. Chill for 2–3 hours.

4 To serve, spoon the gooseberries and syrup on top of the creams.

PASTRY LAYERS WITH
WILD MUSHROOMS AND NORFOLK ASPARAGUS
BLUE CHEESE DRESSING AND SALAD LEAVES

SERVES 4
2 shallots, finely chopped
1 garlic clove, finely chopped
3 tbsp olive oil
225g mixed wild mushrooms
2 tbsp chopped parsley
16 asparagus spears, trimmed to 7.5cm long
young salad leaves
salt and pepper
PASTRY
110g soft plain flour
pinch of cayenne pepper

110g salted butter
175g mature Cheddar, finely grated
1 egg yolk
BLUE CHEESE DRESSING
1 tsp runny honey
1 tsp Dijon mustard
1 tsp red wine vinegar
150ml groundnut or extra virgin olive oil
2 tsp lemon juice
1 shallot, very finely chopped
50g firm Binham Blue cheese, crumbled

1 Begin by making the pastry. Put all the ingredients, with the exception of the egg yolk, in the bowl of a food processor and whiz quickly to combine, then add the egg yolk and process again until the pastry comes together. Divide in half, shape into two balls and wrap individually in cling film. Leave to rest in the fridge for an hour.
2 Preheat the oven to 180°C/gas 4.
3 Roll out one of the pastry balls on a lightly floured surface as thinly as you dare (about 3mm thick is ideal). Make sure you keep moving the pastry to prevent it from sticking. Cut into 12 neat rectangles 7.5cm long and 5cm wide (re-roll any trimmings). Transfer the rectangles to a baking tray lined with baking parchment, leaving a little space between them. Cover with another sheet of baking parchment and place another baking tray on top. I set a couple of bricks on this to weight it down even more. Bake for 20 minutes or until the pastry is golden and crisp. Leave the biscuits to cool and firm on the tray, then transfer to a wire rack and set aside.
4 Next make the dressing. In a bowl whisk together the honey, mustard and a good pinch each of salt and pepper, then whisk in the vinegar. Slowly pour in the oil and lemon juice, whisking constantly. Add the shallot and blue cheese.
5 Heat a frying pan and quickly fry the shallots and garlic in the oil until soft, then add the wild mushrooms and season. Continue cooking over a high heat until the mushrooms soften. Transfer to a bowl and add the chopped parsley. Leave to cool.
6 Cook the asparagus in a pan of boiling water until just tender. Drain and refresh.
7 To serve, lay a biscuit on each plate. Spoon some mushrooms along the biscuit and top with two asparagus spears. Cover with another biscuit and add the remaining mushrooms and asparagus. Put the final biscuit on top. Spoon the dressing around and garnish with some young salad leaves.

178

LASAGNE OF MORSTON LOBSTER
WITH GRUYÈRE CREAM SAUCE

SERVES 4

2 live lobsters, each 700g

1 onion, chopped

large bouquet of soft herbs
  (tarragon, parsley, chervil, dill)

1 lemon, quartered

salt and pepper

LOBSTER SAUCE

a little olive oil and butter

1 large leek, roughly chopped

4 large shallots, roughly chopped

bunch of parsley stalks

lemon juice

250g baby plum tomatoes

1.2 litres fish stock or white chicken stock

100ml double cream

bunch of chives, snipped

PASTA

110g '00' pasta flour or strong
  plain flour

6 egg yolks

1 tsp truffle oil or olive oil

GRUYÈRE CREAM SAUCE

1 shallot, sliced

1 tbsp olive oil

a strip of lemon peel

25ml Noilly Prat vermouth

120ml whipping cream

50g Gruyère cheese, grated

1 First cook the lobsters. Bring a large saucepan of water to the boil with the onion, bouquet garni, lemon and 1 tsp salt. Once boiling, lower in the lobsters (first take off the rubber bands that keep the large claws closed). When the water boils again, cook for 6 minutes. Take the lobsters out and immediately plunge into iced water.

2 Place a lobster on a chopping board. Twist off the large claws and the body and head section from the tail. Using a pair of sturdy scissors carefully snip along the length of the tail shell, then ease the meat away from the shell. Using either the back of a knife or a rolling pin, gently break the shell of the claws, then extract the meat. Once you are satisfied you have extracted everything edible from the first lobster, repeat the procedure with the other lobster. Set all the meat aside. Keep the tail shells and body/head sections (not the claw shells) for the lobster sauce. By the way, if the lobsters have any dark green jelly (coral) in their heads, keep this as it is wonderful added to sauces for colour and flavour.

3 Next make the lobster sauce. Preheat the oven to 150°C/gas 2. Place the lobster tail shells and body/head sections in a roasting tin and roast for about 20 minutes to allow the shells to dry out a little.

4 Meanwhile, heat a little olive oil and butter in a saucepan and sweat the leek and shallots with the parsley stalks over a moderate heat. Add the roasted lobster shells together with some lemon juice, the tomatoes and enough stock to cover. Bring slowly to the boil and simmer gently for 1 hour. Remove from the heat and blitz the whole lot (heads included) in a blender or food processor, then pass the mixture through a sieve into a clean saucepan.

5 Bring to the boil again and simmer to reduce by about half, skimming off any scum. Keep tasting. When the sauce has reached the desired consistency and flavour, whisk in the cream. Check the seasoning. Set aside. Just before serving stir in plenty of snipped chives.

6 To make the pasta, sift the flour and a good pinch of salt into the bowl of a food processor. Lightly beat all the egg yolks with the truffle oil in a jug. Turn on the processor and quickly pour in the egg and oil mixture. As soon as the ingredients come together as a crumbly textured dough, remove from the machine and knead into a ball. Wrap in cling film and leave to rest in the fridge for at least an hour.

7 The next stage requires a pasta machine. Cut the pasta dough into two pieces. Take one of the pieces of dough and, on a lightly floured surface, flatten with your hands. Set the pasta machine on its widest setting and roll through the piece of dough. Fold in half and roll it through the machine again, still on its widest setting. Do this seven times in all. Now set the machine on the next setting and roll through once. Repeat on the next setting, then continue the process up to two notches from the thinnest setting. Lay the resulting long strip of pasta on your work surface. Using a 7.5cm round cutter, cut out discs. Repeat with the other piece of pasta dough. You need 12 discs for the lasagne, although I always cut a couple of extra. Allow the pasta discs to dry out while you make the Gruyère cream sauce.

8 Fry the shallot in the olive oil until softened, then add the lemon peel and Noilly Prat and bring to the boil. Simmer to reduce the liquid by half. Add the cream, bring back to the boil and simmer again to reduce and thicken. Pass through a sieve into another saucepan. Set aside, ready to reheat. Just before serving stir in the Gruyère.

9 Now you are ready to assemble the lasagne. Preheat the oven to 140°C/gas 1. Divide the lobster meat into eight equal portions on a buttered baking tray, giving each one a little claw meat as well as tail meat. Cover each portion of lobster with 3 tbsp of lobster sauce, then cover the tray with cling film. Place in the oven to warm through while you cook the pasta.

10 Drop the pasta discs into a pan of gently boiling salted water. Cook for about 3 minutes, then lift them out with a draining spoon. Quickly season and give them a splash of olive oil.

11 To serve, place a pasta disc in the centre of each warm plate. Place a portion of lobster on top, then cover with another pasta disc. Repeat the lobster and pasta layers, then spoon over the remaining lobster sauce and the Gruyère cream sauce.

180

ROAST NORFOLK DUCKLING
WITH ORANGE SERVED WITH
WITH BUBBLE AND SQUEAK

SERVES 4

1 duckling, about 1.8kg, with giblets
vegetable oil
1 carrot, chopped
1 celery stick, chopped
3 garlic cloves, chopped
2 sprigs of sage
1 tsp soft brown sugar
1 tbsp red wine vinegar
1 large glass of red wine
2 tbsp runny marmalade
a little butter
1 orange, peeled and segmented
salt and pepper

BUBBLE AND SQUEAK

3 large baking potatoes
450g peeled swede, cubed
350g peeled parsnips, chopped
1 Savoy cabbage, leaves separated,
    halved and centre stalk removed
225g salted butter
3 medium-sized English onions,
    thinly sliced
1 garlic clove, chopped

1 Begin by making a good stock. Take the wings from the duck, and chop the giblets, heart and any other bits, except the liver (keep this to use later). Heat a splash of oil in a decent-sized saucepan and gently fry the carrot, celery and garlic with the sage until softened. Add the giblets, wings and other bits from the duck and lightly brown these. Now add the sugar and red wine vinegar and deglaze the pan, then add the red wine and reduce a little. Cover with 600ml of water and bring to the boil, then simmer gently for about 1 hour.

2 While the stock is simmering, prepare the vegetables for the bubble and squeak. Preheat the oven to 200°C/gas 6 and bake the potatoes for 45 minutes to 1 hour. Meanwhile, bring the swede to the boil in salted water, then cover and cook until very tender; drain. Do the same with the parsnips. For the cabbage, blanch the leaves in a pan of boiling water for about 5 minutes, then drain and refresh under cold running water. Squeeze the cabbage to remove any liquid.

3 Heat a frying pan until hot, then add 50g of the butter and fry the onions until they start to colour. Add the garlic, followed by the blanched cabbage leaves and another 50g butter. Turn the heat down to very low and gently stew the cabbage in the onions until soft. Lightly season, then remove from the heat and set aside, ready to reheat for serving.

4 Scoop the flesh from the baked potatoes and push through a sieve or potato ricer, adding a knob of the butter. Push the swede and parsnips through a sieve or ricer, add the remaining butter to them and season. Combine the potato, swede and parsnip in a saucepan, then set aside.

5 Preheat the oven to 200°C/gas 6.

6 Set the duck on a trivet in a roasting tin and score the skin with a sharp knife, trying not to penetrate through into the meat. Season the skin really well. Place in the hot oven and roast for 45 minutes. Some fat will have run out of the bird and you can baste the duck with this. Then brush over the marmalade. Return to the oven and continue roasting for a further 40 minutes, basting occasionally with the fat and residue in the tin. Remove from the oven and allow to rest for a few minutes, then take the legs off the duck. Return these to the oven to finish cooking for a further 15 minutes, if necessary.

7 While the duck is roasting, strain the stock into another pan and reduce by half over a high heat, skimming off any fatty scum that comes to the surface. Then keep reducing the stock to achieve a gravy with the desired consistency and flavour.

8 To finish the bubble and squeak, gently heat through the potato, swede and parsnip mixture and the cabbage and onion mixture.

9 Fry the liver in a little butter, then quickly chop the liver and add to the gravy.

10 To serve, carefully take the duck breasts off the bone. Slice the breasts and arrange on four warm plates with the meat from the legs. Spoon the potato, swede and parsnip mixture on the plates and top with the cabbage and onions. Finally, add the orange segments to the gravy and spoon over the duck.

A classic case of necessity mothering invention, bubble and squeak – named for the sound it made while cooking – combined leftover boiled beef with potatoes and cabbage. This is a more refined, though no less tasty, version of the ultimate comfort food.

182

STEAMED
TREACLE SPONGE PUDDING
WITH CLOTTED CREAM ICE CREAM

SERVES 4
4 tbsp golden syrup
grated zest and juice of 1 orange
175g softened unsalted butter
175g light soft brown sugar
3 eggs, beaten
1 tsp black treacle
175g self-raising flour

CLOTTED CREAM ICE CREAM
300ml clotted cream
150ml milk
5 eggs yolks
115g caster sugar

1 First make the ice cream. Place the cream and milk in a saucepan and heat gently until on the point of boiling (just starting to tremble on top). Meanwhile, whisk the egg yolks with the sugar in a large bowl until well combined. Slowly add the hot cream mixture, continuing to whisk as you do so. Pour the mixture back into the saucepan and cook over a low heat, stirring constantly, until thick enough to coat the back of the spoon. Be careful not to let the mixture get too hot or it might split. Pass through a fine sieve and allow to cool completely.

2 Churn in an ice cream machine to a soft consistency. Transfer to an airtight container and put into the freezer for at least 2 hours. If more convenient, you can make the ice cream the day before. You may find if you freeze it for 24 hours or more, you will need to take it out of the freezer about 20 minutes before serving, otherwise it will be very solid and difficult to serve.

3 Butter the inside of a 1 litre pudding basin. Combine the golden syrup with the orange zest and juice, then pour this into the bottom of the basin. Set aside.

4 Beat the butter and sugar together really well until the mixture is pale, then slowly add the beaten eggs, beating well after each addition. Add the black treacle, followed by the flour, again beating well.

5 Spoon this mixture into the pudding basin and cover with greaseproof paper and foil, pleated across the middle; tie on with string and trim off excess all around. Steam the pudding for 2 hours, checking the water level at regular intervals.

6 To serve, run a knife around the rim of the basin and ease out the pudding on to a large serving plate. Give each portion a good spoonful of ice cream. For extra indulgence, serve with some custard too.

SOUP OF
JERUSALEM ARTICHOKES
WITH NORFOLK PHEASANT

SERVES 4

175g onions, finely sliced
50g salted butter
600ml chicken stock
450g Jerusalem artichokes, peeled
   and finely sliced
pinch of ground mace

600ml milk
2 pheasant breasts, skinned
2 pheasant legs, skinned
½ egg white
6 tbsp double cream
4 slices of smoked streaky bacon
salt and pepper

1 Begin by making the soup. In a large heavy-based saucepan sweat the onions in the butter until softened. Add the stock, artichokes and mace, bring to the boil and simmer until the artichokes are soft. Add the milk and simmer for a few minutes longer, then remove from the heat. Purée the soup in a blender or food processor until smooth, then pass through a sieve into another saucepan. Check the seasoning and set aside.

2 Remove the fillets from the underside of each pheasant breast and set aside. Place the breasts between two pieces of cling film and bash gently with a rolling pin into fairly thin and even rectangular shapes. Set aside.

3 Take the meat from the pheasant legs and blitz with the egg white in a food processor until smooth. I like to push this through a sieve to get rid of any sinews. This isn't essential, but you get a smoother result. Place the puréed meat in a bowl and lightly season, then slowly add the cream, beating well after each addition. Add enough cream to achieve a dolloping consistency. Spoon half the purée along the centre of each flattened breast, then place the reserved fillets on top of this. Roll each flattened breast firmly around the purée to make a sausage, then roll these tightly in cling film and tie each end tightly with string. You can prepare ahead to this stage.

4 Half an hour before you are ready to serve, place the pheasant rolls in a steamer or a saucepan of boiling water and cook for 20–30 minutes. When ready the rolled breast should feel firm to the touch.

5 While the pheasant is cooking grill the bacon until crisp; set aside.

6 Remove the pheasant from the steamer or boiling water and allow to rest for a few minutes. Meanwhile, gently reheat the soup and spoon it into bowls.

7 Slice the pheasant 'sausages' while still in their cling film wrappers, then slip off the film as you arrange the slices on top of the soup. Top each bowl with a piece of crisply grilled bacon and serve immediately.

MORSTON HALL CRAB CAKES
AND TARTARE SAUCE

SERVES 4

225g white crab meat
1 egg yolk, beaten
½ lobe of fresh ginger, finely grated
1 small, mild red chilli, finely chopped
2 tbsp chopped coriander
seasoned plain flour
1 egg, beaten with 80ml milk
Japanese or fine white breadcrumbs
splash of olive oil
knob of butter
salt and pepper
salad leaves, tossed at the very last minute
    with a splash of lemon juice, a small drizzle
    of olive oil and seasoning

TARTARE SAUCE

1 egg
pinch of caster sugar
pinch of English mustard powder
Maldon sea salt
150ml sunflower oil
150ml olive oil
1 tbsp white wine vinegar
1 tbsp lemon juice
2 small shallots, finely chopped
2 tbsp chopped flat-leaf parsley
1 tbsp chopped tarragon
3 small cornichons or 1 small gherkin,
    finely diced

1 In a bowl combine the white crab meat with the beaten egg yolk, ginger, chilli and coriander. Season to taste with salt and pepper. Divide the mixture into eight or 12 equal portions and shape each into a cake. Place the crab cakes on a tray, then put into the freezer for 30 minutes to firm up.

2 Meanwhile, set out three separate bowls, one with seasoned flour, the second with the egg and milk mixture (egg wash) and the third with the breadcrumbs.

3 Remove the crab cakes from the freezer and, one at a time, drop first into the seasoned flour to coat all over; shake off excess flour and dip into the egg wash; shake off any excess egg and turn in the breadcrumbs. Make sure the crab cake is lightly and evenly coated with breadcrumbs before placing it on a tray lined with greaseproof paper. Cover with cling film and refrigerate.

4 To make the tartare sauce, place the egg, sugar, mustard powder and a pinch each of Maldon salt and freshly ground black pepper in a bowl and, using an electric hand mixer on high speed, beat together thoroughly. While beating, slowly drizzle in the sunflower oil, followed by the olive oil and white wine vinegar. Turn off the mixer and stir in the rest of the ingredients, mixing well. Check the seasoning (I prefer flakes of Maldon sea salt and coarsely ground black pepper). This will make more sauce than you need for the dish; keep the remainder in the fridge for up to 5 days.

5 When you are ready to serve, heat a large heavy-based frying pan over a moderate heat. Add a splash of olive oil and a knob of butter, which should foam gently. Place the crab cakes in the pan and fry gently for 4 minutes on each side or until golden.

6 Serve the crab cakes with some tartare sauce and lightly dressed salad leaves.

CASSEROLE OF
NORFOLK SAUSAGES
WITH MASH

SERVES 4

12 Norfolk sausages or other meaty
   pork sausages
2 English onions, thinly sliced
55ml olive oil
175g smoked streaky bacon, finely chopped
24 button mushrooms
1 small glass of red wine
600ml good beef stock
2 baking apples, peeled and diced
   (I use local Bramley's for this)
salt and pepper

MASH

3 decent sized baking potatoes,
   such as Norfolk Pinks or Maris Piper
75g salted butter
2 garlic cloves, crushed
150ml milk
6 tbsp whipping cream
sprig of rosemary
sprig of thyme
a good grating of nutmeg

1 Preheat the oven to 180°C/gas 4.

2 First, for the mash, put the potatoes into the oven to bake for 1–1 1/2 hours, depending on the size of the potatoes.

3 Heat a deep-sided roasting tray on top of the cooker and colour the sausages all over. Remove and set aside, then fry the onions in the olive oil until they just start to caramelise. Add the bacon and mushrooms and continue frying for a couple of minutes. Next add the red wine and, over a high heat, reduce by half. Put the sausages back into the roasting tray and cover with the stock. Bring back to the boil, then place in the oven and cook for 30 minutes (if the sausages are cooking too quickly, cover with foil). Add the diced apple and cook for a further 10 minutes. You should now have a stew consistency with plenty of sauce.

4 While the sausages are in the oven, finish the mashed potato. Combine the butter, garlic, milk, cream and herbs in a saucepan and bring to the boil. Once boiling remove from the heat and leave for 20 minutes for the flavours to develop.

5 Take the baked potatoes from the oven and scoop out the flesh. Pass through a sieve or potato ricer set over a saucepan. Strain the milk and cream mixture, then gradually add to the potato, beating really well with a wooden spoon. Do not pour in the liquid in one swoop, as different varieties of potato vary in how much they will absorb; you want the potato to hold its shape on the plate rather than spread. Taste and season, then add the nutmeg.

6 To serve, spoon the mashed potato on to the centre of the warm plates, top with the sausages and spoon over the sauce, ensuring that each serving has plenty of bacon, apple and mushrooms.

HOT RHUBARB SOUFFLÉ
WITH CUSTARD AND GINGER ICE CREAM

SERVES 4
315g pink rhubarb, trimmed and cut
   into 2.5cm pieces
grated zest of ½ orange
25ml orange juice
20g cornflour, mixed with a little water
110g caster sugar
3 egg whites
sifted icing sugar

vanilla pouring custard made with
   425ml full fat milk, ½ vanilla pod,
   4 egg yolks and 75g caster sugar

GINGER ICE CREAM
150ml whipping cream
250ml milk
50g fresh ginger, peeled and grated
5 egg yolks
75g caster sugar

1 Put the rhubarb in a saucepan with the orange zest and juice and 75ml water. Gently heat until completely soft. Purée in a blender and pass through a fine sieve into a clean pan. Return to the heat, add the cornflour mixture and stir until the purée is very thick. Remove from the heat, place a sheet of cling film directly on top of the purée and set aside.

2 In another pan dissolve 75g of the sugar in 6 tbsp of water over a low heat. Boil to the soft ball stage (115°C on a sugar thermometer). Pour into the warm rhubarb purée and mix well, then gently heat. Transfer to a large bowl and cool completely.

3 Butter four 8.5cm ramekins well with softened unsalted butter, making the brush strokes go upwards so as not to hinder the rising of the soufflé. Chill until set, then repeat the buttering process. Dust well with caster sugar. Return to the fridge.

4 To make the ice cream, put the cream, milk and ginger in a large pan and bring slowly to the boil, stirring frequently. Meanwhile, whisk the egg yolks and sugar in a bowl until pale. Once the cream mixture has come up to the boil, pour over the egg yolks and sugar and whisk together. Strain the custard back into the pan and slowly heat until the custard thickens enough to coat the back of a spoon. Don't allow it to get too hot or it might split. Strain into a bowl and allow to cool completely. When cold, churn in an ice cream machine to a soft consistency, then transfer to an airtight container. Freeze for at least 2 hours. (The ice cream can be made the day before.)

5 Twenty minutes before serving, preheat the oven to 200°C/gas 6.

6 To finish the soufflés, whisk the egg whites until stiff, slowly adding the remaining 25g caster sugar to produce a meringue. Using a slotted spoon, quickly beat one-third of the meringue into the rhubarb purée, then gently fold in the remainder.

7 Spoon into the buttered ramekins. Level the tops and run your thumb around the edge, just inside the rim of the ramekin. Set the ramekins on a baking tray and bake for about 10 minutes or until the soufflés have risen about 2cm above the ramekins.

8 Transfer to plates, dust with icing sugar and add a blob of ginger ice cream alongside. Serve immediately, with the custard to be poured into the soufflés.

CHAPTER SEVEN SCOTLAND

TOM LEWIS & NICK NAIRN

TOM LEWIS & NICK NAIRN

Scottish food is wrested from an unforgiving land. Farmers, fishermen, stockmen rely on resourcefulness, ingenuity and the necessity of invention in a beautiful but harsh landscape ill-served by an unyielding climate. Hardy grains like oats and barley are staples, the rough-hewn delights porridge and haggis are celebrated national dishes.

Porridge, no more than boiled oats and water stirred steadily with a wooden spoon called a spirtle, was made by crofters, traditionally at the beginning of the week, allowed to cool and cut into slices, one each for lunch every day of the week. Ironically, it's fashionable now, its profile boosted by a proven ability to lower cholesterol, a modern menace in Scotland as elsewhere in the developed world, though the modish drizzle of maple syrup that accompanies it now would be a mystery to the impoverished, parochial crofters.

Haggis, which Robert Burns hailed as "Great chieftain o' the pudden race", is one of the world's finest but most unforgiving regional specialities, best kept away from timorous souls who prefer not to know where their food comes from. Sheep's offal, or 'pluck' – including windpipe and lungs – is boiled and minced and mixed with oatmeal and suet. Then the whole rich, spicy concoction is sewn up in a sheep's stomach to be served with 'neeps and tatties', the roasted swede and potatoes that flourish in barely fertile soil.

CATTLE COUNTRY

If the fruit of the soil is limited, life abounds in Scotland's larder, not least in the imposing form of the bulky, black Aberdeen Angus, regarded by many as the finest of all beef cattle breeds. Its optimum blend of fat and muscle, in part a result of Scotland's cool climate, gives it a flavour that is unequalled by any of its rivals.

The history of the Aberdeen Angus goes back to the early 19th century when oft-lauded stockmen like Hugh Watson of Angus, William McCrombie, and the returning Oxford-educated patrician Sir George Macpherson Grant employed newly developed close breeding skills to transform the cattle locals knew as 'doddies' and 'hummlies' into a new breed whose delicious marbled meat soon achieved a worldwide reputation.

Colonies of the creatures were taken by pioneers to the Empire and the United States, and were eventually to come to the rescue of the original Scottish lines, which were threatened with decline during the 1960s – an age that demanded cheap meat with which to pack the shelves of the expanding supermarkets, and saw the widespread import of leaner continental cattle. This emphasis on price-cutting led ultimately to the tragedy of BSE, 'mad cow disease', which decimated much of Britain's beef industry. But the BSE scandal enhanced the reputation of the carefully reared, traceable Aberdeen Angus, which remained untainted, proof that, in the end, quality will always trump quantity. The meat of the Aberdeen Angus has never been more valuable or so highly regarded.

TO THE MEAT MARKET

Every Wednesday for a quarter of a century, butcher Alan Kennedy has been casting an informed eye over the finest exhibits paraded at Forfar's cattle market. Forfar, the county town of Angus and the old capital of the Picts, marks the southern boundary of what Kennedy calls "Britain's finest beef area", stretching north to Aberdeen, within which fifth- and sixth-generation cattle handlers treat their charges with the utmost reverence and care.

"The quality of the handling is reflected in the taste," Kennedy claims. "It's all about husbandry. The cattle are relaxed, they are never stressed. They have plenty of space, and feed on grass, barley, potatoes, natural foods."

Each bull is treated as an individual, growing

at different rates, which is why they are only slaughtered when absolutely ready, at anywhere between 12 and 24 months. Every one is fully traceable. "I can tell you exactly the area, the farm, the bull from where any of my fillet steaks come," says Kennedy. "There's an unspoken trust among everyone connected with the raising of beef here. Everyone knows what happens."

So what should a great steak taste like, I ask Kennedy? "It should have a very slightly gamey taste, a real strength of flavour. That's where hanging is imperative. It needs to be hung for three weeks, so the enzymes break it down, and it gets darker and looks older." And the result? "This is the best steak you can buy anywhere in the world. Serve it plain, pan-fried or grilled medium-rare for about three minutes."

FROM LAND TO SEA

Willie Little rises every morning at three o'clock to check the produce arriving at his fishmongers in Perth. Cod, john dory, redfish, gurnard, squid, prawn, langoustines – the fruit of a chilling, turbulent sea, dependent by the day on the catch of the four boats he buys off, which operate out of the northern fishing port of Scrabster, looking out on the distant form of Orkney.

Little was a chef for 35 years in hotels and restaurants around Perthshire and Angus, so he knows better than most what a chef is looking for. Which is?

"Look at the eyes of the fish," he says. "They should be prominent, popping out. The skin should be gleaming with a film of fresh slime, it should be springy to touch, and the gills should be red. And there should be no smell. Fresh fish do not smell."

Like Kennedy and his cattle handlers, Little is reliant on the skill and care of the men on the trawlers. "Handling is everything. The men on the boats know not to overfill the boxes, and they take

Scottish beef is considered by many to be the finest in the world. Cattleman Derek Morrison sends his animals to market at Forfar.

care when pulling the fish aboard. A bruised fish is no good to anyone."

Little is dependent, too, on the fishermen for what is caught, and in turn chef Tom Lewis is dependent on him. "Tom's menu depends on what I have to offer him, and that depends on what the fishermen offer me. It's a chain of trust."

Little eats fish every day, which may account for his remarkable energy. His favourites tend to be unfashionable species, at least in Britain. "Coley, that's very underrated, tremendously tasty. And hake. The Spanish love it. I think Scots should learn to love it too."

TOM LEWIS

"We don't have the best climate in the world," admits Tom Lewis, head chef at Monachyle Mhor, a hotel that nestles alongside Loch Voil in the genteel highlands of Perthshire, "but we do have great flavours in Scotland. Lots of game in season [Lewis is an able shot], venison, pheasant, duck, fish, of course, and great beef. The thing is to keep it simple. I don't fanny about. I let the flavours do the talking."

Despite his love of Scotland, Lewis was born among a family of farmers near the Welsh market town of Abergavenny. Completely self-taught, he was inspired to cook by his mother, a copy of *Larousse*, and a broadcast of Desert Island Discs featuring Nico Ladenis. Despite having worked as a sheep-shearer in the Antipodes, he reckons that cooking is the hardest job in the world. But for Tom it's reaping rewards.

For ten years now, he has been in the kitchen at Monachyle Mhor, picking up awards for his daily changing menu that's more reliant on the seasons than most. "What fish are cooked depends on what fish are caught," he says. If he shoots one of the deer that roam his 800 hectares, that will make the menu too. The hotel's herb garden is kept in good shape by gardener Black Dan, and nearly everything else comes from within a 19km radius.

But it's not all haute cuisine. Lewis also runs a fish and chip shop in Callander. "Beef dripping for the chips, and fresh fish, a lot more variety than you usually see," Lewis proclaims. "Haddock, sea bass, lemon sole, coley, hake, it's all for sale in the fish and chip shop."

MENU ONE

> Soused Monachyle Roe Deer with a Roasted Beetroot and Horseradish Cream
> West Coast Scallops, Quinoa and Smoked Haddock Kedgeree with Mustard Leaves and a Light Curry Dressing
> Roast Sirloin of Perthshire Highland Beef with Ayrshire Potatoes, Roasted Glamis Asparagus and a Radish Relish
> Classic Summer Pudding with Mixed Scottish Red Berries, a Vanilla and Glenturret Ice Cream and a Shortbread Biscuit

MENU TWO

> Fillet of Perthshire Lamb, Seared Kidney and Balsamic Onions, Rocket and Broad Beans with Arran Mustard Dressing
> Seared Herring in Oatmeal with Celeriac Rémoulade, Garden Cress and Champagne Chive Butter Sauce
> Roasted Breast of Grouse, Balquhidder Chanterelles and Seasonal Vegetables with Sage and Onion Jus
> Black Dan's Honey and Toasted Oatmeal Cranachan with Comrie Strawberries Poached in Pernod and Cinnamon

NICK NAIRN

It was while travelling the world with the Merchant Navy that Nick Nairn had the epiphanal moment that would launch him on his way to becoming one of Scotland's most celebrated chefs. "It was my first satay, in Singapore. Grilled over coals and served with peanut sauce. Fantastic." Inspired by the many and varied flavours experienced on his travels he decided to become a cook. "I was obsessed with the gregarious pleasure of cooking and it seemed a natural progression to earn a living from it."

He opened his first restaurant, Braeval, to great applause in 1986 and, in 1991, became the youngest Scottish chef to gain a Michelin star, an accolade he retained for some 10 years. Yet Nairn's interests have always extended beyond the kitchen into education. His state-of-the-art Cook School, with its stunning architectural design and beautiful lochside location on the Lochend Estate near Stirling, has raised the bar for cook schools in Scotland. It has nurtured skills and appreciation in some 15,000 people since opening in 2000, schooling them in a number of different styles of cuisine. And Nairn works with the Scottish Executive to promote healthy eating, a matter of some urgency in urban Scotland, where obesity and related ill-health is a major problem.

"The real answer lies in a cultural change regarding the value of eating in Scotland," Nairn believes. "Countries such as Finland and Australia have made a real effort to improve people's diets, and we need to do the same. We chefs have a duty *not* to make food exclusive, to keep it simple so that everyone can appreciate good, fresh, seasonal food. We have had a minor food revolution in Britain, but the gulf between the way wealthy and poor people eat is still widening. We need to address that."

MENU ONE
> Roast Langoustine with Spiced Avocado
> Seared Home Smoked Salmon with an Apple and Watercress Salad and Horseradish Cream
> Loin of Roe Venison with Potato Cake, Roast Roots, Creamed Cabbage and Game Gravy
> Hot Blairgowrie Raspberry Soufflé with Malt Whisky, Honey and Oatmeal Ice Cream

MENU TWO
> Home Smoked Salmon with Oatmeal Pancakes, Horseradish and Chive Crème Fraîche
> Lobster Macaroni with Rocket and Parmesan
> Peppered Fillet of Beef with Whisky and Mushroom Sauce
> Rhubarb and Ginger Mousse with Rhubarb Sauce

SOUSED MONACHYLE ROE DEER
WITH A ROASTED BEETROOT AND
HORSERADISH CREAM

SERVES 4
loin of roe deer (see method)
olive oil
1 tbsp tarragon vinegar
salt and pepper
mixed peppery leaves

MARINADE
equal parts red and white wine to cover meat
600g coarse sea salt
bunch of thyme
10 bay leaves
good pinch of ground cloves
3 garlic cloves, crushed
small handful of black peppercorns (20–30)
small handful of small dried chillies (10–12)
4 good strips of orange zest

OATCAKES
350g pinhead oatmeal
350g porridge oats
400g brown flour
125ml extra virgin olive oil
125ml light olive oil

**ROASTED BEETROOT AND
HORSERADISH CREAM**
2 beetroots
1 tbsp olive oil
sprig of thyme
1 good tbsp home-made horseradish
   cream (freshly grated horseradish
   mixed with mayonnaise or
   crème fraîche)
1 shallot, finely chopped

1 To make the marinade, put all the ingredients in a pot and bring to the boil, then remove from the heat and leave until cold. Place the meat in the marinade and leave in a cool place or the fridge for 5–7 days or until the meat feels firm. Drain and pat dry, then wrap in muslin and air dry in a cool place (not the fridge) for 1 week. The venison will serve 15–20 portions; it can be kept in the fridge for up to 2 weeks.

2 Preheat the oven to 170°C/gas 3.

3 To make the oatcakes, mix together all the ingredients with a good pinch of salt, then add about 300ml water until it binds. With a floured rolling pin, roll out the dough to 2–3mm thick. Cut out square shapes and place on a non-stick baking tray. Fold the trimmings back together and roll out and cut again. Bake for 25 minutes or until a pale colour. Cool on a wire rack. This will make quite a lot of oatcakes; they can be kept in an airtight container for up to 2 weeks.

4 Turn the oven up to 180°C/gas 4. Put the beetroots in a small roasting tray and toss with the olive oil, a splash of water and the thyme. Roast for 35–45 minutes, depending on size. When cold, peel and chop. Fold the beetroot into the horseradish cream together with the shallot and add salt and pepper to taste.

5 Mix the tarragon vinegar with 4–5 tbsp olive oil and seasoning to taste.

6 To serve, slice the roe deer very thinly and arrange on the plates. Drizzle with olive oil and add a small grinding of black pepper. Spoon the beetroot cream on top. Toss the salad leaves with the vinaigrette and serve on the side together with the oatcakes.

WEST COAST SCALLOPS
QUINOA AND SMOKED HADDOCK KEDGEREE WITH MUSTARD LEAVES AND A LIGHT CURRY DRESSING

SERVES 4
8 scallops, shelled
olive oil
12 mustard leaves or rocket

KEDGEREE
125g quinoa
½ vegetable stock cube
2 fillets of pale-smoked Scrabster haddock
milk
2 bay leaves
few black peppercorns
4 free range eggs, hard-boiled and chopped
2 shallots, finely chopped
good sprig of parsley, chopped

1 small tsp curry powder
butter
cream
juice of 1 lemon

CURRY DRESSING
1 shallot, finely chopped
1 garlic clove, crushed
1 tsp curry powder
vegetable oil
100ml poaching liquid from the
   haddock, or fish stock
½ glass of white wine
bunch of flat-leaf parsley
2 tbsp double cream

1 First cook the quinoa for the kedgeree in water to cover, with the stock cube, for 8–10 minutes or until tender. Drain and reserve.

2 Poach the haddock in milk to cover with the bay leaves and peppercorns for 3–4 minutes. Drain the fish, reserving the liquid. When it is cool enough to handle, flake the fish, discarding skin and bones. Strain the liquid and make up to 100ml with fish stock or water if necessary. Set the fish and liquid aside.

3 To make the dressing, sweat the shallot with the garlic and curry powder in a little vegetable oil until soft but not brown. Pour over the haddock poaching liquid and add a good glug of white wine and the parsley stalks. Bring to the boil, then reduce by two-thirds. Add the cream and reduce to a sauce consistency. Pass through a sieve into a clean pan and add the chopped parsley tops. Set aside, and reheat for serving.

4 To make the kedgeree, combine the quinoa, haddock, eggs, shallots, parsley and curry powder in a bowl and fold together. Season with salt and pepper. Gently warm through in a pan in some butter, adding enough cream to bind and a good squeeze of lemon to taste. Keep warm.

5 If the scallops are large you can cut them across in half. Heat some olive oil in a frying pan, add the scallops and sear for 1–2 minutes on each side.

6 To serve, spoon some kedgeree into the centre of each warm plate, moulding it in a metal ring. Lift off the ring. Arrange the mustard leaves on the kedgeree. Place a scallop on top with the rest to the side. Drizzle the dressing around.
Illustrated overleaf

ROAST SIRLOIN OF
PERTHSHIRE HIGHLAND BEEF
WITH AYRSHIRE POTATOES, ROASTED GLAMIS ASPARAGUS AND A RADISH RELISH

SERVES 4

12 small new potatoes
duck fat
1kg boned sirloin or ribeye of beef
½ glass of red wine
100ml beef stock
2 tbsp unsalted butter
2 tbsp plain flour
20 asparagus spears
olive oil
12 baby carrots

12 baby turnips
300g fresh peas
salt and pepper

RADISH RELISH

12 red radishes, finely chopped
2 shallots, finely chopped
1 tbsp good-quality aged sherry vinegar
4 tbsp light olive oil, not too peppery

PARSLEY BUTTER

knob of butter
1 heaped tbsp chopped parsley

1 First make the radish relish. Mix all the ingredients together, season with salt and pepper and leave overnight in the fridge.

2 Preheat the oven to 120°C/gas ¼.

3 Cut the top and bottom off each potato to make a barrel shape, then put them in a roasting tray and cover with duck fat. Place in the oven to cook for 25–30 minutes.

4 Meanwhile, make the parsley butter by mashing the ingredients together.

5 When the potatoes are done, remove them from the oven and keep warm. Turn up the oven temperature to 230°C/gas 8.

6 Season the beef, then sear in a hot roasting tin on top of the cooker. Add the red wine. Transfer to the oven and roast for 30–40 minutes, then leave to rest in a warm place for at least 15 minutes. Meanwhile, prepare the gravy and vegetables.

7 Skim excess fat from the juices in the roasting tin, then add the stock. Bring to the boil. Mash the butter with the flour to make a beurre manié. Add this in small pieces to the hot juices, whisking to thicken. Check the seasoning.

8 Put the asparagus in another roasting tin, drizzle with olive oil and season with salt and pepper, then roast for 5–7 minutes. Pop the potatoes into the oven to reheat for about 8 minutes. Cook the carrots, turnips and peas, separately, in boiling salted water until just tender; drain, then toss with the parsley butter.

9 To serve, spoon the mixed vegetables into the centre of the warm plates and arrange the asparagus to the side. Slice the beef and fold over to give height, then place on the vegetables. Stand the potatoes alongside. Pour over the gravy and finish with a good spoonful of radish relish.

West Coast scallops (recipe on page 195)

198 CLASSIC SUMMER PUDDING
WITH MIXED SCOTTISH RED BERRIES
A VANILLA AND GLENTURRET ICE CREAM
AND A SHORTBREAD BISCUIT

SERVES 4

SUMMER PUDDING

1kg mixed red berries in equal quantities
(strawberries, raspberries,
blackcurrants, redcurrants)

250g caster sugar or more to taste

1 ½ gelatine leaves, soaked in cold water for
at least 10 minutes

8 slices of white bread, crusts removed

SHORTBREAD

185g unsalted butter

90g caster sugar

235g plain flour

30g cornflour

good pinch of salt

1 tsp good quality vanilla essence

VANILLA AND GLENTURRET ICE CREAM

750ml double cream

450ml milk

2 vanilla pods, split lengthways

350g caster sugar

15 egg yolks

Glenturret whisky

TO SERVE

red berry coulis

redcurrants

icing sugar (optional)

1 First make the pudding. Put the berries in a thick-based pot, with the strawberries sprinkled with the sugar at the bottom. Very slowly warm through. When still undercooked, remove from the heat.

2 Gently squeeze dry the gelatine leaves, then add them to the warm berries and stir until completely melted. Taste the mixture: if it seems a bit tart, stir in extra caster sugar as required.

3 To mould the puddings you need four metal rings that are 4–6cm diameter and 3–4cm high. Set them on a tray lined with cling film.

4 Cut a disc from each of four of the bread slices to fit the rings. Dip the bread in the berry juices, then press into the bottom of the rings. Spoon in the berries, using a slotted spoon. Cut discs from the remaining bread to fit the top of the rings. Dip these in the rest of the berry juices, then press into place. Cover the puddings and chill in the fridge to set.

5 Preheat the oven to 160°C/gas 3.

6 To make the shortbread, beat the butter and sugar in a bowl until light in colour. Add the remaining ingredients and mix until it binds together. Put in the fridge to cool for 4–5 minutes. Then roll out until about 5mm thick and cut into circles. Place on a non-stick baking tray. Mark with a fork or leave plain. Bake for 5–8 minutes. Cool on a wire rack.

7 For the ice cream, mix the cream and milk in a large pan. Scrape the vanilla seeds from the pods into the pan, then add the pods too and bring slowly to the boil. In a bowl, whisk the sugar with the egg yolks until pale and thick. Pour a little of the hot cream on to the eggs, then pour back into the pan. Cook, whisking constantly, until the custard thickens and will coat the back of a spoon. Pass the custard through a sieve and leave to cool.

8 Churn the cold custard in an ice cream machine. When it starts to freeze add Glenturret to taste (a bloody good pour). When ready, transfer the ice cream to a freezerproof container and put into the freezer.

9 To serve, place a pudding (still in its metal ring) off-centre on each plate (ideally use square plates). Place the shortbread to the side. Lift the ring off the pudding. Pour a little coulis over the top of the pudding and garnish with a few redcurrants. Place the ice cream on top of the shortbread. Finish by sprinkling a little icing sugar over the pudding, if wanted.

Scotland may not be the first place people think of as a fruit-growing region, but wild berries abound, not only in temperate Tayside and Fife, but also in the harsher climes of Grampian and the Highlands, Arran and Ayrshire. The country's long summer days ensure these wild foods have plenty of time to ripen, and intensify their flavour. Too much heat, and they would simply shrivel.

200

FILLET OF PERTHSHIRE LAMB
SEARED KIDNEY AND BALSAMIC ONIONS
ROCKET AND BROAD BEANS
WITH ARRAN MUSTARD DRESSING

SERVES 4
4 fillets of lamb
4 lamb kidneys, cut in half and veins
 and skin removed
olive oil
salt and pepper

BALSAMIC ONIONS
6 red onions, sliced
20ml olive oil
about 200ml balsamic vinegar

ARRAN MUSTARD DRESSING
100ml lamb stock
1–2 tsp coarse grain Arran mustard
 (or other good quality wholegrain
 mustard)

BROAD BEAN AND ROCKET SALAD
2 handfuls of baby broad beans
2 handfuls of rocket

1 Preheat the oven to 230°C/gas 8.

2 First prepare the balsamic onions. Sweat the onions in the olive oil, then pour over enough vinegar just to cover the onions. Slowly cook until the vinegar is almost completely reduced. Season before serving.

3 Meanwhile, sear the lamb fillets and kidneys in a little hot oil in a frying pan for 1–2 minutes on each side. Place in the oven and cook for 2 minutes. Remove and leave to rest before slicing.

4 While the lamb is cooking, make the Arran mustard dressing and salad. Reduce the lamb stock by half, then stir in the mustard. Reduce a little more. Meanwhile, blanch the broad beans in boiling salted water for 2 minutes. Drain and refresh, then pop the beans from their skins. Toss the beans with the rocket and a drizzle of the mustard dressing.

5 To serve, slice each lamb fillet at a 45° angle into three pieces. Spoon the balsamic onions on to each warm plate, arrange the pieces of lamb fillet on the onions and top with the kidneys. Add the broad bean and rocket salad and pour the mustard dressing over or around.

202

SEARED HERRING IN OATMEAL
WITH CELERIAC RÉMOULADE, GARDEN CRESS
AND CHAMPAGNE CHIVE BUTTER SAUCE

SERVES 4

4 plump fillets of herring
100g oatmeal to coat
butter
handful of garden cress lightly dressed
    with a tarragon vinaigrette
salt and pepper

CELERIAC RÉMOULADE

½ head of celeriac
2 heaped tbsp coarse grain Arran mustard
2–3 tbsp mayonnaise to bind

CHAMPAGNE AND CHIVE BUTTER SAUCE

1 large shallot, finely chopped
1 tsp butter
150ml Champagne
1 good tbsp Champagne vinegar
1 tbsp double cream
200g cold unsalted butter, diced
1 tbsp finely chopped chives

1 First make the celeriac rémoulade. Peel and shred the celeriac, then mix with the mustard, salt and pepper and enough mayonnaise to bind. Leave overnight.

2 For the Champagne and chive butter sauce, sweat the shallot in 1 tsp butter, then pour in the Champagne and vinegar. Reduce until almost all the liquid has evaporated. Add the cream and bring back to the boil, then whisk in the diced cold butter, a few pieces at a time. Keep the sauce warm but do not boil. Just before serving add the chives.

3 Fold each herring fillet in half, skin side in, and coat with oatmeal. Pan fry gently in a little bit of butter for 2–3 minutes on each side.

4 To serve, spoon the celeriac rémoulade on the warm plates and top with the cress. Place the fish on this and pour over the butter sauce.

For centuries, oatmeal and herring – the silver darlings – have been staples of the Scottish diet. Together, rich in fibre and Omega-3 oils, they make a delicious dish that's good for heart and brain.

ROASTED BREAST OF GROUSE

BALQUHIDDER CHANTERELLES AND SEASONAL VEGETABLES WITH SAGE AND ONION JUS

SERVES 4

8 breasts of grouse or 4 whole young grouse
olive oil
salt and pepper

SAGE AND ONION JUS

2 shallots, chopped
1–2 garlic cloves, chopped
butter
200ml game stock
4–6 sage leaves
1 tbsp white truffle oil (optional)

SEASONAL VEGETABLES

the best vegetables you can source to complement the greatest of all game birds, according to the season, for example baby carrots, fine green beans, runner beans and new potatoes

SAUTÉED CHANTERELLES

200g fresh chanterelles
good knob of butter
1 garlic clove, sliced

1 Preheat the oven to 230°C/gas 8.

2 Whether using just the breasts of older grouse or whole young birds, sear them on both sides, or all over, in a little hot olive oil in a roasting tin. Then place in the oven. Roast breasts for 2–4 minutes and whole birds for 12–16 minutes. Remove from the oven and leave to rest for 10 minutes before serving.

3 While the grouse are cooking, make the jus. Sweat the shallots and garlic in a little butter, then add the stock and reduce by half. Just before serving, season and add the sage. For a bit of decadence, finish with truffle oil.

4 Cook the seasonal vegetables in boiling salted water.

5 At the last minute, sauté the chanterelles in the butter with the sliced garlic and a touch of salt and pepper.

6 To serve, slice each breast at a 45° angle into three pieces, or carve the breasts and legs from the whole grouse. Arrange the grouse neatly on warm plates with the seasonal vegetables and chanterelles and drizzle over the jus.

204

BLACK DAN'S
HONEY AND TOASTED OATMEAL CRANACHAN
WITH COMRIE STRAWBERRIES POACHED IN PERNOD AND CINNAMON

SERVES 4
3 tbsp oatmeal
150ml milk
3–4 tbsp Black Dan's honey or other
　best quality runny honey
1 small vanilla pod, split lengthways
2 gelatine leaves, soaked in cold water
　for 10 minutes
450ml double cream

POACHED STRAWBERRIES
500g strawberries
1 cinnamon stick
2 ½ tbsp caster sugar
3–4 thumb pours of Pernod

1 Toast the oatmeal in a dry pan for 2–3 minutes, stirring. Set aside.
2 Place the milk and honey in a saucepan and scrape in the seeds from the vanilla pod. Add the pod too, then heat until bubbles start appearing around the edge. Do not boil. Remove from the heat. Gently squeeze dry the gelatine, add to the hot milk and stir until completely melted. Stir in the cream. Pass through a sieve into a jug.
3 Divide the toasted oatmeal among four dariole moulds. Slowly pour in the honey cream mixture. Leave to set in the fridge for 4–5 hours.
4 To prepare the strawberries, combine all the ingredients in a heatproof bowl and cover with cling film. Set over a pan of boiling water and cook for 8–10 minutes. Every now and again, carefully tilt the bowl to swirl the juice over the strawberries. Remove from the hot water and leave to cool.
5 To serve, dip each mould into warm (not hot) water and count to five, then turn out on to a plate. Spoon the poached strawberries around the cranachan.

Cranachan is also known as 'cream crowdie' in Scotland, after the soft local cheese – crowdie – which was used instead of cream. This version is named in honour of Tom Lewis's gardener, Black Dan Campbell.

ROAST LANGOUSTINE
WITH SPICED AVOCADO

SERVES 4

12 live medium-sized langoustines

4 tbsp olive oil

salad leaves dressed with olive oil and
    lemon juice, to serve

salt and pepper

LANGOUSTINE OIL (OPTIONAL)

350g langoustine shells (heads and claws)

2 tbsp olive oil

1 celery stick, roughly chopped

40g bulb fennel, cut into small sections

50g carrots, cut into chunks

30g leek, cut into chunks

1 tsp tomato purée

80ml fish stock

250g tomatoes, roughly chopped

1/4 tsp coriander seeds

1/2 tsp fennel seeds

1/4 tsp cumin seeds

2 sprigs of thyme

2 large sprigs of basil

peeled zest of 1/2 lemon

about 500ml light fruity olive oil

SPICED AVOCADO

1 large, ripe Hass avocado, peeled,
    stoned and chopped

1 red lombok chilli, very finely chopped

2 tsp Thai fish sauce

grated zest and juice of 1/2 lime

3 tbsp chopped coriander

1 tbsp sunflower oil

1 Preheat the oven to 220°C/gas 7.

2 First make the langoustine oil. Roughly chop the langoustine shells. Place in
a roasting tray along with the langoustine heads and toss with 1 tbsp of the olive
oil. Roast for 12–15 minutes.

3 Meanwhile, put the vegetables in a saucepan with 1 tbsp olive oil and lightly brown
over a moderate heat for 4–5 minutes, adding the tomato purée towards the end of
cooking. Remove from the heat.

4 Add the shells to the vegetables. Set the roasting tray over a moderate heat.
When hot, add the fish stock and stir to deglaze. Pour this liquid over the shells
in the saucepan. Add the tomatoes, spices, herbs and lemon zest with enough
fruity oil to almost cover the shells. Bring to a gentle simmer and cook for about
20 minutes. Allow to cool, then leave in the fridge overnight.

5 The following day, bring the oil to a simmer again over a moderate heat and
cook for 15 minutes. Allow to cool slightly, then pass through a fine sieve or muslin.
The oil can be kept in the fridge for 2–3 days or frozen for longer storage.

6 Combine the ingredients for the spiced avocado in a bowl. Cover and leave at
room temperature for 1 hour to allow the flavours to merge and mingle.

7 Preheat the oven to 220°C/gas 7.

8 Rub the langoustines with some olive oil and place them in a roasting tin.
Roast for 7–8 minutes. Allow to cool.

9 Carefully remove the tails and shell, then cut the langoustines in half lengthways. Scoop out all the soft brown meat from the heads (this is similar to the brown meat on a lobster). To do this, turn the heads upside down and lift off the pelvis and legs to leave a soft cup full of brown goo, which you can scrape out. Be careful not to scrape so hard that you remove the hard stomach as well. Add this brown meat to the spiced avocado and combine well.

10 To assemble, set a metal ring in the centre of each plate. Place two langoustine halves, flat-side down, at the bottom of each ring, then cover with a spoonful of spiced avocado. Add another two langoustine halves, more avocado and a final pair of langoustine halves. Press down gently so that it all merges together; the avocado acts like a cement to hold the langoustine together in a tower. Carefully remove the rings and top each tower with a small ball of salad. Finish with a drizzle of langoustine oil, if using.

Illustrated left

SEARED HOME SMOKED SALMON
WITH AN APPLE AND WATERCRESS SALAD
AND HORSERADISH CREAM

SERVES 4

4 thick pieces of best quality smoked organic salmon, each 85–90g (look for a darker smoke and fish that has not been brined)

sunflower oil

salt

NICK NAIRN COOK SCHOOL OATMEAL BREAD (OPTIONAL)

21g milk powder

610ml lukewarm water

40g fresh yeast

21g caster sugar

500g strong white flour

500g brown flour

100g pinhead oatmeal

18g salt

50ml virgin olive oil

APPLE AND WATERCRESS SALAD

125g white cabbage, very finely shredded

2 tbsp rice wine vinegar

1 tsp caster sugar

½ red chilli, finely sliced

2 spring onions, finely sliced at an angle

½ apple (we use James Grieve), skin on, grated

lime juice to taste

80g watercress, thick stalks removed, or organic mustard greens

HORSERADISH CREAM

3 tbsp mayonnaise (shop bought is fine)

3 tbsp freshly grated horseradish

2 tbsp crème fraîche

1 tsp freshly squeezed lemon juice

1 If making the oatmeal bread, whisk the milk powder into the warm water, then add the yeast and sugar and stir gently. Leave to stand for 10 minutes to give the yeast time to activate.

2 Sift the flours, oatmeal and salt into a large bowl and mix lightly. Add the yeast mixture, stirring all the time. Add the oil, again stirring constantly, and mix into a dough. Knead for 10 minutes (6–8 minutes in a mixer).

3 Lightly oil a big bowl. Place the dough in the bowl, cover with cling film or a damp cloth and leave to prove at room temperature until doubled in size.

4 Remove from the bowl and re-mix, knocking the air out. Form into individual loaves. You should get about four. Place these loaves on a baking sheet lined with baking parchment. Place the baking sheet in a bin bag and blow air into it. Scrunch up the end, catching the air inside, to make a sort of tent for your loaves to sit in. Allow them to double in size once more.

5 Preheat the oven to 200°C/gas 6.

6 Remove the bin bag. Lightly score the tops of the loaves and dust with flour. Bake for 40–50 minutes or until the bread sounds hollow when tapped on the base. Cool.

7 For the salad, mix the shredded cabbage with the rice wine vinegar, sugar and a pinch of salt. Leave to marinate for 40 minutes at room temperature.

8 Then add the chilli, spring onions, apple, lime juice and salt to taste, and stir in well. Using a fork will help to mix all the components evenly together. Divide the salad into four portions and arrange on the left side of each of four plates.

9 Prepare the horseradish cream by combining all the ingredients in a bowl and mixing well.

10 At the last minute, flash fry the smoked salmon in a little hot sunflower oil for about 30 seconds on each side. Place the watercress on the cabbage salad and top with the smoked salmon. Place a blob of horseradish cream to the side. Serve immediately, with the oatmeal bread.

LOIN OF ROE VENISON
WITH POTATO CAKE, ROAST ROOTS
CREAMED CABBAGE AND GAME GRAVY

SERVES 4

4 tbsp goose fat

100g carrot, cut into 1cm dice

100g parsnip, cut into 1cm dice

100g celeriac, cut into 1cm dice

100g beetroot, cut into 1cm dice

sprig of thyme

1 garlic clove, lightly crushed

20g butter

4 pieces of roe deer saddle with rib bone
   still attached, each 120g

60ml red wine

30ml red wine vinegar

40ml fruit vinegar

200ml light brown chicken stock

250g Savoy cabbage, finely shredded,
   blanched for 2 minutes, refreshed and drained

4 tbsp double cream

salt and pepper

GAME GRAVY

600g venison rib bones

25g unsalted butter

200g venison trimmings, chopped

4 shallots, finely sliced

8 button mushrooms, sliced

1 garlic clove, crushed

1 bay leaf

sprig of thyme

6 white peppercorns, crushed

30ml red wine vinegar

120ml Port

120ml red wine

700ml brown chicken or game stock

1 tsp redcurrant jelly

1 tsp arrowroot

POTATO CAKES

400g peeled Golden Wonder potatoes

10 tbsp goose fat

1 Preheat the oven to 180°C/gas 4.

2 First make the game gravy. Roast the venison bones for 45 minutes. Meanwhile, heat a medium-sized saucepan, add the butter and venison trimmings and caramelise for 20 minutes. Add the shallots, mushrooms, garlic, bay leaf, thyme, and crushed peppercorns. Gently fry for 5–10 minutes or until golden brown.

3 Pour in the red wine vinegar, followed by the Port and red wine. Boil until a thick, syrupy glaze is achieved. Add the stock, redcurrant jelly and roasted bones and simmer for 45 minutes.

4 Pass through a fine sieve into a small, clean pan and boil again to reduce by half. Thicken with arrowroot, then check the seasoning and set aside. Reheat for serving. (This makes more gravy than you need for this dish; keep the rest in the refrigerator or freeze it.)

5 Next make the potato cakes. Grate the potatoes on the coarse side of a box grater, then place them in a clean tea towel and squeeze out the liquid. Put the potatoes in a bowl, add 2 tbsp of the goose fat and season with salt and pepper. Mix well.

6 Heat four 10cm blini pans. Add 2 tbsp goose fat to each, then divide the potato mix among them, pressing down gently. Cook until crisp and golden on the base, then carefully turn over and continue cooking until the other side is golden and the

potatoes are tender. (Alternatively you can make one big cake in a 25cm non-stick frying pan and cut into quarters for serving.) Place in a low oven to keep warm.

7 Heat 2 tbsp goose fat in a heavy-bottomed frying pan and pan-roast the diced vegetables with the thyme and garlic for 15–20 minutes or until coloured and cooked through. Transfer to an ovenproof dish and place in the oven to keep warm.

8 Heat the remaining 2 tbsp goose fat with the butter in the frying pan, then sear the venison until it is well coloured and cooked medium rare. Remove the venison from the pan and place it somewhere warm to relax. This will allow the juices that have been drawn out of the centre to return.

9 Pour out the fat from the pan, return it to a high heat and deglaze with the wine and vinegars. Boil fast to reduce, then add the stock and reduce again by one-quarter to really intensify the flavours. Strain this jus and keep warm.

10 Reheat the cabbage, adding the cream, and season with salt and pepper.

11 To serve, place a pile of cabbage in the centre of each warm plate. Add the potato cakes on top and place the roasted vegetables around the outside. Position the venison on the potato cakes, and pour over the reduced jus. Drizzle the game gravy around the outside of the plates.

HOT BLAIRGOWRIE
RASPBERRY SOUFFLÉ
WITH MALT WHISKY, HONEY AND OATMEAL ICE CREAM

SERVES 4
400g raspberries
1 tbsp lemon juice
100g caster sugar
2 tsp crème de framboise
7g cornflour (about 1 tsp)
icing sugar
170g egg whites (about 6)
pinch of cream of tartar

ICE CREAM
500ml double cream
½ vanilla pod
2 ½ tbsp clear honey
1 tbsp glucose
4 egg yolks
30g oatmeal
10g icing sugar, sifted
1 ½ tbsp Glengoyne malt whisky

1 First, prepare the custard for the ice cream. Pour the cream into a thick-based pan and place over a moderate heat. Split the vanilla pod lengthways and lightly scrape out the seeds into the cream. Add the vanilla pod too, and the honey and glucose. Bring the cream to a calm simmer, then remove from the heat and let stand for at least 10 minutes, to infuse.

2 Lightly whisk the egg yolks in a bowl. Pour some of the warm cream over the yolks and mix well, then return this mixture to the remaining cream and combine. Set the pan over a moderate heat and cook, stirring constantly (from side to side to ensure that the mixture in the centre of the pan is being moved as well as the edges) until the mixture starts to thicken and will coat the back of the spoon. Take care not to allow it to become too hot or the egg will curdle and the custard will become lumpy (if this happens, press through a fine mesh sieve to remove lumps). Immediately pass through a coarse sieve into a clean cold bowl. Cover the surface of the custard with cling film to prevent a skin from forming and leave to cool.

3 Press the raspberries through a fine sieve to produce 180g of purée. Put this into a thick-bottomed pan, add the lemon juice and reduce down to a thick jam, stirring from time to time and being careful not let it catch and burn.

4 Put 45g of the sugar in a separate pan. Melt it, then boil until it becomes a thick syrup (121°C on a sugar thermometer). To test without a thermometer, dip a teaspoon into the syrup and then quickly into cold water. You should be able to roll the cooling syrup into a ball between your fingers. Be careful as the syrup is hot! When it has reached the right point, stir the hot syrup into the raspberry jam.

5 Mix the framboise and cornflour together and stir into the jam over the heat. This will help the jam to thicken. Turn the jam into a small bowl, sprinkle the surface with icing sugar and cover closely with cling film. This can all be done the day before and kept in the fridge. Return the jam to room temperature before using.

6 Preheat the grill to moderate.

7 To finish the ice cream, spread the oatmeal on a baking tray, lightly dust with about one-third of the icing sugar and place under the grill. Cook for a couple of minutes, then turn the oatmeal and sprinkle with more icing sugar. Place back under the grill for another 2 minutes, then repeat the process. Alternatively, cook the oatmeal and sugar in a dry frying pan, stirring constantly. In the end, the oatmeal should be light, golden brown with a crisp, sugary crust. Allow to cool completely.

8 Churn the custard in an ice cream machine, stirring in the cool, caramelised oatmeal and whisky once the ice cream has thickened. Remove the ice cream to a clean container and place in the freezer. If making ahead of time (the ice cream can be kept in the freezer for 3 weeks), scoop four balls of ice cream and freeze them on a tray. Allow to soften in the fridge for 30 minutes before serving.

9 When ready to serve, preheat the oven to 180°C/gas 4. Whisk the egg whites with the cream of tartar until you can form soft peaks, then fold in the remaining caster sugar, taking care not to overmix. Lightly fold the whites into the jam, leaving thin traces of white visible in the mixture. Spoon into four buttered and sugared large ramekins, place these on a baking tray and bake for 10 minutes.

10 Transfer the ramekins to plates. Dust the hot soufflés with icing sugar, make a small hole in the top and place a ball of ice cream inside. Serve immediately.

HOME SMOKED SALMON
WITH OATMEAL PANCAKES, HORSERADISH AND CHIVE CRÈME FRAÎCHE

SERVES 4

350g best quality smoked organic salmon,
  cut into 16 thin slices
salad leaves dressed with olive oil and
  lemon juice
4 tsp Avruga caviar
sprigs of chervil or dill
salt and pepper

OATMEAL PANCAKES

70g pinhead oatmeal
85g plain flour
10g caster sugar
170ml tepid milk
10g fresh yeast
2 egg whites
chopped soft herbs such as dill or chervil
olive oil

CHIVE CRÈME FRAÎCHE

60g good quality crème fraîche
2 tbsp creamed horseradish
chopped chives
lemon juice

1 To make the pancake batter, mix together the oatmeal, flour and a pinch of salt in a stainless steel bowl. Add the sugar to the warm milk and crumble in the yeast, mixing thoroughly, then pour the milk mixture into the flour mixture and gently stir together. When well mixed, cover with cling film and keep in a warm place until the batter has doubled in size.

2 Meanwhile, put the crème fraîche in a bowl and mix in the creamed horseradish. Add the chives and lemon juice and season to taste.

3 Whisk the egg whites to a soft peak, then fold a small amount into the batter to loosen it. Fold in the rest of the egg whites together with the herbs.

4 Heat an 8–10cm blini pan and add a little olive oil. Add a 50ml ladle of batter and cook for 3–4 minutes or until the thick pancake is golden on the base. Flip over, then cook until golden on the other side. Remove and keep warm in a low oven while you cooked the remaining pancakes (you will make five, so will have one extra to enjoy).

5 To serve, place a warm pancake on each plate. Top each pancake with a spoonful of chive crème fraîche and then with salad leaves. Carefully arrange four thin slices of smoked salmon on the leaves, then add a twist of black pepper and 1 tsp of Avruga caviar. Garnish with chervil or dill.

LOBSTER MACARONI
WITH ROCKET AND PARMESAN

SERVES 4
2 large cooked lobsters, each about 400g
200g macaroni or similar pasta shape
250g rocket leaves
50g Parmesan, freshly grated
Maldon sea salt and pepper
extra freshly grated Parmesan or
    Parmesan shavings, to serve

LOBSTER SAUCE
olive oil
1 tbsp tomato purée
2 tbsp brandy
600ml lobster or langoustine stock
200ml double cream

1 To prepare the lobsters, pull off the large claws and set aside. Place the lobster on a chopping board and uncurl the tail so that the lobster is straight. Using a large sharp knife split the lobster in half, cutting through the head towards the tail. Open out and remove the little 'plastic' stomach sac in the head; discard. Carefully remove the tail meat and dice it. Crack the claws, fish out the meat and pull out the cartilage. Dice the meat and add to the tail meat. (You can add any coral or roe you find and the brownish head meat to the sauce.)

2 Preheat the oven to 220°C/gas 7.

3 To make the lobster sauce, chop the lobster legs into two or three sections and place them in a roasting tray with all of the shells. Toss the legs and shells in a little olive oil, then roast in the oven for 10 minutes.

4 Remove the tray from the oven and set over a moderate heat. Add the tomato purée to the shells and stir well, then brown for a minute or so. Add the brandy and flame it to toast the shells a little more. Pour the lobster stock over the shells, stirring and scraping with a wooden spoon to lift any sediment. Simmer for 10 minutes.

5 Strain the stock through a fine sieve into a saucepan. Bring to a simmer and allow the stock to reduce by four-fifths. Stir in the cream and return to a simmer, then let the sauce reduce by half. It will be really thick and intense at this stage. Keep warm or reduce a bit more if you think it needs it.

6 Cook the pasta in plenty of boiling salted water for 8–12 minutes or until al dente, depending on the pasta size.

7 Meanwhile, roughly chop half the rocket and stir into the sauce together with the Parmesan. Taste and season with salt and pepper, then fold in the diced lobster.

8 Drain the pasta really well, return to the hot pan and mix with the lobster sauce.

9 To serve, spoon the lobster macaroni into warm soup plates and top each serving with a handful of the remaining rocket leaves and a sprinkling of Parmesan.

PEPPERED FILLET OF BEEF
WITH WHISKY AND MUSHROOM SAUCE

SERVES 4

3 tbsp black peppercorns
4 fillet steaks, each about 175g
4 tsp Dijon mustard
2 tbsp sunflower oil
50g butter

200g fresh ceps, sliced into chunks
50ml blended whisky
8 tbsp beef stock
4 tbsp double cream
Maldon sea salt and pepper

1 Crush the peppercorns coarsely in a mortar and pestle or grind using a pepper grinder on a coarse setting. Alternatively, you can grind the pepper in a spice mill, but you must then tip the pepper into a fine sieve and shake out all the powder. This is very important because the powder will make the steaks far too spicy.

2 Spread the peppercorns over a small plate. Smear both sides of the steaks with the Dijon mustard, then coat them in the crushed peppercorns. Season the steaks with salt. If you add the salt before this stage it draws out the moisture, preventing the pepper from sticking to the meat.

3 Heat a large, heavy-bottomed frying pan until nice and hot. Add the sunflower oil and then the steaks, and brown both sides, turning once only. Don't fiddle with the steaks once they are in the pan or the peppercorn crust will fall off – the aim is to produce a good crusty coating on each surface.

4 Now add the butter and allow it to colour a nut brown, but don't let it burn. Add the ceps and work around in the butter. As the mushrooms start to absorb the juices, turn the steaks again and allow them to cook for 3–4 more minutes on each side, turning once or twice and moving them around the pan to make sure the whole surface has plenty of colour and the edges of the meat are well seared. Transfer the steaks to a baking tray and set aside in a warm place.

5 Add the whisky to the pan and cook over a very high heat for 1 minute to boil off the alcohol. A word of warning – the whisky is likely to burst into flames. If this worries you, have a large lid handy to whack on the pan. Add the stock and reduce until really thick, then pour in the cream. Reduce again, scraping and stirring together any gooey bits from the bottom of the pan. When it boils fiercely, it's ready.

6 To serve, pour any juices from the resting meat back into the sauce and place a steak on each warm plate. Spoon the sauce with the mushrooms over the steak.

RHUBARB AND GINGER MOUSSE
WITH RHUBARB SAUCE

SERVES 8

900g fresh pink rhubarb, trimmed and cut into chunks
4 'balls' stem ginger in syrup, drained (keep the syrup)
200g + 3 tbsp sugar
4 egg whites
4 gelatine leaves, soaked in cold water for at least 10 minutes
300ml double cream

1 Put the rhubarb into a pan with 2–3 tbsp of water and simmer for 10–15 minutes or until soft and pulpy. Blitz with half the stem ginger in a blender until you have a nice, smooth purée (this is best done in two batches). Pass through a sieve. Measure out 600ml of purée and put it to one side. The remaining purée will be used to make a rhubarb and ginger sauce.

2 Dissolve the 200g sugar in a little water over a high heat and boil the resulting syrup down to the soft ball stage (115°C on a sugar thermometer). Remove from the heat. Whisk the egg whites in a bowl and, when they start to thicken up, slowly pour on the hot sugar syrup. Continue to whisk for 3 minutes or until doubled in bulk and a firm meringue is formed.

3 In a medium-sized saucepan, warm through the 600ml rhubarb purée (do not let it boil). Gently squeeze dry the gelatine leaves, then add to the purée and stir until completely melted. Pour the purée onto the meringue and fold in until fully incorporated and there are no streaks of white.

4 Whip the cream into a soft peak and fold it into the meringue mix. This is your mousse. Pour it into a large jug – this makes it easier to fill the moulds. Pour the mousse into eight dariole moulds that are 6cm deep and 6cm wide. Leave to set overnight in the fridge.

5 Take 8 tbsp of the remaining rhubarb and ginger purée and combine it in a pan with the remaining 3 tbsp sugar and 4 tbsp ginger syrup. Bring to the boil and boil for 1 minute, then remove from the heat. When cool, cover and chill. Cut the remaining ginger into fine shreds, cover and set aside.

6 To serve, dip the dariole moulds in hot water for 15–20 seconds, then turn out the mousses on to chilled plates. Spoon the rhubarb and ginger sauce around them and top with some shredded ginger.

The recent revolution that has taken place in British and Irish food production has received an enormous boost from the growth of the internet. In a perfect marriage of tradition and technology, many of the finest foods in Britain, once local preserves, are available nationwide, often with next day delivery, at the push of a key. The following directory lists the cream of producers who, unless stated, deliver mail order.

MEAT, POULTRY AND GAME

Alternative Meats Ltd
Hough Farm, Weston-under-Redcastle
Shropshire SY4 5LR
Tel: 01948 840130 Fax: 01948 840003
www.alternativemeats.co.uk
ostrich, venison, wild boar, rose veal,
British game and poultry

Aran Lamb
Cwmonnen Farm, Llanuchllyn
Bala, Gwynedd LL23 7UG
Tel: 01678 540603 Fax: 01678 540603
www.aran-lamb.co.uk
certified organic Welsh mountain lamb

The Ark Chicken Company
Babylon Lane, Silverton, Exeter
Devon EX5 4DT Tel/Fax: 01392 860430
traditional free-range poultry from slow growing breeds, including chicken, geese, turkey, quail and corn-fed guinea fowl; the birds are housed in moveable arks (also available for sale), which means they can be regularly moved on to fresh pasture. Overnight delivery. Suppliers to Antony Worrall Thompson and Michael Caines. Regulars at farmers' markets in Dorset, Somerset and Devon

Billfields Food Company Ltd
Unit 2 and 3, 57 Sandgate Street
London SE15 1LE
Tel: 0870 770 6920 Fax: 020 7358 9292
www.billfields.co.uk
speciality beef from Glen Fyne on the
west coast of Scotland

Border County Foods
The Old Vicarage, Crosby-on-Eden
Cumbria CA6 4QZ
Tel: 01228 573500 Fax: 01228 573501
www.cumberland-sausage.net
creators of wonderful Cumberland sausage,
the Old County Original

Brown Cow Organics
Perridge Farm, Pilton
Shepton Mallet, Somerset BA4 4EW
Tel: 01749 890298 Fax: 01749 890298
www.browncoworganics.co.uk
award-winning organic beef, pork, poultry, dairy, vegetables and fruit, produced either on or within close proximity of the farm

Bury Black Pudding Company
PO Box 300, Bury, Lancashire BL9 0YK
Tel: 01617 970689
www.buryblackpuddings.co.uk
superb traditional Lancashire black puddings

Cranborne Farms Traditional Meats
Dorset BH21 5PS
Tel: 01725 517168 Fax: 01725 517787
www.cranborne.co.uk
rare breed pork, beef and lamb from the
Marquess of Salisbury's estate

David Lishman, Lishmans of Ilkley
23-27 Leeds Road, Ilkley
West Yorkshire LS29 8DP
Tel: 01943 609436 Fax: 01943 603809
david@lishmans.fsbusiness.co.uk
breeds Saddleback and British Lop pigs, and has twice won the National Champion of Champions award for sausages; also sells Belted Galloway beef

Daylesford Organic Farmshop
Daylesford, near Kingham
Gloucestershire GL56 0YG
Tel: 01608 731700 Fax: 01608 731701
www.daylesfordorganic.com
handmade cheeses, breads, cakes and biscuits; fresh organic meat from an estate in Staffordshire

Denhay Farms Ltd
Broadoak, Bridport, Dorset DT6 5NP
Tel: 01308 458963 Fax: 01308 424846
www.denhay.co.uk
dry-cured bacon, air-dried ham and cured meat sausages as well as West Country farmhouse cheddar

Donald Russell Direct
Harlaw Industrial Estate, Inverurie
Aberdeenshire AB51 4FR
Tel: 01467 629666 Fax: 01467 629432
www.donaldrusselldirect.com
Royal Warrant butcher

Eastbrook Farms Organic Meat
The Calf House, Cues Lane, Bishopstone
Swindon, Wiltshire SN6 8PL
Tel: 01793 790340 Fax: 01793 791239
www.helenbrowningorganics.co.uk
established in 1989, the Helen Browning's brand is also available in selected supermarkets

Edwards of Conwy
18 High Street, Conwy
North Wales LL32 8DE
Tel: 01492 592443 Fax: 01492 592220
www.edwardsofconwy.co.uk
Ieuan Edwards' highest quality Welsh meat

The Ellel Free Range Poultry Company
The Stables, Ellel Grange, Galgate
Nr Lancaster, Lancashire LA2 0HN
Tel: 01524 751200 Fax: 01524 752648
www.ellelfreerangepoultry.co.uk

excellent poultry producer supplying the public and some of the finest restaurants and hotels in London and the UK

Everleigh Pheasantry and Wiltshire Partridges
Old Rectory Farm, Everleigh, Marlborough
Wiltshire SN8 3EY
Tel: 01264 850344 Fax: 01264 850834
www.pheasants.co.uk
one of the largest game farms in the UK, which also produces fresh Wiltshire meat, cut as required, bacon, hams, salami, dairy products from Wiltshire and Somerset; fresh fish is for sale on Thursdays, Fridays and Saturdays

Farmer Sharp
Diamond Buildings, Pennington Lane
Lindal in Furness, Cumbria LA12 0LA
Tel: 01229 588299 Fax: 01229 583496
www.farmersharp.co.uk
Andrew Sharp is the public face of 27 co-operating farmers in the Lake District who produce some of the finest quality cattle and sheep the area has to offer; from these Herdwick sheep and Galloway cattle, lamb, mutton and well-hung beef is produced. Has a stall in Borough Market

Fellbred Direct
Crooklands Road, Milnthorpe, Cumbria LA7 7LR
Tel: 01539 563232 Fax: 01539 563737
www.fellbred.co.uk
premium quality meats from the fells and dales of the Lake District; North West Producer of the year award winner 2002-2005

Finnebrogue Estate
Killyleagh Road, Downpatrick, Co Down BT30 9BL
Tel: 028 4461 7525 Fax: 028 4461 3185
www.finnebrogue.com
Denis Lynn's company is regarded by many top chefs as the producer of the best venison in the world

Fletchers
Reediehill Deer Farm
Auchtermuchty, Fife KY14 7HS
Tel: 01337 828369 Fax: 01337 827001
www.seriouslygoodvenison.co.uk
Dr John Fletcher is one of the country's foremost experts in deer management; quality of produce recognised by a Queen's Award for Export

The Ginger Pig
8-10 Moxon Street, Marylebone, London W1U 4EW
Tel: 020 7935 7788
Tim and Anne Wilson's shop with large range of gourmet sausages

Goodman's Geese
Walsgrove Farm, Great Witley
Worcestershire WR6 6JJ
Tel: 01299 896272 Fax: 01299 896907
www.goodmansgeese.co.uk
geese and bronze turkeys fed on all-natural foods with no additives or growth promoters

Graig Farm Organics
Dolau, Llandrindod Wells, Powys LD1 5TL
Tel: 01597 851655 Fax: 01597 851991
www.graigfarm.co.uk
huge range of organic produce including meat, local game and goat meat, as well as non-food items; all their meat and dairy products are produced in the UK – as locally to Graig Farm (in the Welsh Marches) as possible

Happy Meats Ltd
Bank House Farm, Stanford Bridge
Worcestershire WR6 6RU
Tel: 01886 812485
www.happymeats.co.uk
specialist producer of free range, rare breed meat; traditional old British and Irish breeds of pig, lamb and cattle are reared outside on chemical-free food

Hazel Brow Farm
Low Row, Richmond, North Yorkshire DL11 6NE
Tel: 01748 886224
www.hazelbrow.co.uk
lamb reared naturally on the herb-rich pastures and wild heather moors of the Pennine Dales Environmentally Sensitive Area

Heal Farm
Kings Nympton, Devon EX37 9TB
Tel: 01769 574341 Fax: 01769 572839
www.healfarm.co.uk
rare breed pigs and other meats and poultry

Higher Hacknell Farm
Burrington, Umberleigh, Devon EX37 9LX
Tel/Fax: 01769 560909
www.higherhacknell.co.uk
produce from mixed farm in North Devon with cattle, sheep and chickens

Hindon Organic Farm
Nr Minehead, Exmoor, Somerset TA24 8SH
Tel: 01643 705244
www.hindonfarm.co.uk
produce from organic hill farm in Exmoor

Holly Tree Farm
Chester Road, Over Tabley, Nr Knutsford
Cheshire WA16 0EU
Tel: 01565 651835
www.hollytreefarmshop.co.uk
meat with traceability, freshness and quality, guarantees on animal welfare and consumer safety, local produce

John Robinson Family Butcher
High Street, Stockbridge, Hampshire SO20 6HF
Tel: 01264 810609 Fax: 01264 810957
hang their own meat and butcher it, cure bacon, hand-make sausages with local ingredients, plus faggots, pies and ready meals; local deliveries

Langley Chase Organic Farm
Mrs Jane Kallaway, The Farm Office
Langley Chase Organic Farm
Kington Langley, Wiltshire SN15 5PW
Tel/Fax: 01249 750095
www.langleychase.co.uk
award-winning rare breed organic lamb

Lucies Farm Ltd
Whitecroft, Colletts Green
Worcestershire WR2 4RY Tel: 01905 830380
www.luciesfarm.co.uk
produce Scottish Kobe beef, a unique fusion of Japanese and Scottish traditions; their pedigree Highland cattle are fed a diet of beer (from the local St George's microbrewery) and grain, and are massaged regularly with sake

McCartney's Family Butchers
56–58 Main Street, Moira, Co Down BT67 0LQ
Tel: 02892 611422 Fax: 02892 613533
www.mccartneysofmoira.co.uk
most famous for award-winning sausages, family butchers who have been in business for over 100 years; sausages are hand-linked and made with natural skins

Musks Ltd
4 Goodwin Business Park
Newmarket, Suffolk CB8 7SQ
Tel: 01638 662626 Fax: 01638 662424
www.musks.com
producers of a Newmarket sausage, unchanged since the days of Queen Victoria; handmade with care in small batches, the sausages are free from colouring and additives

Northfield Farm
Whissendine Lane, Cold Overton
Oakham, Rutland LE15 7QF
Tel: 01664 474271 Fax: 01664 474669
www.northfieldfarm.com
premium quality beef, lamb and pork; licensed dealer in game, and also supply free-range geese and turkeys for Thanksgiving and Christmas. Large range of predominantly British cheeses. Have a stall in Borough Market

Northumbrian Quality Meats
Monkridge Hill Farm, West Woodburn
Hexham, Northumberland NE48 2TU
Tel: 01434 270184 Fax: 01434 270320
www.northumbrian-organic-meat.co.uk
finest quality organic meats

Orkney Organic Meat
New Holland Farm, Holm, Orkney KW17 2SA
Tel: 01856 781345 Fax: 01856 781750
www.orkneyorganicmeat.co.uk
organic Aberdeen Angus beef and Orkney organic lamb; also rare breed pigs

Pentre House
Leighton, Welshpool, Powys SY21 8HL
Tel: 01938 553430
www.pentrepigs.co.uk
traditional free range Berkshire, Tamworth and Kune Kune pigs; whole and half pigs available, plus the usual cuts, bacon, sausages and offal (including cheeks, heads and trotters)

Pheasant Hill Farm Shop
3 Bridge Street Link, Comber, Co Down BT23 5YH
Tel: 028 9187 8470
www.pheasantshill.co.uk
rare breed meats, organic meat and poultry; dry-cured bacon, ham, specialist sausages

Pipers Farm
Cullompton, Devon EX15 1SD
Tel: 01392 881380 Fax: 01392 881600
www.pipersfarm.com
native breeds, reared on grass or cereal, grown slowly and allowed to reach natural maturity; five National Awards for excellence

Providence Farm
Crosspark Cross, Holsworthy, Devon EX22 6JW
Tel/Fax: 01409 254421
www.providencefarm.co.uk
fine organic meats since 1989

The Real Meat Company
Warminster, Wiltshire BA12 0HR
Tel: 01985 840562 Fax: 01985 841005
www.realmeat.co.uk
meat, poultry, ham, bacon and eggs produced under the edict "Flavour Without Equal, Welfare Without Compromise"

Rhug Estate
Corwen, Denbighshire LL21 0EH
Tel: 01490 413000 Fax: 01490 413300
www.rhugorganic.com
family estate belonging to Lord Newborough; various organic meats and produce

Richard Woodall
Lane End, Waberthwaite (near Millom)
Cumbria LA19 5YJ
Tel: 01229 717237 or 717386
Fax: 01229 717007
www.richardwoodall.com
run by seventh and eighth generation family members, and renowned for its traditionally cured hams, bacon and sausages; Royal Warrant holder, they supply ham and bacon to the Queen on a weekly basis. First company in the UK to produce a Parma-style ham

RS Ireland
Pudsville II, Glentop Works, Stacksteads
Bacup, Lancashire OL13 0NH
Tel: 01706 872172 Fax: 01706 872101
www.rsireland.co.uk
fine black pudding

Seldom Seen Farm
Billesdon, Leicestershire LE7 9FA
Tel: 0116 259 6742 Fax: 0116 259 6626
www.seldomseenfarm.co.uk
geese hung for 10 days and on sale from November through to Christmas, all oven ready, complete with giblets and a chunk of goose butter-yellow fat; in November they also prepare the Three Bird Roast, a goose stuffed with a chicken, stuffed with a pheasant and the whole thing layered up with homemade pork and orange stuffing

Sheepdrove Organic Farm
Warren Farm, Lambourn, Berkshire RG17 7UU
Tel: 01488 71659 Fax: 01488 72677
www.sheepdrove.com
specialist in mail order organic meat, with a very extensive site including guides to various meats and cuts and recipes

Sillfield Farm
Endmoor, Kendal, Cumbria LA8 0HZ
Tel: 015395 67609 Fax: 015395 67483
www.sillfield.co.uk
Peter Gott keeps free range wild boar and
rare breed pigs; has just recently added
some Herdwick sheep and pedigree
poultry to his stock

Somerset Organics
Bittescombe Manor, Upton, Wiveliscombe
Taunton, Somerset TA4 2DA
Tel: 01398 371387 Fax: 01398 371413
www.somersetfarmdirect.co.uk
online farm shop

Swaddles Green Farm
Hare Lane, Buckland St Mary
Chard, Somerset TA20 3JR
Tel: 08454 561768 Fax: 01460 234591
www.swaddles.co.uk
award-winning green back bacon
and lamb joints

Tatton Park
Knutsford, Cheshire WA16 6NQ
Tel: 01625 534435
www.tattonpark.org.uk
venison from 1,000 acres of beautiful parkland
managed, maintained and financed by Cheshire
County Council on behalf of the National Trust

Traditional Devonshire Meats
Locks Park Farm, Hatherleigh, Okehampton
Devon EX20 3LZ Tel: 01837 810416
www.traditionaldevonmeats.co.uk
organic beef from Devon Red Rubies, and lamb
from Dartmoor Whiteface sheep

Weatherall Foods Ltd
Crochmore House, Irongray, Dumfries DG2 9SF
Tel: 01387 730326 Fax: 01387 730682
www.blackface.co.uk
lamb, haggis, pork, oven-ready grouse, partridge,
bronze turkeys and venison from the heather hills
of Scotland

Well Hung Meat
Tordean Farm, Dean Prior, Buckfastleigh
Devon TQ11 0LY Tel: 0845 230 3131
www.wellhungmeat.com
organic meat, winner of four Soil Association
Organic Food Awards

Welsh Hook Meat Centre
Woodfield, Withybush Road
Haverfordwest, Pembrokeshire SA62 4BW
Tel: 01437 768876 Fax: 01437 768877
www.welsh-organic-meat.co.uk
well-hung organic and non-organic meat
and poultry from Welsh farmers; halal meat
also available

The Wild Meat Company
Low Road, Sweffling
Saxmundham, Suffolk IP17 2BU
Tel: 01728 663211 Fax:01728 663294
www.wildmeat.co.uk
wild game

FISH

Andy Race Fish Merchants Ltd
Mallaig, Inverness-shire PH41 4PX
Tel: 01687 462626 Fax: 01687 462060
www.andyrace.com
peat-smoked salmon, Mallaig kippers and a variety
of high quality smoked fish and shellfish – with no
resort to dyes; plus selected fresh fish

Brown and Forrest
Bowdens Farm, Hambridge, Somerset TA10 0BP
Tel: 01458 250875 Fax: 01458 253475
www.smokedeel.co.uk
use wood-fired smoking systems with beech
and apple for eel, oak for salmon and trout

Colchester Oyster Fishery
Pyefleet Quay, Mersea Island, Essex CO5 8UN
Tel: 01206 384141 Fax: 01206 383758
www.colchesteroysterfishery.com
boasts oyster beds with a history dating
back to 1189

Cornish Cuisine
The Smokehouse, Islington Wharf
Penryn, Cornwall TR10 8AT
Tel/Fax: 01326 376244
www.smokedsalmon-ltd.com
small commercial smokehouse

Cornish Fish Direct
The Pilchard Works, Newlyn
Penzance, Cornwall TR18 5QH
Tel: 01736 332 112 Fax: 01736 332 442
www.cornishfish.co.uk
fresh Cornish fish, individually prepared and
portioned; pilchards and sardines a speciality

Direct Seafoods Ltd
1 Crown Court, Severalls Industrial Estate
Colchester, Essex CO4 9TZ
Tel: 0870 770 6922 Fax: 01206 751851
www.directseafoods.co.uk

The Fish Shop
Weston's, 5a Westgate Street
Blakeney, Norfolk NR25 7RQ
Tel: 01263 741112
www.westonsofblakeney.co.uk
Willie Weston's superb store;
supplier to Galton Blackiston

The Fish Society
6 Scotlands Close, Haslemere, Surrey GU27 3AE
Tel: 0800 279 3474 Fax: 01428 642513
www.thefishsociety.co.uk
Dover sole, turbot, lobster, kippers, prawns
and 200 other species

FishWorks plc
17 Belmont, Bath BA1 5DZ
Tel: 0800 052 3717 Fax: 01225 465126
www.fishworks.co.uk
from Newlyn fish market, Cornwall, sea bass,
brill, turbot, Dover sole, skate, scallops and
mussels, plus five smoked seafoods

Flatfield Flyfishing
Sydare, Ballinamallard
Co Fermanagh BT94 2DU
Tel/Fax: 028 6638 8184
Mobile: 07808 204401
michaelshortt@pagi.org

Forman and Field
30a Marshgate Lane, London E15 2NH
Tel: 020 8221 3939 Fax: 020 8221 3940
www.formanandfield.com
century-old artisan business and the last salmon
smokery in East London; specialises in traditional
British produce from small, independent producers

Furness Fish and Game Supplies
Stockbridge Lane, Off Daltongate
Ulverston, Cumbria LA12 7GB
Tel: 01229 585037 Fax: 01229 582485
www.morecambebayshrimps.com
family business started by owner Les Salisbury who
has been fishing for shrimps since he was a boy,
going out on horse and cart

H Forman and Son
30a Marshgate Lane, London E15 2NH
Tel: 020 8221 3939
www.formans.co.uk
smoked and fresh fish products

The Hand-Made Fish Co
Bigton, Shetland ZE2 9JF
Tel: 01950 422214 Fax: 01950 422238
www.handmadefish.co.uk
variety of fresh, wild-caught sea fish and organic
farmed fish smoked in pure Scottish hardwoods,
malt whisky barrel staves and peat

Island Seafare Limited
Alfred Pier, Port St Mary, Isle of Man IM9 5EF
Tel: 01624 834494 Fax: 01624 835550
www.islandseafare.co.uk
gourmet seafood, fresh fish, shellfish and
smoked salmon

Loch Fyne Oysters
Clachan, Carindow, Argyll PA26 8BL
Tel: 01499 600264 Fax: 01499 600234
www.loch-fyne.co.uk
quality fresh and smoked seafood, shellfish,
meat and game

Matthew Stevens and Son Ltd
Back Road East, St Ives, Cornwall TR26 3AR
Tel: 01736 799392 Fax: 01736 799441
www.mstevensandson.co.uk
fresh fish from South West harbours of Mevagissey,
Looe, Newlyn and St Ives; also freshwater crayfish

Scott's Road
Hatston, Kirkwall, Orkney KW15 1GR
Tel: 01856 873317/417 Fax: 01856 874960
www.jollyfish.co.uk
pickled, salted and smoked fish

Severn and Wye Smokery Ltd
Walmore Hill, Minsterworth
Gloucestershire GL2 8LA
Tel: 01452 760190
www.salmon-smokers.com
fine quality smoked foods; supplier
to Antony Worrall Thompson

Southport Seafoods
11 Shellfield Road, Marshside
Southport, Lancashire PR9 9US
Tel/Fax: 01704 505 822
www.pottedshrimps.co.uk
specialist shrimpers

Steve Hatt Fishmongers
88–90 Essex Road, London N1 8LU
Tel: 020 7226 3963
one of London's finest fishmongers, now
in its fourth generation, with own smokehouse
at the rear of the shop; seasonal game includes
grouse and venison

Tregida Smokehouse
Trelash, Warbstow
Launceston, Cornwall PL15 8RL
Tel: 01840 261785 Fax: 01840 261775
www.tregidasmokehouse.co.uk
traditional Cornish oak-smoked fish, meat,
game and cheese, free from artificial additives
and flavourings

The Whitstable Shellfish Company
Westmeads Road, Whitstable, Kent CT5 1LW
Tel: 01227 282375
www.whitstable-shellfish.co.uk
fresh oysters in season

CHEESE

Bath Soft Cheese
Park Farm, Kelston, Bath BA1 9AG
Tel: 01225 331601
www.parkfarm.co.uk
Gold Medal winner at the British Cheese Awards;
highest quality produce from Britain and Europe

Buffalo House
Bury Farm, Mill Road, Slapton
Leighton Buzzard, Bedfordshire LU7 9BT
Tel: 01525 220256
www.buffalogold.com
buffalo meat, 'mozzarella' and milk

Butlers Farmhouse Cheeses
Unit 1, Shay Lane, Longridge
Preston, Lancashire PR3 3BT
Tel: 01772 781500 Fax: 01722 782521
www.butlerscheeses.co.uk
supplier to Simon Rimmer and creators
of the unique blue cheese called Blacksticks
Blue, plus a range of fresh and brie-style
cheeses made from goat's, cow's, sheep's
and buffalo milk

Caws Cenarth Cheese
Glyneithinog Farm, Pontseli, Boncath
Dyfed SA37 0LH Tel: 01239 710432
www.cawscenarth.co.uk
small family enterprise that led revival
of Welsh farmhouse cheeses

Cheese Cellar
4 Lion Yard, Tremadoc Road
London SW4 7NQ
Tel: 020 7501 0600 Fax: 020 7627 2048
www.cheesecellar.co.uk
huge range of specialist cheeses

The Fine Cheese Company
29 and 31 Walcot Street, Bath BA1 5BN
Tel: 01225 448748 Fax: 01225 318905
www.finecheese.co.uk
magnificent range of up to 150 cheeses,
plus charcuterie, bread and utensils

La Fromagerie
2–4 Moxon Street, London W1U 4EW
Tel: 020 7935 0341 Fax: 020 7935 6245
www.lafromagerie.co.uk
emphasis on French cheeses but still
a formidable range of British produce

Hamish Johnston
48 Northcote Road, London SW11 1PA
Tel: 020 7738 0741
www.hamishjohnston.com
emphasis on British cheeses, plus biscuits, chutney,
butters, creams and other interesting ingredients

Lower Lightwood Farm
Cotheridge, Worcestershire WR6 5LT
Tel/Fax: 01905 333468
www.lightwoodcheese.co.uk
presence at farmers' markets in Worcestershire,
Warwickshire, Herefordshire and Gloucestershire

Neal's Yard Dairy
17 Shorts Gardens, Covent Garden
London WC2H 9UP Tel: 020 7240 5700
www.nealsyarddairy.co.uk
pioneering company with a very wide range
of British and Irish cheeses

Pant Mawr Farmhouse Cheeses
Pant Mawr Farm, Rosebush, Clynderwen
Pembrokeshire SA66 7QU
Tel: 01437 532627 Fax: 01437 532627
www.pantmawrcheeses.co.uk
Welsh farmhouse cheeses

Rippon Cheese Stores
26 Upper Tachbrook Street, London SW1V 1SW
Tel: 020 7931 0628/0668 Fax: 020 7828 2368
www.ripponcheese.com
around 500 types of cheese

Teddington Cheese
42 Station Road, Teddington
Middlesex TW11 9AA
Tel: 020 8977 6868 Fax: 020 8977 1141
www.teddingtoncheese.co.uk
cheeses from all over Britain and Europe matured
on premises, cut and served when in peak condition

Mrs Temple Cheese
Copys Green Farm, Wighton
Norfolk NR23 1NY Tel: 01328 820224
cmt@mrstemplescheese.co.uk
suppliers of cheese to Galton Blackiston

Wester Lawrenceton Farm
Forres, Moray IV36 3RH
Tel: 01309 676566
sweet milk cheese from unpasteurised organic milk
of Ayrshire cows; at farmers' markets and specialist
cheese shops throughout Scotland

SWEETS AND PRESERVES

L'Artisan du Chocolat Ltd
89 Lower Sloane Street
London SW1 W8DA
Tel: 020 7824 8365 Fax: 020 7730 6139
www.artisanduchocolat.com
"The Bentley of chocolate", according
to Gordon Ramsay

Cartmel Village Shop
The Square, Cartmel, Cumbria LA11 6QB
Tel (office): 015395 58300
Tel (shop): 015395 36280
Fax: 015395 58507
www.stickytoffeepudding.co.uk

Cocoa Central
Commercial Road, Swanage, Dorset BH19 1DF
Tel: 01929 421777 Fax: 01929 422748
www.chococo.co.uk

Dowsons Dairies Ltd
Hawkshaw Farm, Longsight Road
Clayton-le-Dale, Blackburn
Lancashire BB2 7JA
Tel: 01254 812407 Fax: 01254 814476
www.mrsdowsons.co.uk
black pudding ice cream!

The Hive Honey Shop
93 Northcote Road, London SW11 6PL
Tel: 020 7924 6233 Fax: 020 7640 0552
www.thehivehoneyshop.co.uk
one of a handful of commercial beekeepers,
with 65 different British honeys

Mrs Huddleston's
Lodge Hill House, Great Brickhill
Buckinghamshire MK17 9AY
Tel: 01525 261868
www.mrshuddleston.com
whole fruit conserves and jams, citrus marmalades,
mature chutneys, fruit relishes, English wine jellies
and ice cream sauces

James Chocolate
Laighton Lane, Evercreech
Shepton Mallet, Somerset BA4 6LQ
Tel: 01749 831330 Fax: 01749 831370
www.bar-chocolat.com
handmade chocolates

Montezuma's Chocolates
Birdham Business Park, Birdham Road
Chichester, West Sussex PO20 7BT
Tel: 0845 450 6304 Fax: 0845 450 6305
www.montezumas.co.uk
handmade chocolates

Rococo Chocolates
321 Kings Road, London SW3 5EP
Tel: 020 7352 5857
www.rococochocolates.com
fine organic chocolate with imaginative
ingredients such as sea salt

Sarah Nelson's Grasmere Ginger Bread
Church Cottage, Grasmere
Ambleside, Cumbria LA22 9SW
Tel: 015394 35428 Fax: 015394 35155
www.grasmeregingerbread.co.uk
fine Cumbrian confectionery

Wendy Brandon Handmade Preserves
Felin Wen, Boncath, Pembrokeshire SA37 0JR
Tel: 01239 841568 Fax: 01239 841746
www.wendybrandon.co.uk
fine jams, marmalades and chutneys

FRUIT AND VEGETABLES

Abel and Cole Ltd
8–15 MGI Estate, Milkwood Road
London SE24 0JF Tel: 08452 626262
www.abel-cole.co.uk
fresh organic fruit and veg, organic meat,
sustainably sourced fish, most from UK farms

Baxters Fruiterers
Borough High Street, London SE1 9AH
Tel: 020 7403 0311

Boxfresh Organics
Unit 5C, Rodenhurst Business Park
Rodington, Shropshire SY4 4QU
Tel: 01952 770006 Mobile: 07786 918322
www.boxfreshorganics.co.uk
certified organic produce including free
range eggs, apple juice and poultry; varies
week to week according to what's in season

Crapes Fruit Farm
Aldham, nr Colchester, Essex CO6 3RR
Tel/Fax: 01206 212375
andrew.tann1@virgin.net
over 150 varieties of apples grown in
a 12.5-hectare orchard

Dolphin Sea Vegetable Company
Unit 54 Glenwood Centre
Springbank Industrial Estate
Belfast 17 0QL
Tel: 02890 617512 Fax: 02890 430220
www.irishseaweeds.com
harvest, process and sell sea vegetables; also
do a range of seaweed cosmetics. Worldwide
mail order

Dragon Orchard
Dragon House, Putley
Ledbury, Herefordshire HR8 2RG
Tel: 01531 670071 Fax: 01531 670811
www.dragonorchard.co.uk
fine apples from a traditional English orchard

Organic Doorstep
125 Strabane Road, Castlederg
Co Tyrone BT81 7JD
Tel (order free phone): 0800 783 5656
Tel (other enquiries): 028 816 79989
Fax: 028 816 79820
www.organicdoorstep.co.uk
organic local produce from Northern Ireland

Riverford Organic Vegetables Ltd
Wash Barn, Buckfastleigh, Devon TQ11 0LD
Tel: 0845 600 2311 Fax: 01803 762718
www.riverford.co.uk
over 85 different vegetables, most of them
delivered the day after picking

River Nene Organic Vegetables
Stanley's Farm, Peterborough PE7 3TW
Tel: 0845 078 6868
www.rivernene.co.uk
organic vegetables box scheme delivering to
homes in the Midlands and Eastern counties

Turnips Distributing
Borough Market, Borough High Street
London SE1 9AH Tel: 020 7357 8356

FA Secretts Ltd
Hurst Farm, Chapel Lane, Milford
Godalming, Surrey GU8 5HU
Tel: 01483 520529 Fax: 01483 520501
www.secretts.co.uk
third generation family business set in the
heart of the Surrey countryside selling an extensive
range of herbs, fruit, vegetables and salads

BREAD

Baker and Spice
41 Denyer Street, London SW3 2LX
Tel: 020 7589 4734
www.bakerandspice.com
artisan baker of traditional British breads,
baked without additives

Elizabeth Botham and Sons Ltd
35/39 Skinner St, Whitby
North Yorkshire YO21 3AH
Tel: 01947 602823 Fax: 01947 820269
www.botham.co.uk
North Yorkshire cakes, hampers, biscuits and
plum bread

Carley's of Cornwall Ltd
34–36 St Austell Street, Truro
Cornwall TR1 1SE Tel: 01872 277686
www.carleys.co.uk

Common Loaf Bakery
Stentwood Farm, Dunkeswell
Devon EX14 4RW Tel: 01823 681213
www.commonloaf.com

Ditty's Bakery
44 Main Street, Castledawson
Co Antrim BT45 8AB
Tel: 028 794 68243 Fax: 028 794 68967
www.dittysbakery.com
guardian of traditional Irish baking; in business
for over 40 years

Hobbs House
Unit 6, Chipping Edge Industrial Estate
Hatters Lane, Chipping Sodbury
Bristol BS37 6AA
Tel: 01454 321629 Fax: 01454 329757
www.hobbshousebakery.co.uk

Jungs
6 The Broadway, Beaconsfield
Buckinghamshire HP9 2PD
Tel: 01494 673070 Fax: 01494 681070
www.hpjung.com
founded by a German Konditor meister; produces
a wide range of quality breads and cakes

Otterton Mill Bakery
Budleigh Salterton
Otterton, East Devon EX9 7HG
Tel/Fax: 01395 568031
www.ottertonmill.com

The Patisserie
38 Station Road, Stoke D'Abernon
Cobham, Surrey KT11 3HZ
Tel: 01932 863926
www.thepatisserie.co.uk
bread and pastries baked using traditional
methods and ingredients

St Martin's Bakery
Moo Green, St Martin's
Isles of Scilly TR25 0QL
Tel: 01720 423444
www.stmartinsbakery.co.uk

Strawberry Hill
Newent, Gloucestershire GL18 1LH
Tel: 01531 828181 Fax: 01531 828151
www.authenticbread.co.uk
founded in 1995 to keep alive traditional
baking methods and produce

CHEFS' DIRECTORY

Galton Blackiston is Head Chef at Morston Hall Hotel
and Restaurant
Morston Hall, Holt, Norfolk NR 25 7AA
(01623 741041; www.morstonhall.com)

John Burton Race is Head Chef at The New Angel
2 South Embankment, Dartmouth, Devon TQ6 9BH
(01803 839425; www.thenewangel.co.uk)

Michael Caines is Head Chef at Gidleigh Park
Chagford, Devon TQ13 8HH (01647 432367; www.gidleigh.com)
Michael Caines' Restaurant, Café Bar and Wells House Tavern
at ABode Exeter at The Royal Clarence, Cathedral Yard, Exeter,
Devon EX1 1HD (01392 223638; www.abodehotels.co.uk/exeter)
Michael Caines at the Bristol Marriott Royal Hotel, College Green,
Bristol BS1 5TA (0117 9105309; www.michaelcaines.com/bristol)
Michael Caines' Fine Dining Restaurant, Café Bar and Vibe Bar
at ABode Glasgow, 129 Bath Street, Glasgow G2 2SZ
(0141 221 6789; www.abodehotels.co.uk/glasgow)

Richard Corrigan is Head Chef at Lindsay House
21 Romilly Street, London W1D 5AF
(020 7439 0450; www.lindsayhouse.co.uk)
Bentley's Oyster Bar and Grill, 11–15 Swallow Street,
London W1B 4DG (020 7734 4756)

Angela Hartnett is Executive Chef at The Connaught
Carlos Place, London W1Y 6AL
(020 7592 1222; www.the-connaught.co.uk)

Atul Kochhar is Chef-Owner of Benares
12a Berkeley Square House, Berkeley Square, London W1J 6BS
(020 7629 8886; www.benaresrestaurant.com)

Tom Lewis is Head Chef at Monachyle Mhor
Balquhidder, Perthshire FK19 8PQ
(01877 384622: www.monachylemhor.com)

Nick Nairn Cook School
Port of Menteith, Stirling FK8 3JZ
(01877 389900; www.nicknairncookschool.com)

Paul Rankin is Chef Patron at Cayenne
7 Ascot House, Shaftesbury Square, Belfast BT2 7DB
(028 9033 1532; www.rankingroup.co.uk/cayenne.php)
Roscoff Brasserie, 7–11 Linenhall Street, Belfast BT2 8AA
(028 9031 1150; www.rankingroup.co.uk/roscoff.php)
Rain City, 3335 Malone Road, Belfast BT9 6RU
(028 9068 2929; www.rankingroup.co.uk/rain_city.php)
Branches of Café Paul Rankin are at Fountain Street, Belfast
(028 9031 5090); Arthur Street, Belfast (028 9031 0108);
Castlecourt Shopping Centre, Belfast (028 9024 8411);
Lisburn Road, Belfast (028 9066 8350);
Belfast International Airport (028 9445 4992);
High Street Mall, Portadown (028 3839 8818);
Junction One International Outlet Centre, Antrim (028 9446 0370);
Bow Street, Lisburn (028 9262 9045);
Dundrum Town Centre, Dublin (00353 1 2963105).

Gary Rhodes is Head Chef at Rhodes Twenty Four
Tower 42, 25 Old Broad Street, London EC2N 1HQ
(020 7877 7703; www.rhodes24.co.uk)
Rhodes W1, The Cumberland, Great Cumberland Place,
London W1A 4RS (020 7479 3938; www.garyrhodes.com)

Simon Rimmer is Chef Patron at Green's
43 Lapwing Lane, West Didsbury, Manchester M20 8NT
(0161 434 4259)

Marcus Wareing is Head Chef at The Savoy Grill
Strand, London WC2R 0EU (020 7592 1600)
Pétrus, The Berkeley, Wilton Place, Knightsbridge,
London SW1X 7RL (020 7235 1200)

Bryn Williams is Executive Sous Chef at The Orrery
55 Marylebone High Street, London W1U 5RB (020 7616 8000)

Antony Worrall Thompson is Chef Patron at Notting Grill
123a Clarendon Road, London W11 4JG
(020 7229 1500; www.awtonline.co.uk)
Kew Grill, 10b Kew Green, Richmond, Surrey TW9 3BH
(020 8948 4433)
The Angel Coaching Inn and Grill, High Street, Heytesbury,
Nr Warminster, Wiltshire BA12 0ED
(01985 840931; www.theangelheytesbury.co.uk)
Greyhound Free House and Grill, Gallowstree Road,
Rotherfield Peppard, Oxon RG9 56HT

INDEX

ACKNOWLEDGEMENTS

Dorling Kindersley would like to thank the following:

Alex, Emma, Saskia, Brianne, Katrin and Jim at Smith & Gilmour; Stephen Parkins-Knight, food stylist, for preparing and presenting recipes for the camera; Noel Murphy for location photography, Dan Jones for food photography and Fabio Alberti for photographic assistance; Divertimenti for loan of props; Alan Kennedy, Rosie Rose, Derek Morrison, Bob Kennard, David and Christine Pugh, Anthony Buscomb, Denis Lynn, Willie Weston, Tony Batchelor and Neil Robson for their help with location photography; Jackie Baker, Sophie Seiden, Vanessa Land and Annina Vogel at Optomen Television; and Hilary Bird for the index